Finding Faith Today

Finding Faith Today

BRYAN P. STONE

CASCADE *Books* • Eugene, Oregon

FINDING FAITH TODAY

Copyright © 2018 Bryan P. Stone. All rights reserved. Except for brief quotations in critical publications or reviews, no part of this book may be reproduced in any manner without prior written permission from the publisher. Write: Permissions, Wipf and Stock Publishers, 199 W. 8th Ave., Suite 3, Eugene, OR 97401.

Cascade Books
An Imprint of Wipf and Stock Publishers
199 W. 8th Ave., Suite 3
Eugene, OR 97401

www.wipfandstock.com

PAPERBACK ISBN: 978-1-5326-5146-5
HARDCOVER ISBN: 978-1-5326-5147-2
EBOOK ISBN: 978-1-5326-5148-9

Cataloguing-in-Publication data:

Names: Stone, Bryan P., author.

Title: Finding faith today / Bryan P. Stone.

Description: Eugene, OR: Cascade Books, 2018 | Includes bibliographical references.

Identifiers: ISBN 978-1-5326-5146-5 (paperback) | ISBN 978-1-5326-5147-2 (hardcover) | ISBN 978-1-5326-5148-9 (ebook)

Subjects: LCSH: Religions. | Religions—Statistics.

Classification: BL80.3 S74 2018 (paperback) | BL80.3 (ebook)

10/30/18

Contents

Introduction | vii

1 Christians | 1

2 Christians: Setting Out on the Journey | 7

3 Christians: The Journey | 22

4 Christians: Factors Leading to Faith | 48

5 Christians: Is There a Change? | 92

6 Judaism | 112

7 Buddhism | 142

8 Islam | 170

9 Unitarian Universalists and Quakers | 186

   Excursus on Hinduism, Jainism, and Sikhism | 208

10 Concluding Observations | 212

Appendix A—Christian Representation in the Survey | 217

Appendix B—Factors in Coming to Faith by Tradition | 219

Appendix C—Changes in Attitudes and Positions on Social Issues | 222

Appendix D—Most Important Feature of the Congregation | 226

Appendix E—Active Seekers or Drawn in by Others Without Actively Seeking? | 228

Appendix F—Significance of Changes | 230

Bibliography | 233

Introduction

How do persons come to faith in our time? Do they set out seeking to adopt a faith? Or does the faith adopt them? Is it a journey? Or is it more like a sudden conversion? Is *faith* even the right word? Are friends and relatives most important to the process? Do clergy matter? Are books, television, or films significant factors? What sorts of values, practices, and lifestyles tend to change for those who newly come to faith? What, if any, are the substantial differences in how one comes to faith among Christians, Jews, Muslims, Buddhists, Unitarian Universalists, or persons of other religious traditions? The Finding Faith Today Project is a nationwide research project that attempts to answer these and other questions.

It was around 2003 that I first learned from a British student named Julian Gotobed about the Finding Faith Today study that Bishop John Finney had undertaken in England in 1990. Julian had come to Boston University School of Theology to study, and over the years as I pondered with him Finney's findings (published in 1992 in the book *Finding Faith Today: How Does It Happen?*), we wondered if a similar study might be feasible in the US some twenty-five years later. Finney had begun research into the question of how persons become Christians in the 1980s, first interviewing around 400 people and then employing a questionnaire more widely. But surprisingly little research has been done since then on this subject. The current Finding Faith Today project (we chose to keep the same name as Finney's project) is an expansion and follow-up of that study.

In 2012, I worked with student researchers at Boston University School of Theology to pilot such a study in three US cities: Los Angeles, Boston, and St. Louis. The cities were chosen given their rich social and religious diversity and their spread across the United States geographically. As with Finney's approach, we initially designed a survey for pastors that gathered information about their congregations and asked them for names of persons in their churches who had made a new faith commitment or recommitment in the past year or so. Unlike Finney, I am not a bishop, and getting pastors to participate in the study, much less send us names of new Christians in their care, proved exceptionally difficult. The fact that pastors themselves had to take the survey as part of the process ended up creating a bottleneck in gaining access to those who were the most important sources of the study: persons who had newly come to faith or had recently returned to faith. While that initial pilot project was limited (108 pastors and only forty-four new Christians completed the survey), it gave us valuable information about the process of coming to faith, and it helped us rethink the survey instrument along with the process of accessing study subjects.

The following year, we set out to undertake the study with a national scope, and rather than asking clergy to take the survey and send us names, we simply asked them to pass along the survey (or the web link to it) to those adults in their churches, age eighteen or older,[1] who had recently made a new faith commitment, recommitment, or profession of faith, or who had experienced what they understood to be a conversion. The nationwide study took place over several years and also included a multi-religious dimension not present in Finney's original study, so that we could compare the ways persons from different religious traditions come to faith. In the survey instructions, we recognized that for some persons this new commitment might be more like a return to faith or an activation of the religion into which they were born. We also recognized that how one describes this new commitment or conversion will vary from tradition to tradition and person to person. Sometimes the language of conversion is inadequate to describe the way people take up religious practice, as with Buddhism. Moreover, some people who take up Buddhism continue to consider themselves Christians, or adherents of other religious traditions. As with Finney, we did not begin with a definition of "Christian" (or of "Jewish," "Buddhist," etc.), but allowed respondents to self-identify. In fact, one of the fascinating and highly important findings of our study is the relationship between what it means to be any of these and how one goes about finding faith. Evangelicals, for example, prioritize certain things in describing what it means to be a Christian that are not at all the same as what Mainline Protestants prioritize. These differences shape how one comes to faith in those two Christian traditions in pretty remarkable ways.

In addition to survey data, we also conducted interviews and focus groups with persons across the country. Our study concentrates on how persons come to faith, how they understand the faith to which they have

---

1. There are strict laws around research with subjects under the age of eighteen that make studying them complicated. It can be done, but we chose to concentrate on adults in this study. Bishop Finney studied persons sixteen and older.

committed themselves, what they understand to be the most important factors during the process, and any changes in values, practices, or lifestyle that accompany this new commitment. Throughout this book, I have stuck closely with the exact wording of their responses and I have generally not tried to refine or alter their grammar. I leave things in their own words as much as possible so that readers can get a sense of the texture of their responses. We received 1,788 responses: 64 percent of those were from the largest Christian groups—Black, Evangelical, and Mainline Protestants; Roman Catholics; and Orthodox. The remaining 36 percent were primarily from Jews, Buddhists, Muslims, Quakers, and Unitarian Universalists, with a small number of responses from Hindus, Sikhs, and others.

I spend more time in the following chapters on those traditions from which we received a substantial number of responses. For example, only a handful of Jains, Sikhs, Hindus, and persons from traditions such as Wicca, Bahá'í, Unity, Humanism, or Paganism participated in our study, so we were unable to add much to existing knowledge about those traditions. Likewise, the Church of Scientology, the Jehovah's Witnesses, and the Church of Christ of Latter Day Saints (Mormons) were not able to assist us in gaining access to any of their recent converts, despite repeated attempts, so those faith traditions will not be represented here. Nonetheless, the end result is, we think, a fascinating and largely representative portrait of American religious life.

The first and largest part of the book focuses on Christians, who now make up a little over 70 percent of the US population, and compares our findings with those of Finney's study at several key points. It also compares Christians from the three largest traditions in the United States (Catholic, Evangelical Protestant, and Mainline Protestant) with one another. The second part of the book explores ways one comes to faith or practice in other religious traditions, examining those paths on their own terms and in relation to other traditions.

A project such as this that has taken place over several years and that has attempted to dig deep into faith traditions across the United States relied heavily on the assistance of many persons, most of them students at Boston University. I am thankful to the School of Theology and to Dean Mary Elizabeth Moore for support of the project, and to the Center for Practical Theology for its funding and staff assistance. In particular, I am thankful to the following persons for their assistance throughout the project.

Xochitl Alvizo	Michelle Ashley	Chris Broadwell
Ashley Anderson	Stephanie Arel	Simrat Dhaliwal
Greta Appleton	Sarah Bradley	Johnny Gall

Yara Gonzalez-Justiniano	Jaeguen Lee	EunJoo Park
Julian Gotobed	Min Hyoung Lee	Miracle Ryder
Melinda Hicks	Landis Masnor	Molly Simpson
Kathryn House	Erin McKinney	Rebecca Smith
Blake Fox	Brady Moses	Danielle Stecher
Kaitlyn Martin Fox	Kaci Norman	Adam Wallis
Emily Kleidon	Lauren Osga	Caitlin White

1

Christians

WHO PARTICIPATED IN THE STUDY?

1,149 CHRISTIAN ADULTS (AGE eighteen and older) participated in the on-line survey. Among those, the median age was 46, with a slightly younger median age for Evangelicals (43) than for Catholics (46) and Mainline Protestants (49). The age distributions in our study (Figure 1.1) compare fairly well to national demographics, though with a slightly younger cohort of respondents in our study. The Pew Research Center's 2014 Religious Landscape Study (the most recent such study to date) found the median age of all Christian adults to be 49 (up from 46 in 2007).[1] While the median age of our respondents is similar to that study, it is worth noting that the average age of Christians is rising (a trend that does not bode well for the future of Christianity in the US). At the same time, younger persons are increasingly unaffiliated (those who are now often called the "nones"). The average age of those unaffiliated is 36.

1. Pew, "America's Changing Religious Landscape," 50. Their study also showed that the median age of mainline Protestant adults is 52 and the median age of Evangelical and Catholic adults is 49.

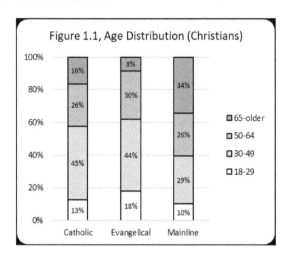

Figure 1.1, Age Distribution (Christians)

Participants in our study had a much higher level of education than the US general public (Figure 1.2). While 76 percent of Christian respondents had a college or graduate degree, that is true for only 29 percent of the US general public.[2] We know that higher education rates correlate with higher wages, mobility, and civic participation rates, so one has to take those factors into account when assessing the results of our study.

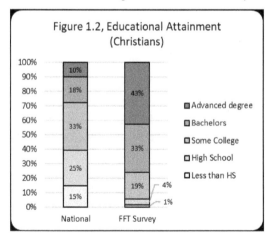

Figure 1.2, Educational Attainment (Christians)

One of the fascinating lessons learned from this study is the extent of significant differences among Christians in the United States. Indeed, that is a theme that will run throughout this entire book. The narrative of how people become Christians in the United States has multiple story lines. One of the reasons I distinguish throughout the book between the

2. Pew, "A Portrait of Jewish Americans," 42.

largest Christian family groups—Roman Catholic, Evangelical Protestant, and Mainline Protestant—is that the differences between them are striking. Christians share much in common; but their differences at key points might lead a researcher to believe she is studying different world religions at times. Even among Protestants, there are large differences, and so throughout the study I draw distinctions between Evangelical and Mainline Protestants. At times, I note unique features of Christian groups who do not always fit easily into these three large categories, but it is difficult to make substantial conclusions from our data about, for example, Orthodox Christians because of their relatively low response rates in our survey (only thirteen of the 1,149 Christians surveyed said they were Orthodox). Historically Black Protestants also have several unique features, but while 3 percent of our Christian respondents identified as Black or African American, most of those were in Evangelical or Mainline denominations so that our data does not allow us to parse out those features more closely. At times, though, the differences between those groups and other Christian groups are worth noting. At times, it is possible to group Roman Catholics and Orthodox together when their responses warrant that, as they sometimes do. But we have not identified them as distinct categories when the sample size was insufficient to draw larger conclusions.

The terms *Mainline* and *Evangelical* are sociological categories used to distinguish theological and other historic characteristics among Protestants in the United States. While Mainline denominations were once the largest and most influential group in the United States, their numbers have been almost halved in the last half century so that only about 12–15 percent of the US population now affiliates with Mainline denominations.[3] These include the American Baptist Churches, the Christian Church (Disciples of Christ), the Episcopal Church, the Evangelical Lutheran Church in America, the Presbyterian Church (USA), Religious Society of Friends (Quakers), the Reformed Church in America, the United Church of Christ, and the United Methodist Church. Mainline denominations have tended to be more progressive in their stances on social issues and have historically been proponents of the ecumenical movement, symbolized in their memberships in the National Council of Churches. Evangelical Christians, by contrast, tend to be more conservative on social issues and emphasize the authority of Scripture, the need for conversion (often expressed in the term "born again"), the importance of evangelizing others, and several doctrinal affirmations related to Christ and his work. The National Association of Evangelicals is a body comprised of forty denominations along with

3. Stetzer, "23 Easters," para. 8.

congregations, schools, and other organizations, many of them having no particular denominational ties.

Figure 1.3 summarizes the representation from the primary Christian traditions in the US in our current Finding Faith Today study as compared to US averages more generally. A full list of denominational representation by Christian family can be found in Appendix A.

Figure 1.3, Christian Representation		
	Percent of US Christians[A]	FFT Survey Responses
Evangelical Protestant	36%	31%
Catholic	29%	20%
Mainline Protestant	21%	36%
Historically Black	9%	1%
Orthodox	<1%	1%
Other Christian	4%	0%
Unknown	N/A	11%

A. Pew, "America's Changing Religious Landscape," 4.

While it is clear from this chart that in relation to national averages Mainline Protestants are over-represented in our study and Roman Catholics and Evangelicals are somewhat under-represented, the responses of each Christian family are analyzed separately throughout the book so as not to distort the overall picture of how Christians come to faith in the United States. There is plenty of data from each group to allow us to paint an accurate picture of how Christians come to faith within those distinct traditions as well as within the Christian tradition as a whole. About 10 percent of the respondents did not identify their denominational or family tradition, but indicated only that they were Christians. While we have good reason to suspect that most of those individuals are Evangelicals, given that Evangelicals do not always affiliate with a denomination, we cannot know for sure. Their data is included at key points along the way.

HOW DID CHRISTIANS SIGNAL THEIR FAITH?

We asked Christians in our study how they signaled their new faith commitment or recommitment. Not surprisingly, there were significant differences among the major Christian traditions at this point. Evangelical and Black Protestants mentioned baptism most often (47 percent) followed by church membership (32 percent) or some form of public declaration, reaffirmation, or testimony. Other markers included confirmation, prayer, baptism in the Holy Spirit, speaking in tongues, and church attendance.

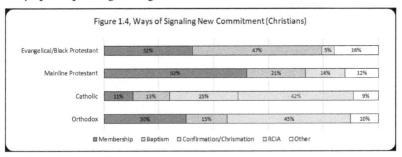

Figure 1.4, Ways of Signaling New Commitment (Christians)

For Mainline Protestants, the situation is somewhat reversed with membership (52 percent) cited most often followed by a much smaller number who cited baptism (21 percent). In addition, a good number identified confirmation (14 percent) as a marker, demonstrating the ongoing strength of that practice in Mainline denominations (though it also remains important among some Evangelical groups and denominations). For Orthodox Christians, almost all respondents identified the dual rituals of baptism and chrismation (also called confirmation) that culminate a process of catechesis.

The situation of Roman Catholics is unique given the importance of the Rite of Christian Initiation of Adults (RCIA) for those not baptized as infants, baptized in another Christian church, or baptized but never given religious instruction in the Catholic Church. The RCIA process includes several stages that include study, discussion, prayer, and rites that take place in the context of the Mass. Close to half (42 percent) of Roman Catholic respondents identified the RCIA as the most important signal of their new commitment. Another 25 percent cited confirmation and 13 percent claimed it was their baptism. Other responses included confession, church attendance, and the Roman Catholic "welcome back" program, an initiative begun in 2008 to evangelize, reclaim, and welcome back lapsed Catholics.

Much has been made of the drift by Catholics away from the church of their birth (though Catholics actually have one of the highest retention rates among religions in the US) or the fact that most Catholics (77 percent) do not regularly attend Mass.[4] And yet several outreach programs aimed at welcoming inactive Catholics are making a difference. One such program is "Landings," which provides a safe community of support and "reconciliation process" for persons such as Laura, in her thirties, who had not been

---

4. Center for Applied Research in the Apostolate, "Statistics," line 42.

to church much since her first communion. Laura's experience is similar to many Catholics in our study. She needed a place where she could ask questions, voice her apprehensions, and learn more about Catholicism.[5] After participating in Landings, she enrolled in RCIA at St. Charles Borromeo Church in Arlington, Virginia, and eventually became a team leader for the next Landings group.

---

5. Peterson, "You Can Go Home Again."

2

Christians: Setting Out on the Journey

WHAT IS A CHRISTIAN?

Is a Christian a person who lives in a particular way? Believes certain things? Experiences God in some distinct way? Or perhaps has made some noteworthy set of life commitments? There may be no question more important to this study than the question of what a person making a new commitment to Christian faith understands a Christian to be. Our survey left the question open without providing a list of choices so that persons would not be steered in any one direction. Understandably, a few of the respondents were unsure about what it means to be a Christian, but those were actually quite rare. The vast majority answered the question with confidence and a good degree of clarity, even if that meant offering fairly standard jargon and Christian language.

Answers to the question vary significantly by Christian tradition. Two-thirds of Mainline Protestants focus their answer on a pattern of living, character, or actions, such as the 49-year-old librarian, who put it this way:

> *Mostly conducting yourself with tolerance and treating others with respect and dignity. Loving your neighbor.*

A 28-year-old fundraiser saw being a Christian as:

> *. . . being a good and kind person who treats others the way they want to be treated and is welcoming and receptive to everyone they meet.*

Of course, many people in the world aspire to live out the Golden Rule: "do to others as you would have them do to you" (Luke 6:31), and not Mainline Protestants only. But what we heard confirms a pattern of what sociologist of religion Nancy Ammerman has called "Golden Rule" Christianity that is well represented among Mainline Protestants. People sometimes distinguish Mainline Protestants from Evangelical Protestants by claiming that the latter are characterized by ideological certainty in relation to traditional Christian beliefs (about the Bible, Christ's atoning death, the virgin birth, the second coming, etc.) while the former are the exact opposite—ideologically less committed to certainty and more skeptical where such beliefs are concerned. But as Ammerman puts it (and our results support this), many Mainline Protestants are "best defined not by ideology, but by practices. Their own measure of Christianity is right living more than right believing. . . . these Christians are characterized by a basic 'Golden Rule' morality and a sense of compassion for those in need."[1]

We did not ask many questions about the content of the religious beliefs of the participants in this study, as that was not our focus. But the contrast is sharp between Mainline Protestants and Evangelical Protestants when it comes to the question of whether lifestyle or belief is most important in defining what it means to be a Christian. While two-thirds of Mainline Protestants focus on actions or lifestyle, only one-third (35 percent) of Evangelicals place the emphasis there, preferring instead to concentrate on beliefs (23 percent) or on commitment, trust, faith, devotion, and putting God first (20 percent). A significant number of Evangelicals, moreover, construe being a Christian as having a relationship with Jesus (or God) or accepting Jesus as one's savior (14 percent). They are much less likely to talk about what that means in terms of lifestyle or action. So, for example, a 26-year-old technician who identifies as an Evangelical summarized what many other Evangelical participants in our study said in describing what it means to be a Christian:

> To accept Christ as your lord and savior. And to believe that he died on the cross for our sins and that he rose from the dead. And will be back.

Or as this 66-year-old insurance servicer put it,

> Accepting Jesus Christ in your heart as your Lord and Savior. Knowing that he is always with you to get you through everything.

1. Ammerman, "Golden Rule Christianity," 197.

Evangelicals are three times as likely as Catholics or Mainline Protestants to speak of what it means to be a Christian in terms of forgiveness of sins, accepting Jesus as lord or as personal savior, or asking Jesus into one's heart. While only a small number of Evangelicals (3 percent) center their answer on being a witness or example to reach others with the gospel, even that small percentage is twice as much as Mainline Protestants and Roman Catholics.

Clearly, what it means to find faith varies greatly among Christians, as Figure 2.1 summarizes. For some, faith is primarily a matter of belief; for others, it is a matter of trust, devotion, and relationship with God, or Christ; and for others it is more a matter of lifestyle, action, and practices.

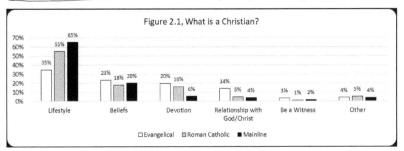

Figure 2.1, What is a Christian?

Roman Catholics are likewise distinctive in the way they describe what it means to be a Christian. Over half (55 percent) understand that as primarily a matter of lifestyle and actions, with a focus on being "Christ-like," and in this respect they are more like Mainline Protestants than Evangelicals. Yet the percentage of Roman Catholics who focus on trust, worship, and devotion is almost three times that of Mainline Protestants, and in that respect more like Evangelicals. The nature of that devotion and trust, however, varies greatly between Evangelicals and Catholics. In answering the question of what it means to be a Christian, Evangelicals lean significantly more toward the language of personal commitment, and accentuate trust, surrender, submission of one's will, and acceptance of Christ's sacrifice, including even a frequent protest against "works-righteousness." Catholics, by contrast, tend to frame their devotion in terms of a spirituality that is more communal, ecclesial, liturgical, mystical, or worked out in practices. The following are typical responses from Catholics, as examples:

> *To hope for, and pray for, my inner unity to Jesus in His prayer and faithful self-offering, to others and to the Father.*
> *Live in the light of Christ, seeking to adhere to his lessons and spread his message.*
> *That we have come to Christ's table and accepted his offering of forgiveness of our sins via Jesus's sacrifice.*

To be able to serve God and the community.

*To be a human person, to follow the teachings of the Holy
catholic and apostolic church, to know and to love God.*

Now contrast those responses with the following responses, typical of
Evangelicals:

*I think being a Christian is when you give your life over to God
and allow him to be the sole driver. He sent his son to die for our
sins, he sacrificed so much for us because he loves us and we are
his children.*

*It means living your life to honor and please God by allowing
Him to live through me and surrendering my will for His will. I
also want to express here my calling to share my faith with others
unashamedly and hopefully become a stronger witness and testimony day by day.*

*It means that I have bowed my will to Christ and gave Him
the right to be my King, and have devoted myself to expanding
His Kingdom.*

*Trusting God to have control over your life and being fully
committed to him.*

For all three groups, around one-fifth focus consistently on beliefs,
so the real differences cannot be located there (even if Evangelicals are a
bit more likely to focus on beliefs). Rather, the primary differences come
down to how much emphasis is placed on lifestyle and actions. In the case
of Evangelicals, the emphasis placed on having a relationship with Christ
is especially prominent (14 percent as compared to just 4 to 5 percent for
Mainline Protestants and Catholics) and ends up displacing the emphasis
on lifestyle and actions found among other Christians.

In his 1992 study of new Christians in England, Finney reported that
"nearly all defined a Christian, not so much by what he or she believed, but
in terms of friendship and the effect of faith upon their own life."[2] That was
not at all the case in our study, where being a friend was mentioned by only
one person. At the same time, our study found that relationships are indeed
central, and Finney's observation that faith is to be understood in terms of
a three-way relationship with God, with other people, and with one's self
holds true for the subjects of our study as well.

In chapter 5, I will outline the changes that becoming a Christian has
made in the lives of our respondents. Of course, these changes are necessarily a matter of self-reporting (we did not go around checking up on them!).
But the reader will see that the differences among Christian traditions are

2. Finney, *Finding Faith Today*, 20.

pronounced and bear great similarity to the answers about what it means to be a Christian summed up here.

HOW THE PARTICIPANTS SAW THEMSELVES

A small number (about 2 percent) of the Christian-identified respondents claimed they were not sure if they were Christians. This may seem odd, since they must first have answered that they had made a new Christian faith commitment or recommitment. But in most cases, there were lingering questions or doubts about Christ's nature, the Trinity, or other church teachings, and thus a reticence to apply the Christian label to themselves. In other cases, the respondents were hesitant to claim the label because they understood their own faith commitment to be personal rather than institutional or out of compliance with mainstream Christianity, and thus defying definition or identification as Christian. Others did not want to be defined by any one religion, or they had interests in multiple religious identities. One honest individual reported simply, "I haven't sold my worldly goods and given the proceeds to the poor."

According to a 32-year-old Roman Catholic,

> *I know I just became an official Roman Catholic, but during Lent I started re-thinking and becoming confused about the role of Christ in my life. I feel like I can become connected with God but I am dubious about the Father-Son-Spirit relationship.*

A 54-year-old Evangelical said:

> *While I follow Christ's teachings, I do not believe in the basic Christian tenets regarding the virgin birth and Christ's resurrection. I believe that Christ was one of the most important teachers in history, like the Buddha or Gandhi. Hence, while I think of myself as a follower of Christ, I think most people would not see me as "Christian" in the traditional sense.*

And a 68-year-old Mainline Protestant put her reservations this way:

> *So many definitions of "Christian." Many do not apply. Many I would want nothing to do with. I'm searching for a definition that may fit my beliefs and with which I may be comfortable.*

Though the group of those who made a new faith commitment but are still "unsure" if they are Christians is small, they represent an important contingency of persons who are still living into what that commitment means. Indeed, they may never fit quite comfortably into what some see as orthodox Christianity. They help us remember that, while Jesus is recorded as saying "the gate is narrow and the road is hard that leads to life" (Matt 7:14), not all Christians understand that narrow gate to consist of a narrow range of beliefs. It is also important to remember, however, that some of the respondents made their new commitment up to three years prior to their participation in our study. They may well have experienced changes and doubts, or they may even have begun to reconsider that commitment.

WERE THEY CHRISTIANS BEFORE THIS NEW COMMITMENT?

But what of the 98 percent of Christians who still identify as Christians? The first thing that must be said about people who make a new Christian faith commitment is that most of them have always thought of themselves, at least nominally, as Christians. Something new has recently happened to them, signaled through membership, a profession of faith, baptism, or some ritual of initiation that triggered their participation in this study. But most (about two-thirds) always thought of themselves as Christians. The exception to this is Evangelicals.

Figure 2.2 shows the ratio of persons within each of the major Christian traditions who (a) have always thought of themselves as Christians (at least nominally), (b) have not always thought of themselves as Christians and are first-time converts to the Christian faith, and (c) have not always thought of themselves as Christians but are returning to the Christian faith. Even among those who have always thought of themselves as Christians, this does not mean that they have always thought of themselves as fully committed. The vast majority of respondents (between 80 to 90 percent), regardless of tradition, understand themselves to have been less committed prior to their new commitment.

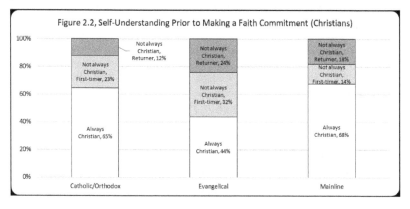

Figure 2.2, Self-Understanding Prior to Making a Faith Commitment (Christians)

Remarkably, 65 percent of Roman Catholics and 68 percent of Main-line Protestants have always understood themselves to be Christians, though their new faith commitment clearly represents some further step or a deeper dedication. Only 44 percent of Evangelicals, by contrast, have always thought of themselves as Christians. That should not be surprising since we find more Evangelicals who converted to Christianity from something else or from no religious affiliation at all, given their focus on evangelization and conversion. At the same time, the number of Evangelicals who have always thought of themselves as Christians is still twice as high as those in Finney's study twenty-five years ago in England. Finney did not use the word "Evangelical," so it is difficult to compare. But he did identify a group similar to what we now call Evangelicals in the US, comprised of New Church, Baptist, and "ecumenical" congregations. The differences between our study and his at this point illustrate the complexity of the word *Evangelical* when moving between the US and other contexts. The fact that so many Evangelicals have always thought of themselves as Christians prior to their faith commitment, moreover, may also illustrate how pervasive is a kind of "nominal Evangelicalism" in the United States. Evangelicalism has a long history and powerful cultural resonance in the US, especially in the "Bible Belt," where persons might grow up identifying with Evangelical faith even without ever having made a public faith commitment. The cultural force that is Evangelicalism in the US does not have strict parallels in many other countries of the world where nominal Christianity might be more closely associated with a state church, such as Anglicanism in England.

Finney cautioned in 1992 that "we cannot assume that people see themselves as not Christian—even if they do not go to church."[3] That continues to be true in the United States today, where there is still a high level of nominal Christianity, especially in the backgrounds of those who end up making a faith commitment. At the same time, we should not conclude more from this than the evidence warrants. All signs point to the decline of nominal Christianity in the US, as the number of those who identify as Christians continues to drop, while those with no religious affiliation (the "nones") continue to grow and now comprise about 23 percent of the population.[4]

3. Ibid., 23.
4. Pew, "America's Changing Religious Landscape," 4.

Those Who Have Not Always Thought of Themselves as Christians

When we look more closely at those who have not always understood themselves to be Christians and for whom something new and significant has occurred in terms of their self-identification, we find further important differences by tradition. Well over half of Catholics and Evangelicals in that category describe themselves as coming to faith for the first time rather than returning after a period of disaffiliation. For Mainline Protestants in this group, by contrast, these numbers are reversed. When making a new faith commitment, most of those who have not always thought of themselves as Christians are returning after a period of disaffiliation.

On one hand, then, Catholics and Mainline Protestants who make a new faith commitment share a propensity to understand themselves as always having been Christians throughout their lives—just not as committed. On the other hand, among those who did not understand themselves previously to be Christians, Catholics bear more resemblance to Evangelicals in sharing a propensity to be first-timers rather than returners. Mainline Protestants stand out, then, as a group with a higher level of Christianity (of at least a nominal variety) in their DNA. They tend to understand themselves more than others as always having been Christians. And among those who have not always been Christians, more Mainline Protestants tend to be returners rather than first-timers.

Only a few respondents (no more than about 5 percent of those who understood themselves as having become Christians for the first time) indicate that they had been adherents of other religions prior to making their new commitment, though several Evangelicals included Catholicism as a non-Christian religion, which increased their relative percentage slightly. About half of all first-time Christians understand themselves to have had no religion prior to this new commitment (about 36 percent) or to have been agnostic (about 16 percent). A few spoke of themselves as seekers, as spiritual, or as those who believed in God but were not Christians.

While it is important to highlight the differences among branches of the Christian tradition in reflecting on how persons come to faith, any Christian, church, or ministry reaching out to others should be aware of the impressive diversity in how people think of themselves. To affirm Finney's original observation, just because persons do not go to church does not mean they do not understand themselves to be Christians. This fact, placed alongside the large and growing number of persons without any Christian background, indicates that there is no "one-size-fits-all" form of Christian outreach that is best suited to the US context. While those with no religious commitment or background may be increasing as a percentage of the population, there are still a large number of persons in the US who do not think of themselves as coming to Christian faith from outside it.

COMING TO FAITH—A GRADUAL OR SUDDEN EXPERIENCE?

One of the most interesting aspects of how persons come to faith is the length of time it takes. When asked if they understood their recent commitment to be sudden enough that they could put a date on it or whether they understood it to be a more gradual process, a solid majority of Christians claim it was more gradual than sudden (Figure 2.3). Indeed, sudden conversions comprise a clear minority of cases across the board.

Figure 2.3, Was the New Commitment to Faith Sudden or Gradual? (Christians)		
	Evangelicals	Non-Evangelicals
Gradual	65%	79%
Sudden	35%	21%

Those who have always considered themselves to be Christians are more likely to describe their commitment as gradual. While they recently made a distinct and public faith commitment, they had been journeying on the Christian road for some time. By contrast, a more sudden conversion corresponds more highly to not always thinking of oneself as a Christian prior to that conversion.

Compared to other Christians, significantly more Evangelicals understand their experience of coming to faith as sudden. Given Evangelicals' greater attention to conversion and the experience of being "born again," this is to be expected. At the same time, it is much more common than not for all Christians, including Evangelicals, to experience coming to faith as a journey.

If we look at how long it took these gradualists to come to faith, the median across all Christian traditions is three years. At the same time, survey respondents reported it taking anywhere from a month to fifty years. A significant number of respondents from all Christian traditions (14 percent of Evangelicals, 22 percent of all others) could not quantify the length of the process at all, but instead answered that the process is an ongoing or lifelong one. For Evangelicals, however, the journey tends to be shorter than it is for other Christians. Evangelicals who think of their conversion as a journey are three times more likely than other Christians to identify that journey as lasting less than a year.[5] That is certainly consistent with their greater emphasis on conversion and being "born again."

Age as a factor

Age is a factor here, and though most younger persons still understand their journey to be gradual, persons aged 18 to 24 are more likely than persons over 24 to report their faith commitment as sudden (Figure 2.4). Some social psychological research has associated sudden conversion with relational transitions and attachment insecurities, which could help explain this to some extent.[6] At the same time, we also know that religious parents who are closely related to their children tend to produce religious children, so we should not conclude from these studies that persons come to faith only out of relational insecurities and crises. It may well be true, however, that relational transitions that are more characteristic of young adulthood contribute to the experience of sudden conversion.

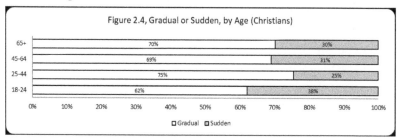

Figure 2.4, Gradual or Sudden, by Age (Christians)

Age	Gradual	Sudden
65+	70%	30%
45-64	69%	31%
25-44	75%	25%
18-24	62%	38%

- The median age at which gradualists began their journey is 30 for Evangelicals, 32 for Catholics, and 35 for Mainline Protestants.

- The median age for sudden commitments or conversions is 33 for Evangelicals, 41 for Mainline Protestants, and 44 for Catholics.[7]

In considering age as a factor in how suddenly or slowly one makes a new commitment to Christian faith, it is important to remind ourselves that

5. Nineteen percent of Evangelicals identified the process as lasting less than a year as compared to only 7 percent of Mainline and Black Protestants and only 5 percent of Roman Catholics.

6. Other studies that have examined how attachment patterns affect both the likelihood and speed of conversion are Granqvist and Hagekull, "Religiousness"; Granqvist and Kirkpatrick, "Religious conversion"; and Kirkpatrick, "God as a Substitute."

7. In Finney's study, the average age for "gradualists" was 30 and for sudden conversions was nearly 36; a bit younger than our respondents in both cases (Finney, *Finding Faith Today*, 25).

this survey sought responses only from adults 18 or older. It could be that sudden conversions are much more likely among persons under age 18. The National Association of Evangelicals (NAE), for example, reports that 11 is the median age for those who become born again, and they speak of a "4/14 Window" when evangelization is optimal—that is, between the ages of 4 and 14.[8] That reporting, based on Barna Group research, focuses on "born again" conversions of an evangelical type, so it may not apply across the board. But other studies have also shown that the average age of conversion to Christianity is earlier than age 18, so those conversions would not be captured in our study.[9]

Two observations are important here. First, we must admit that there are many conversions our study does not capture, including more sudden conversions that happen prior to age 18. Secondly, by focusing narrowly on a certain type of conversion, as the NAE does, it misses a significant number of persons who come to faith in other ways.

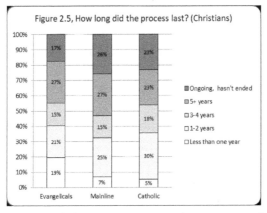

Figure 2.5, How long did the process last? (Christians)

The stereotype of the average person becoming a Christian in a moment of sudden awakening or conversion is for the most part false. It happens, of course, but not for most adults in the US. The preoccupation with getting quick results, moreover, may even be unhealthy considering the kinds of changes in life patterns, practices, commitments, beliefs, and purpose that often end up accompanying conversion. Without forgetting the reality that some people do make sudden and life-altering commitments and decisions, clearly those who want to aid others in coming to faith need to take seriously how they might come alongside those who are on a journey of faith, nourishing and nurturing them by understanding faith as a process

8. National Association of Evangelicals, "When Americans Become Christians," para. 2. See also Kennedy, "The 4–14 Window."

9. See Poston, "The Adult Gospel."

of cultivating habits, practices, convictions, and dispositions of character over time. Indeed, it is doubtful that the notion of faith as a "decision" is as accurate as it is sometimes made out to be by those who focus on securing conversions. More often than not, persons look back at their journeys of faith in key moments of commitment (baptism, confirmation, membership) and marvel at the way the path unfolded—not so much as an act of their will, decision, or understanding, but as a process of formation by a community of persons who have loved and influenced them over time.

PREVIOUS RELIGIOUS COMMITMENT

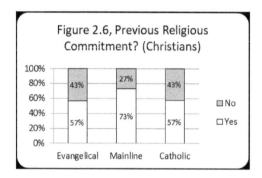

Figure 2.6, Previous Religious Commitment? (Christians)

Most Christians making a new faith commitment have made a previous religious commitment at some point in their lives (Figure 2.6). While a little over half (57 percent) of all Evangelicals and Catholics have made a previous religious commitment, interestingly, a significantly higher percentage of Mainline Protestants report having done so (73 percent).[10] This is likely because of the larger number of Mainline Protestants who leave the church in the first place, and so create a larger pool of those who have some religious experience to which they can look back. A 2014 Pew Religious Landscape Study, for example, found that the retention rate for Mainline Protestants is one of the lowest of any religious tradition (only 45 percent of those raised in Mainline Protestant churches continues to identify with it on into adulthood).[11] That same study found that for every one convert to Mainline Protestant groups, 1.7 people converted away. For Evangelicals, by contrast, for every person who left, 1.2 people converted in.

Of those who have made previous religious commitments, about half of all Evangelicals made those commitments in Evangelical churches and

10. Orthodox respondents were far more likely to have made previous commitments also (83 percent), but the sample size was insufficient to draw larger conclusions.

11. Pew, "America's Changing Religious Landscape," 39.

about half of all Mainline Protestants made them in Mainline churches (Figure 2.7). Catholics who made previous commitments come from Catholic, Evangelical, and Mainline traditions equally. Only a very few persons come to Christian faith from other religious traditions.

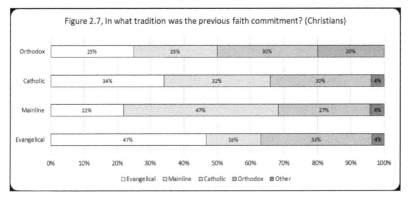

Figure 2.7, In what tradition was the previous faith commitment? (Christians)

The high percentages of those in our study who have made previous commitments is consistent with two recent reports from the Pew Research Center. The first, a 2009 report from the Pew Forum on Religion and Public Life, found that "about half of American adults have changed religious affiliation at least once during their lives."[12] This study was focused on the fluidity of religious affiliation, and so it does not intersect precisely with our study (since ours is focused only on those who have recently made a new faith commitment), but its findings provide important context for understanding our data. According to the Pew report, "Americans change religious affiliation early and often."[13] Forty-four percent of the US population do not currently belong to their childhood faith, and even among the other 56 percent, one in six had a different faith than their current one at some point in their life (Figure 2.8).[14] That represents considerable movement in religious affiliation. We know that the largest group of changers are those who have shifted to unaffiliated, so it makes sense that there would be a sizeable pool of persons—whether shifting from one religious family to another, or shifting from unaffiliated to affiliated—who can point to an earlier religious background or experience.[15]

12. Pew, "Faith in Flux," 1.

13. Ibid.

14. Ibid.

15. While 7 percent of Americans were raised unaffiliated, 16 percent now claim to be unaffiliated with any particular religion. Ibid., 8.

Figure 2.8, Changing Faiths[A]	
	Share of US Population (%)
Do not currently belong to childhood faith	44
· Raised Catholic, now unaffiliated	4
· Raised Catholic, now Protestant	5
· Raised Protestant, now unaffiliated	7
· Raised Protestant, now different Protestant faith	15
· Raised unaffiliated, now affiliated	4
· Other change in religious affiliation	9
Same faith as childhood	56
· Changed faith at some point	9
· Have not changed faith	47
Total	100

A. Pew, "Faith in Flux," 1.

The second Pew Research Center report worth mentioning at this point is the previously mentioned study in 2014, which found that, while the number of those without religious affiliation (the "nones") is growing dramatically, about eight in ten adult "nones" were raised in a religion, while the remaining 21 percent come from religiously unaffiliated backgrounds.[16] All of these data combined paint a picture of a fluid religious landscape in which many persons were raised in religious traditions but often became unaffiliated. Our study found that a sizeable number of those making new faith commitments are those who return to a faith tradition, though not necessarily the one in which they were raised.

EARLIER INVOLVEMENTS IN CHURCH

Only one-fourth of all Christians say they had no involvement in any organization or activity associated with the church during their youth. By contrast, 68 percent have participated in some form of Sunday school or Bible study, 44 percent have participated in a youth group, 16 percent have engaged in camping or scouting programs associated with a church, and 14 percent attended a religious school. These percentages vary little by Christian tradition or denomination, and are summarized in Figure 2.9. Participants in our study frequently told stories about the importance of those involvements, though these tended to be less important in shaping

16. Pew, "America's Changing Religious Landscape," 39.

their current commitment and had more to do with the overall journey that led up to the commitment.

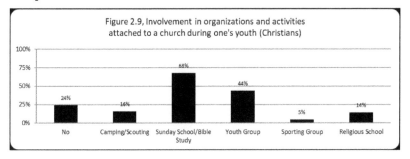

Figure 2.9, Involvement in organizations and activities attached to a church during one's youth (Christians)

INSTRUCTION IN THE FAITH

Among Christians, there are pronounced differences in the importance of catechesis and instruction in the faith as part of the conversion and recommitment process. These intersect closely with the very meaning of faith and salvation among Christian traditions discussed previously. For Catholics, coming to faith is becoming part of a church, a liturgical tradition, and a way of life ordered by practices, so that conversion is the acquisition of that way of life. One has to learn how to become a Catholic Christian. Almost all (90 percent) Catholics report attending instructional classes as part of the conversion process. For Evangelicals, on the other end of the spectrum, conversion is more about acceptance of Christ as one's personal savior. For many Evangelicals, this can be done in a moment of time and does not always require catechesis and training, at least at the moment of decision. Only 56 percent of Evangelicals report attending such classes. Over two-thirds of Mainline Evangelicals report attending instructional classes, which demonstrates the continued importance of catechesis and training in that tradition. For Christians of all stripes, there is virtually no difference in how they viewed the importance of such classes when they did take them—a remarkable 96 to 98 percent found them helpful.

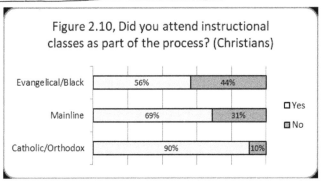

Figure 2.10, Did you attend instructional classes as part of the process? (Christians)

3

Christians: The Journey

WHY DID THEY DO IT?

Among the most important questions to be asked and answered in exploring why people make a new faith commitment is *why*? Why did they decide to make this new declaration or commitment? While Christians provided a staggering variety of answers to this question, their answers tend to cluster around a few types of responses, though with important differences among the major Christian traditions. In chapter 4, we will explore the primary factors involved in making a faith commitment, and there is certainly some overlap between the responses there *(what were the primary and supporting factors in your coming to faith?)* and the responses here *(why did you do it?)*. Yet answers to the question "why?" have a slightly different cast to them, and are more likely to focus on key incidents that primed the decision or led to the experience of coming to faith.

The top two sets of responses to the question of "why?" have to do with (a) one's desire to grow and take next steps in a faith journey, including making a public and/or fuller commitment, and (b) the influence and appeal of a congregation or those within the congregation such as the minister and other key persons.

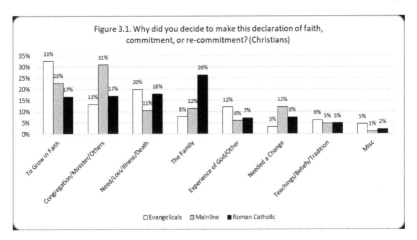

Figure 3.1. Why did you decide to make this declaration of faith, commitment, or re-commitment? (Christians)

Growing in the faith and "going public"

Many of those who make a new faith commitment or recommitment do so as way of marking publicly what has happened to them—whether that is a conversion experience or a new and significant step in their journey of faith. Their responses to the question of why they made this new commitment cluster around the desire to grow in faith or to "go public" with their faith. One out of three Evangelicals mentioned this first set of responses. Their response rate was significantly more frequent than we found in other Christian traditions, though it was the second most frequently mentioned response by Mainline Protestants (at 23 percent), whose responses were spread out more evenly among other types of answers. Here are some of the typical ways of expressing this reason for making a new faith commitment, taken from among the respondents in the study:

> To "make official" putting down roots in a new church denomination and congregation after several years of searching. Also to feel more fully involved in the church's activities and life.

> To formally break from the Catholic Church and have a formal ceremony to indicate my commitment to a new denomination.

> I had always considered myself a Christian, just hadn't had an opportunity to be baptized.

> To symbolize the profession of my faith in Christ Jesus. That my life is no longer my own and I've been cleansed of my sins and now want to follow Jesus no matter the cost.

I felt moved by the Holy Spirit to openly declare my belief and faith in Jesus Christ as my savior. As belief grew from logical to spiritual, making a declaration became important to me.

The Congregation

In answer to the question of why persons made a new faith commitment, another of the most popular answers had to do with the congregation. This was the favorite among Mainline Protestants, who gravitated in this direction almost twice as often as Catholics and well over twice as often as Evangelicals. The frequency of this response is a testament to the influence and importance among Mainline Protestants (and a significant number of other Christians) of congregations, their programs and outreach, their members and ministers. Many of the persons who talked about the importance of the congregation used language like "fit," "acceptance," "welcome," and "comfort." Others cited their desire to participate more fully in the congregation they had already been attending as the reason for their decision.

I had been attending the local [church] for about 6 years and had never formally become a member. I felt that it was time to "jump in" rather than stand on the edge of this community, mainly out of respect and obligation for the members of the church.

The communion and community of my new faith helps me feel completely accepted and loved for who I am and where I am in my life and relationship by and with God.

I found a church who was progressive and open minded enough that religion felt "real" again.

I wanted to be a part of the community. The people in this church were friendly. The pastor made a point to greet me every week and get to know me and my family.

I have been wanting to make a re-commitment to my faith for a long time now and as a lesbian in a 17-year relationship with my partner we have not felt welcomed in most churches until we found this one.

Adversity, Loss, and Need

The third most frequent set of responses (about 16 percent of all responses) focused on adversity, loss, or need as leading them to this new commitment.

About half of the persons whose responses are included in this third category talked about <u>something missing or empty in their lives.</u> Many spoke about being on a quest to find purpose, peace, and direction while others were looking to satisfy some need—whether spiritual or relational.

> *To continue a search for truth, purpose and meaning in life.*

> *Something was missing from my life and it was a calling to come back to the church.*

> *There was an enormous hole in my life.*

> *I needed a sense of direction for my faith, more than just a spirituality.*

Evangelicals were far more likely to express this need in explicitly religious terms such as a need for God, Christ, salvation, or freedom from sin and guilt.

> *I understood and came to know that I was a sinner and there was a divide between me and God and I wanted to surrender and give my life to him.*

> *I need Christ in my life.*

> *I understood what Jesus did at the cross for me and wanted to have my sins forgiven so I can spend eternity with Him.*

While half of the respondents in this third category focused on filling a void, satisfying a need, or looking for direction and meaning, the other half talked about coming to faith in relation to a crisis, trauma, illness, accident, unemployment, divorce, addiction, death, or other loss in their lives.

> *I had always wanted to be a member of the Catholic Church but never followed through with it. I faced a life-threatening illness and decided to move ahead with it.*

> *I lost my husband to cancer and felt guided by the Holy Spirit to convert.*

> *A need for God in my life because of past abuse, rejection, and drug abuse. I didn't want to go back to a lifestyle of pain and I knew God was my only way out.*

> *My oldest child died suddenly and I found my comfort in God and my church family. So I repented and came back to my faith.*

> *I was at a crossroads in my life. Something needed changing and I determined that it was me. My marriage was in trouble and I, alone, could not fix or repair it.*

The Family

One in four Catholics said the reason they took this new step was for the sake of the family, to promote unity in the family, or because of the influence of the family. That is twice the number of Mainline Protestants in that category and over three times the number of Evangelicals. We should not conclude from this that the family is unimportant as a motivator for other Christians, but clearly for Catholics coming to faith is often motivated by family-oriented considerations.

> I felt ready to declare my faith after marrying a strong Christian man who showed me how God works in his life and how he could work in mine as well.

> Having a child and wanting her to be baptized and to have a church community was the main motivation.

> Preparing for marriage. Wanted my marriage and life to be as blessed as my grandparents' was. Wondered what their secret was. Most important thing of all to them was their faith in Christ.

> We have a young family and wanted to provide them with spiritual guidance, we saw joining a church as a good way to do that. I did it because my parents wanted me to do it.

Direct Call from God or Other Experience

When asked why they made this new faith commitment, an average of 8 percent of all respondents talked about coming to faith in response to a direct call from God or some spiritual experience in their lives.

> God was speaking to me to be baptized. It was my way of knowing that God was in my heart and I had found my perfect church home.

> I was inspired to re-affirm my faith after working through the Twelve Steps of Alcoholics Anonymous and having a spiritual awakening.

> I was moved to by the Holy Spirit who worked through the beautiful worship music that filled my heart with joy and the direct, articulate messages from our lead pastor.

> After one of my bad dreams I felt like I received a message that I need to clean my body from all sins and be reborn to be closer with God.

I felt at home. I felt Jesus had been calling me home to the Catholic Church for a long time. I felt at peace with the Eucharist.

I had a profound religious experience where I for a brief moment felt the raw power of God guiding to the church. It was wonderful and terrifying.

Needed a Change

Another 8 percent (on average) had recently moved to a new city or just wanted something new in their lives. In some cases, they were dissatisfied with their present church or faith tradition, or wanted to get back to the faith of their earlier years.

Recently moved to this area and feel it is very important to belong to a faith community where we live.

The church I was attending did not satisfy my spiritual needs.

I have always had faith and been committed to my church but left the Roman Catholic church due to disagreeing with certain social issues and feeling judged.

Finally fully retired and looking for new ways to repurpose my life. There was a big void in my life as I entered full retirement and I really felt the need to return to my roots in the church.

Lastly, an average of 5 percent of all respondents said the reason they made their new commitment was because of the teachings of the Bible or some new understanding or belief at which they had arrived. Some of these folks also mentioned the importance of their own particular Christian tradition or denomination.

I didn't grow up in church, but when presented with the Gospel of Jesus Christ, I found the message of the Christian Faith and sacrifice of a just and loving God compelling. Through receiving forgiveness for my sins by God's grace through faith, I have found that my life is filled with joy.

Because I believe Jesus died for me, and I believe in the Bible and what it teaches; so I knew it to be the right thing to do.

THE "GRADUALISTS"—IMPORTANT INCIDENTS ALONG THE WAY

In the remainder of this chapter, I will distinguish between the "gradual-ists" and the "conversionists," to borrow language from Finney's previous study. Recall that about two out of three Evangelicals and four out of five non-Evangelicals claim to have come to faith gradually. We asked those who experienced coming to faith as a gradual process whether there were any particularly important incidents during their journey. Most said yes, and their answers were remarkably diverse but paint a picture of persons going through significant life changes, experiencing the acceptance and inclusion of a congregation, or being influenced by key persons in their lives. About half of all responses from the gradualists had a more or less positive tone to them, while roughly a quarter referenced distressing circumstances such as divorce, addiction, death, job loss, prison, or illness. While the question asked for key "incidents," the answers often reference a process of change comprised of numerous incidents over time. Bear in mind that the percent-ages listed below are from among the gradualists only, not the total pool of Christian respondents in the study. Also, the percentages included with each category below do not add up to 100 percent since persons were en-couraged to identify multiple incidents if they wished.

The influence of a congregation (19 percent)

We know from our respondents that coming to faith over a long period frequently includes the support and nurture of a local congregation. In fact, about one in five gradualists mention the importance of a local church or faith community. Finding the right faith community provides a home for faith and a company of travelers on the road one is traveling. Words most often used to describe that community were *welcoming, open, inspiring, home, loving, supporting,* and *the right one for me.* Gradualists also describe their congregations as places where they feel engaged, comfortable, and challenged, and as a place where they can share their journey with others. A good number of the responses that mentioned the influence of a lo-cal church also mentioned the importance of rituals or sacraments, such as communion. Those types of responses were more frequently given by Catholics and members of traditions with an emphasis on liturgy and sacra-ment, as one might expect.

> *Coming across an amazing church that welcomed up with open arms and finding a priest whom we love and respect.*

Finding a Roman Catholic Mass offered to gays and lesbians.

I found a church that inspired my walk and my growth.

I [once] kept my faith within me, and now I have a home in which to share it and share the company of others.

I found the love a support of a church family that loves me for me, supports me in everything I do and encourages me to step out of my comfort zone.

Bereavement (10 percent)

One out of ten of all gradualists mentioned the death of a loved one and how that ended up serving as a catalyst or significant event for re-thinking life and its meaning.

My mother died prior to this and opened my eyes to a real eternity.

Going through the death of 2 grandparents. Also beginning to think about my parent's eventual deaths and the desire to have my own children. The concept of the circle of life was very meaningful to me during this time.

The death of my sister at a young age sparked a lot of questions and thinking that focused me on spirituality.

Mother committed suicide.

I was dealing with my grief over a traumatic miscarriage.

Marriage, engagement, partnering (9 percent)

The influence of a partner, spouse, or fiancé can often serve as the key stimulus in the process of coming to faith. At other times, it is not so much the influence of that partner but rather the very experience of getting married and starting a new life together that prompts the desire for a unified faith commitment.

I met and married my husband, who is a Roman Catholic.

Met my fiancé. We became serious and started to discuss faith and its importance in our future and in our future kids' lives.

*My partner (from a different Christian tradition) and I were look-
ing for a church that could be a middle way for us.*

Childbirth and the influence of children (8 percent)

For some persons, having children is a time to rethink life's priorities and
the importance of God and matters of faith. At times, taking children to
church or watching them as they take steps of faith can be influential on the
parents or relatives.

*As we expected our first child, my wife and I wanted to bring our
daughter up in the church.*

The birth of my son started my desire to be closer to God.

*Our daughter asking to become involved in the church and com-
mitting herself*

Spiritual Incidents and Journeying (8 percent)

A good number of those responding to this question chose to describe what
was happening along the way in almost wholly religious or spiritual terms,
or as a growing awareness of spiritual need. For some it was a sense of being
at peace or being blessed. Others described a period of God speaking to
them, "working on their hearts," revealing Godself, or calling them—often
through prayer, Scripture, or the lives of others. Some spoke of encountering God or Jesus while others described a new self-understanding or mindfulness. While most persons who cited incidents of a more spiritual nature
described their experience in positive terms, there was also a minority of
persons who used the language of darkness, confusion, brokenness, depression, trials, and anger.

Church-related events (7 percent)

Christian gradualists cited an impressive list of conferences, retreats, study
groups, formation programs, camps, and special services that are a reminder
of the important role of church and parachurch programs in Christian outreach and formation. Some were formal initiation programs like the Rite of
Christian Initiation for Adults (RCIA) in the Roman Catholic Church (see

more on that below) or other denominational initiation and confirmation programs. Most often mentioned were church-based small groups, such as Bible study or other study groups, recovery groups, youth groups, inquirers classes, and even church sporting groups. A good number of persons mentioned the importance of mission trips and community service programs in their process of growing in faith.

> *Another powerful point during this time is when I was invited to attend a Catholic retreat—Cursillo. This particular retreat, my first as an adult, was another turning point for me in understanding God's immense love and forgiveness for me (and others) as well as the love of an active Christian community of believers.*

> *I had attended a mom's group bible study and the topic was Grace. It hit me that that was what I was missing from life. I felt like everything I had in life was perfect, yet why wasn't I happy? I pondered the message for several months and that's when it came to me. I wanted to commit my life to Christ. I've never felt better!*

> *The educational class that I took at the Episcopal Church was very informative and the priest that taught the class was so helpful and made me feel so welcome.*

> *Working in a soup kitchen for the poor.*

> *Conversations with my friend about religion; being invited to join the church men's softball team; my children's involvement in Sunday school and youth group.*

Divorce (6 percent)

Marriage, cited earlier, was mentioned by a sizeable number of respondents, but so also were divorce and other romantic break-ups, which often have the consequence of leaving persons contemplating a new start, including a new spiritual start. In a few cases, the divorce was included in or the result of the decision to grow in faith, especially when the marriage was reported as an abusive one. In some other cases, marital problems were a catalyst that drove persons to faith.

> *I was widowed . . . ; then in an abusive relationship and marriage for 12 years, [then] divorced. . . . After a period of despair and depression, I found myself living alone, making new friends, exercising and getting healthy and becoming contented. This was part of my process of "reformation."*

During my divorce I began this process. I began a relationship with someone who was very committed and helped to reignite the desire for me.

The influence of friends, family, Christians, or other individuals (6 percent)

Those on a gradual journey of faith mentioned a number of persons who had influenced them along the way. Some of these influential persons intentionally provided advice and support, but others were influences without ever trying, and instead were simply present as exemplars of faith.

Reading the Bible for the first time and being mentored by my employer who was a very strong Christian. . . . He was truly a mentor to me as I attempted to study the Bible. My mother-in-law was also a great influence as she too lived by the word of God and was a very fine example to me as well as a wonderful advisor when I had questions regarding my studies.

Regularly exposed to people whose lives were different than mine. I desired what they had. A personal relationship with Jesus Christ was the difference.

I met a neighbor who was quite devout and, from my perspective, seemed to live within the Christian faith. She, without trying, nudged me off the proverbial fence I had been sitting on for such a long time.

I met my best friend who is Muslim and wears a hijab. She brought me closer to my own faith.

Contact with a minister (3 percent)

To the above group, we should add the influence of a minister or priest. In chapter 4, I will give more attention to the importance of clergy as a factor in how people come to faith.

Reading and Study (4 percent)

Several persons mentioned reading and study as central to their journey, and half of those in this category mentioned the Bible. Other sources include both early church writings and contemporary religious literature. For some individuals, the reading was conducted more like a search for answers and often involved reading Scripture or, in some cases, literature from other religious traditions while on the quest.

> *Attended a bible study that answered many questions and got into more parts of the bible that were now causing me to be disturbed. Also pointed out things that I hadn't seen before.*

> *Reading the Bible cover to cover using the study application guide. By year's end, I was a Believer.*

> *. . . a gradual process of learning about Christianity and what I was "signing up" for. What does it mean? What are the values? What do I make of the Bible and what can I understand from it?*

Health-related problems, addictions (4 percent)

Health problems, aging, accidents, surgeries, and cancer surface frequently as important incidents on the way. These were often cited as the respondent's own problems, but just as often they were related to close friends and loved ones. A third of the respondents in this category mentioned addictions to drugs and alcohol. All of these situations, while they frequently yielded opportunities to reexamine one's life, also led to other stresses related to relationship problems and the loss of employment and income.

Other life changes (4 percent)

Persons experiencing coming to faith as a gradual process also mentioned a variety of other life changes such as relocating, travel, unemployment, finding a new job, going to college, aging or retiring, and, for a few, being arrested or going to prison.

Other Responses

There were incidents contained in the responses from the gradualists that don't really fit in any one of the categories above, yet they reveal the remarkable range of incidents that make up one's journey to faith. Some of those include spending time at a monastery, infighting or scandal in one's home church or religious family that led the person to look elsewhere, family dysfunction, loss of one's business, or coming out as gay or lesbian.

Individuals and congregations who hope to reach out to, travel alongside, or support persons undertaking a journey of faith would do well to understand the complexity of that journey and its inevitable variability. Though we can paint a fairly coherent picture of the kinds of incidents most likely to be important to people who gradually come to faith, it is impossible to predict ahead of time what might lead any one person to rethink the direction of his or her life.

THE CONVERSIONISTS—WHAT WAS HAPPENING AT THE TIME?

If we now change gears and ask what was happening in the lives of those who reported coming to faith more suddenly, we find some similarities in responses but also some conspicuous differences. As with the gradualists, many of these persons emphasize the adversity or troubles they were facing at the time, while others emphasize that which more positively drew them into the experience.

The influence of a congregation (20 percent)

Just as in the case of those who came to faith gradually, one in five conversionists mention the importance of a local congregation or faith community as the context or catalyst for their conversion.

I attended the Requiem Mass on All Saints Day in November, 2012. I had been participating in RCIA, but that was the moment at which I clearly decided to become a Catholic. I had been searching spiritually for a context in which to frame grief, joy, and the extremes of emotion, and experienced peace during that Mass in a way I had not before.

I had been looking to get back into church for a few years, but had difficulty finding a church that my family felt comfortable being a part of. Was recently invited to attend this church and accepted. Within three weeks of attending, I felt God calling to me and it was time. I approached the pastor after the service and asked him to pray with me and that I wanted to be saved. It was done immediately. After attending a class to get oriented to the church, I asked to be baptized as soon as possible.

My husband and I had just moved 230 miles for a new job (which I had prayed for), and we had talked about wanting to find a new church. So we volunteered to help at this church to deliver beds to needy kids and they said we should come to a service. So we went to the church service and I felt happier that I had went. We went the next week and during the sermon it felt like God touched my shoulder and gave me peace, I started crying and my husband was worried but I told him it was a good kind of cry. I felt so light and happy that I thought I might burst. I have never felt that way before and I can't even remember what the sermon was about but I believe that I found God that day.

I decided to attend a Quaker Meeting. The silence awakened me and hearing the wisdom of others broadened my perspective. Also, everyone was friendly but genuine.

Situations of despair, need, or experiencing life as out of control (17 percent)

Some people found themselves in troubling or desperate situations, looking for direction, feeling confused, or needing strength, community, or God. Several persons used even stronger language, such as *feeling empty, hitting rock bottom*, or experiencing their lives as *out of control*.

Felt an emptiness inside me. I knew there was something more I should do with my life and felt that only God could fill that void. Sitting at church with a friend that had invited me, I couldn't stop myself when the preacher asked for people to come down front to be saved. Was the best decision I have ever made.

I got to a point where I had nowhere else to go and knew without God I couldn't do it.

Divorce, financial ruin and major depression led me into AA, and from there I was spiritually reconnected to my faith.

I had hit rock bottom and I prayed for God to help me and He whispered to me, "Child, you need to call on me all the time and not just when you need help."

Was considering suicide. God called out to me. This turned my life around. Started a full commitment to Christ.

Encounter with or Experience of God, or the Divine (10 percent)

One out of ten Christians who experience coming to faith suddenly describe their conversion less with reference to various social situations or personal influences, and more to the direct action of God, or the divine. These respondents describe their encounters as moments of conviction, repentance, salvation, and transformation.

> That night . . . God convicted me of my sin and showed me that I was a sinner before God and needing to be born again. Then the Holy Spirit drew me to the altar where I bowed before God, repenting of my sin and believed the gospel message of Christ and was gloriously and wonderfully saved by God's grace. My life at that moment changed and has been progressively changing ever since!!!!!

> I was driving to a job and just knew I had to accept Christ and be born again. It truly was a "gut" feeling.

> I was watching the interaction between Pope Francis and a child on television, the Holy Spirit touched my heart and I knew immediately that I needed to return to the church. It was his modeling of Christ, his spirit and genuine love for all.

> I drank a lot one night in college, and then I heard a voice from up above telling me that I needed to be saved and commit to Christ. I decided to become Christian for the sake of my being a more humble, graceful person.

> I experienced an intervention from Mary in the form of The Virgin of Guadalupe in 2008.

> I have felt the touch of the Holy Spirit through my body at least four, maybe five times in my life so far! I have always known my heart lives for God the father Jesus his son and the love of all by the touch of the Holy Spirit.

Evangelistic event, group, or class (6 percent)

Evangelistic events, programs, classes, and church groups comprise a small percentage of incidents that proved key to those experiencing a more sudden conversion, but are nonetheless important to consider.

> I became involved with a group of young adult Quakers who were exploring the roots of our faith. I found Christ in the appropriate

*context, which had always escaped me beforehand. My eyes were
finally opened and I began regular bible study on my own.*

*I went to a conference with my Campus Ministry in February,
. . . and during that we had many different rallies where we heard
the gospel each time. It was on the second night where I felt like I
could relate very well to the talk that he was giving, as he was in a
Fraternity, and I am in a Sorority. It was that night that I realized
that the gospel applies to all people, no matter how bad or broken
we are.*

I made a commitment to Jesus at a crusade.

I accepted Jesus into my heart at a Young Life camp.

Bereavement (5 percent)

As with the "gradualists," the conversionists were sometimes led to a new
faith decision or commitment after experiencing the death of a loved one.

My longtime boyfriend was murdered.

*My husband died very suddenly at home. I attended a grief group
at a nearby church and that caused me to move back into my faith.*

*My Grandfather asked me near the time of his death if I knew that
I was saved. I answered that I did without thinking about it. This
question though stirred my thinking. After he died I knew that I
had only been saved before because I had felt talked into it and the
need for "fire insurance" from Hell. Nine days after my Grandfather died I could no longer handle it and knew that I would never
see him again if I didn't change my life. I was saved that day.*

Influence of family member(s) (5 percent)

The influence of family members was cited by a small percentage of conversionists, and in some cases that amounted simply to a request that one
go to church. In other cases, this took the form of an invitation to go *with* a
member of the family. About a third of these references to the influence of a
family member focus on a spouse or partner.

*My husband kept asking me to become Catholic because he want-
ed all of us to be together if we were to pass away. I also wanted to
become Catholic for myself and our children.*

*Visiting with my cousins and they were witnessing to me and I
answered the call.*

*Came to live with daughter and son-in-law who are believers
and living current lives in a Christ like walk. Started discussing
life and practices and began to pray and start reading the bible
again. Started attending church services with them over the past 6
months and felt the desire to recommit my life to Jesus.*

Influence of minister (often through sermons) (4 percent)

Several of those converting to faith more suddenly cited the influence of
their minister. Most often that influence was described with reference to the
clergyperson's preaching.

*I was emotionally broken. I was attending church for two years
and wasn't really getting anywhere. I found myself going less and
less. I notified my pastor about wanting to talk to him. We sched-
uled a meeting. During the talk he said something about God
being at a table with all of His gifts laid out and that I simply
had to sit down to receive those gifts. Now looking back, it kind
of seems like a selfish perspective. But I don't know why. I just
imagined God sitting there with a smile and open arms. I realized I needed Him at that moment. After that I professed my faith
in Jesus Christ in my pastor's car, in front of a Denny's, and got
baptized a few weeks later.*

*The pastor gave a sermon one Sunday and it just clicked that being
baptized was something I wanted to do. To show that I am committed to God, that I had waited long enough and I was unaware
as to why I was waiting.*

Influence of Others (4 percent)

Respondents also cited non-clergypersons as having a key role in the experience of coming to faith suddenly.

*A close friend of mine had come to Christ and seeing how God had
changed him made me want what he had found.*

My friend . . . asked if I suddenly died and didn't have a chance to accept Jesus Christ as my personal God and savior, where would my soul go? So I asked my pastor at that time to be baptized.

I met a stranger on a plane that shared his faith and at the time I was a new age believer and believed in a God but I didn't believe the bible was the word of God and I was skeptical of the Christian religion and didn't want to be a part of any church. After my encounter with this man, I had an overwhelming desire to know Jesus. I have been on fire ever since.

Evangelistic material (4 percent)

A few persons mentioned radio shows, religious books, television shows, and one mentioned the film *The Passion of the Christ*.

Marriage problems/divorce (4 percent)

As with the 6 percent of gradualists who mentioned marital and relational problems as key incidents along the way, 4 percent of the conversionists found divorce or marriage problems the catalyst for their new commitment.

I had recently been divorced and was just at a point that I KNEW that God was making His presence felt again.

My marriage was ending. I was running two departments at work. My health was poor. My friend asked me, "What are you doing for yourself?" and I had no answer. I began exercising and praying. I remembered the joy I felt in college when I used to take an early admission student to Mass, so I started attending a Catholic church. I felt compelled to go every week. During the Mass, I would tear up with joy. I found peace.

I went through a divorce and it broke me. I turned to the Lord and He changed my life.

A new understanding or decision (4 percent)

A small percentage of respondents spoke less of particular circumstances that contributed to their coming to faith and instead focused on the new understanding they reached or decision they made.

Came to believe in Christ as my savior.

I heard the Good News about Jesus and understood that I had sin and would go to hell if I had died without making a profession of faith in Jesus Christ. I believe what the Bible says about Jesus is true and that he will save me.

Basically, I finally recognized how God was working in my life. . . . How hard he had been trying to get through to me in so many different ways. And finally I decided to take notice.

Became more enlightened.

Other factors

A host of other incidents and influences were cited by conversionists as key factors or catalysts in their coming to faith. For some, prayer, dreams, or visions made the difference. For others, reading the Bible was cited as the most important factor at the time. Life changes such as loss of a job, retirement, or having children were mentioned by several respondents, while others identified situations where they were trying to overcome addictions or where a loved one was facing some sort of major surgery or life-threatening illness. While those who spoke of addictions all spoke of their own personal struggles, interestingly no respondents who mentioned health crises spoke about their own health issues. It was always the illness of a loved one that was the most important catalyst leading to their conversion.

For both those who come to faith gradually and those who see it as happening suddenly enough such that they could put a date on it, the influence of a congregation was mentioned most often in reciting what was happening at the time. That fact alone ought to be a wake-up call both for congregations (who need to take seriously their influence) and for those who tend to see evangelism as primarily a matter of campaigns, programs, and gimmicks, or as focused on the use of mass media. Relationships with other humans, often over long periods of time, matter tremendously. While experiences of despair, loss, need, struggle, and lack of purpose are more frequently associated with more sudden faith commitments than with more gradual journeys, for both groups the context for coming to faith is just as likely one of more positive questing, conversation, and constructive influences rather than a mere reaction to desperation or pain.

EXTERNAL CIRCUMSTANCES

In order to get a fuller picture of what was happening to Christians when they were making this new faith commitment, we asked both about their states of mind and about any significant external circumstances at the time. In response to the question, "was anything particularly important happening in your life?" over a third of the responses pointed to loss or suffering, often of a quite serious nature. Yet given the fact that, for most persons, coming to faith is experienced gradually as a journey over time, it is not surprising that many of the responses include a variety of circumstances, some more positive and some more negative, during that time. While 21 percent could not identify anything in particular that was worthy of mention, the most common responses were:

- 14 percent—Searching for meaning and purpose or trying to grow spiritually and in other ways

- 12 percent —Trauma, depression, loneliness, identity questions, or the experience of life spinning out of control

- 12 percent—Experiencing life transitions (for example: college/graduate school, graduating, retirement, job changes, or facing an "empty nest")

- 10 percent—Divorce or other marital and relationship problems

- 9 percent—Having children or grandchildren

- 9 percent—Bereavement

- 8 percent—Getting engaged or married

- 8 percent—Dealing with illness, injury, accident, or addictions

INTERNAL STATE OF MIND

We asked about the state of mind of our participants at the time they made their new commitment. Their responses were divided about equally between states of mind that could reasonably be considered negative or undesirable, on one hand, and more neutral or positive, fulfilled states of mind, on the other hand. Responses fell broadly into the following three types:

More negatively tending responses

- 24 percent—depressed and unhappy

- 11 percent—confused and anxious
- 5 percent—lost, unfulfilled, missing something

Questing or open responses

- 19 percent—questioning, searching, or open

Neutral or positively tending responses

- 27 percent—content and happy
- 8 percent—focused, clear, certain, determined
- 6 percent—normal, nothing stands out

In the first grouping above, we can see that about 40 percent of all Christians described themselves as having been unhappy or in need of help at the time. In several cases, the depression and loneliness were quite severe, and a few even described themselves as suicidal. Quite often, the incidents I have already outlined above had a close and causal relationship to experiences of loss, loneliness, depression, and anxiety. Only a very few persons used the language of guilt or sinfulness to describe their state, and this is consistent with the fact that very few Christians in our study described coming to faith with words like *repentance* or *forgiveness*—only 6 percent of the conversionists (almost all of them Evangelicals) and less than 1 percent of the gradualists. What Finney wrote twenty-five years ago is true of the persons in our study as well: "The picture of guilt-ridden, self-accusatory people finding psychological release by turning to Christianity is sometimes painted. If it is true at all, it is true for only a small minority—the great majority of the stories which the participants told did not fit this pattern."[1]

By contrast with those who were hurting or unhappy, 41 percent expressed no dissatisfaction with their lives at the time and the majority of those persons used positive terms such as *content, peaceful, positive,* or *happy*. The middle 19 percent described themselves as *questioning, searching,* or *open,* but not especially *unhappy, hurting,* or *confused*. They had simply reached points in their lives where they were receptive to, if not searching for, faith.

1. Finney, *Finding Faith Today*, 34.

PRAYER

Prayer is a largely accepted practice for most of those who make a new faith commitment, with over one-half reporting that they prayed daily or weekly at that time. According to research undertaken by the Pew Research Center in the US context, 45 percent of all persons and 55 percent of all Christians claim to pray daily—much higher than the percentages reported in our study (Figure 3.2).[2] Of course, our question asks about prayer prior to one's new faith commitment in order to understand the background to their experience.

The fact that Mainline Protestants report having prayed much more frequently than Evangelicals prior to their new commitment makes sense if we remember that Evangelicals are more likely to have come to faith suddenly and from outside of any awareness of Christian belonging. Mainline Protestants, by contrast, are more likely to have always understood themselves as Christians, at least nominally, and as coming to faith gradually. Perhaps it is not surprising, then, that they would report higher rates of daily and weekly prayer. All in all, fewer than a quarter of all respondents report that they had never or seldom prayed prior to their new commitment.

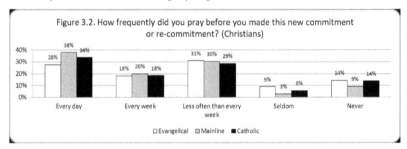

Figure 3.2. How frequently did you pray before you made this new commitment or re-commitment? (Christians)

CONSCIOUSNESS OF GOD

We also asked persons how much they had thought about God prior to making their commitment, and, as Figure 3.3 shows, about 9 out of 10 persons had. Between 40 to 50 percent had thought a great deal about God. In chapter 5, we will look more closely at how their understanding of God changed during this time.

---

2. Pew, "5 Facts about Prayer," para. 5. Interestingly, in Bishop Finney's study in the UK, only 25 percent of respondents reported to have prayed daily and 15 percent weekly. Finney, *Finding Faith Today*, 34.

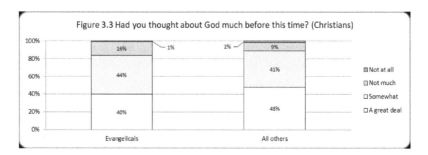

Figure 3.3 Had you thought about God much before this time? (Christians)

DRAWN IN BY OTHERS OR ACTIVE SEEKERS?

One of the striking conclusions of the study was the confirmation that persons who come to faith tend to consider themselves active seekers in the process rather than persons who were drawn in by others without actively seeking. More than 8 out of 10 new (or recommitted) Christians say they were "somewhat" or "very much" actively seeking (Figure 3.4). There are, of course, external influences and invitations from others, but most individuals who end up making a faith commitment characterize themselves as actively carrying out a quest and are less likely to describe themselves as having been drawn in by others without actively seeking. Indeed, less than half of all Christians in the study describe themselves as drawn in by others without actively seeking.

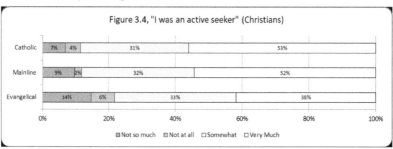

Figure 3.4, "I was an active seeker" (Christians)

Exceptions to this are Evangelicals, who we know tend to be highly motivated to bring others to Christian faith. For them, the situation is mixed. While it is true that most Evangelicals consider themselves to have been active seekers, that number is lower than with other Christians and, likewise, the number of Evangelicals who understand themselves to have been drawn in by others rather than actively seeking is far greater than other Christian groups (60 percent of Evangelicals in contrast to 45 percent of others). In fact, 10 percent of Evangelicals claim to have been both "very much" actively seeking and, at the same time, "very much" drawn in by others without actively seeking.[3]

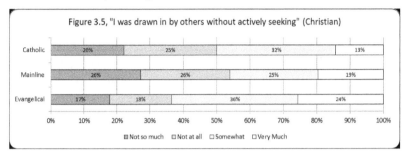

Figure 3.5, "I was drawn in by others without actively seeking" (Christian)

RELIGIOUS OR SPIRITUAL?

The fact that the majority of those we studied thought of themselves as actively seeking does not mean that they belong to the category of "religious seekers" documented by Wade Clark Roof.[4] Roof studied baby boomers (those born between 1946 to 1964) and found that they were increasingly turning to religious questing and spiritual seeking, though not necessarily to organized religion. This is the group that often claims to be "spiritual but not religious." But that kind of seeking is not the same kind we asked about in this study. The fact that all the persons we studied made faith commitments in the context of a church (that is where we went to look for them in the first place) meant that there was already some positive connection to organized religion. For the most part (almost two-thirds of Mainline Protestants and Catholics), the Christians in our study had no problem thinking of themselves as "both spiritual and religious" (Figure 3.6), even if Evangelicals were a little less likely than others to do so. It is worth noting that Catholics and Orthodox are far more willing than others to describe themselves simply as "religious."

3. As compared to just 2 percent of Catholics and 4 percent of Mainline Protestants, who chose "very much" to both questions.

4. Roof, *A Generation of Seekers*.

Figure 3.6, "Religious" or "Spiritual"? (Christians)					
	"Religious"	"Spiritual but not Religious"	"Both Spiritual and Religious"	"Neither Spiritual nor Religious"	"Don't know"
Evangelical	15%	26%	49%	2%	8%
Mainline	15%	14%	62%	1%	8%
Catholic/ Orthodox	25%	6%	62%	2%	5%

We learned that there are important generational dynamics at work in these responses. Recent studies show that millennials (those born between 1981 to 1997) do not fit easily in the "spiritual but not religious" category, and that is true of our study as well, at least for non-Evangelicals. As Christian Smith says:

> Very, very few American adolescents appear to be caught up in the much discussed phenomenon of "spiritual seeking" by "spiritual but not religious" seekers on a quest for higher meaning. . . . Contrary to popular perceptions, the vast majority of American adolescents are not spiritual seekers or questers of the type often described by journalists and some scholars, but are instead mostly orientated toward and engaged in conventional religious traditions and communities.[5]

While Smith's findings are consistent with what we heard from Mainline and Catholic respondents in our study, Evangelicals are, again, an exception. Evangelical millennials are four to five times as likely as their Mainline or Catholic counterparts to refer to themselves as "spiritual but not religious" (Figure 3.7). But then Evangelicals from the baby boomer (1946 to 1964) and silent (1928 to 1945) generations are also much more likely to choose "spiritual but not religious." This may be due to the greater tendency among Evangelicals to accentuate a spirituality of the heart and an inward relationship with Christ and to play down external and more formal elements associated with the label "religious" (liturgy, vestments, episcopacy, iconography, etc.). The following is a summary of how persons in each of the three traditions responded to the question by age group.

5. Smith, *Soul Searching*, 27.

Figure 3.7, "Religious" or "Spiritual"? (Christians, by Generation)					
Catholics	"Religious"	"Spiritual but not Religious"	"Both Spiritual and Religious"	"Neither Spiritual nor Religious"	"Don't know"
Greatest (before 1928)	0%	0%	100%	0%	0%
Silents (1928–1945)	13%	13%	60%	7%	7%
Baby Boomers (1946–1964)	18%	3%	69%	3%	6%
Gen X (1965–1980)	18%	10%	67%	2%	3%
Millennials (1981–1997)	41%	6%	47%	0%	6%
Mainline Protestants	"Religious"	"Spiritual but not Religious"	"Both Spiritual and Religious"	"Neither Spiritual nor Religious"	"Don't know"
Greatest (before 1928)	0%	0%	0%	0%	100%
Silents (1928–1945)	4%	4%	74%	4%	13%
Baby Boomers (1946–1964)	11%	15%	68%	1%	6%
Gen X (1965–1980)	18%	21%	53%	0%	7%
Millennials (1981–1997)	23%	7%	62%	0%	8%
Evangelical Protestants	"Religious"	"Spiritual but not Religious"	"Both Spiritual and Religious"	"Neither Spiritual nor Religious"	"Don't know"
Greatest (before 1928)	0%	0%	0%	0%	0%
Silents (1928–1945)	7%	29%	43%	0%	14%
Baby Boomers (1946–1964)	20%	27%	45%	1%	7%
Gen X (1965–1980)	14%	18%	55%	3%	9%
Millennials (1981–1997)	11%	30%	49%	3%	7%

The journey to faith for Christians is varied, complex, and shaped deeply by what persons (and their faith communities) think it means to be a Christian in the first place. No one can predict the kinds of incidents or influences along the way that will matter to everyone, or even most persons. At the same time, it is possible to trace the primary and supporting factors that tend to show up with great regularity in the reporting of people who are returning or newly coming to faith. To those factors we now turn our attention in chapter 4.

4

Christians: Factors Leading to Faith

THE PREVIOUS CHAPTERS HAVE described some of the most important circumstances and incidents associated with the way Christians come to a new faith commitment in the United States. We also asked these Christians to identify what they understood to be the most important factors in coming to faith. We suspected that people we interacted with (especially Christians) would likely identify God, Christ, or the Holy Spirit as a key factor, but we wanted to know what other factors they took as primary (even if they understood those factors as mediating God's activity in their lives). Thus, we asked the question, "What or who (other than God) played the largest part in your commitment or recommitment?" (Figure 4.1).

We first asked persons to identify the main factor among fourteen possibilities. Secondly, we gave them the opportunity to identify as many "supporting factors" as they wished from among those same possibilities (the totals for those answers, therefore, could exceed 100 percent). We also invited the respondents to write in their own choice if we had not listed it already as a possibility. We used the same thirteen factors that Bishop Finney had used, which he had developed on the basis of his own prior research. In this way, we would be able to make comparisons with his data. But we also added one other factor that was not on his original survey: "a particular congregation or faith community." That was added based on my own preliminary research, and indeed it was selected by a great many of the respondents. In addition to making choices about primary and supporting factors, we also asked persons to comment on *why* each factor was important. Their stories provide a rich account of why and how Christians come to faith in the United States.

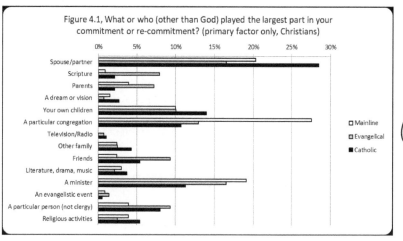

Figure 4.1, What or who (other than God) played the largest part in your commitment or re-commitment? (primary factor only, Christians)

The picture painted in Figure 4.1 is that of the importance of personal connection in the experience of coming to faith. For all the importance of evangelistic programs, events, tracts, literature, and music, and despite the emphasis that television and radio personalities place on their ministries as crucial to reaching the world evangelistically, about three-quarters (74 percent) of all Christians identify a spouse or partner (21 percent), a congregation (16 percent), a minister (15 percent), a parent or other family member (8 percent), a friend (65 percent), or some other person (8 percent) as the primary factor in coming to faith.[1]

Another 11 percent of Christians come to faith for the sake of their children, though I have not included that in the 76 percent figure because this has less to do with the direct influence of children on their parents and more to do with parents wanting to raise their children in the context of the church and Christian faith. If, however, we add children to the list of personal influences, the total rises to a staggering 86 percent of all Christians. The data show especially the importance of spouse or partner, congregation, and minister, about which I will provide further commentary below. It is striking that only 1 percent of respondents identify television and radio as the primary factor, and among Mainline Protestants, not even one person out of 324 Mainline respondents claimed these media as the primary factor. Appendix B includes summary charts that show how the data breakdown by Christian tradition.

1. Note that these percentages are weighted to reflect the proportionate number of Evangelical Protestants, Catholic, and Mainline Protestants in the United States and are not just the total of all responses in our survey (recalling that our survey is disproportionately represented by Mainline Protestants).

Figure 4.2 illustrates how things look when we combine the primary factor with all other supporting factors. Here Scripture grows in prominence, but otherwise the data support the same conclusion—people reach people. At the same time, there are pronounced differences by Christian tradition—for example, the importance of Scripture for Evangelicals or the importance of the congregation for Mainline Protestants.

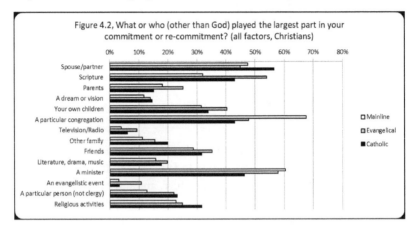

Figure 4.2, What or who (other than God) played the largest part in your commitment or re-commitment? (all factors, Christians)

THE FAMILY

Spouse or Partner

The influence of spouses and partners on those coming to faith is considerable, and congregations would do well to take seriously how they might support persons whose spouses may be considering the journey of faith. Twenty-eight percent of Roman Catholics, 20 percent of Mainline Protestants, and 17 percent of Evangelicals identify their spouse as the *primary* factor in coming to faith. This number is significantly higher than the 11 percent that Finney found in England twenty-five years ago. An additional 27 to 28 percent of Christians today cite their spouse or partner as a *supporting* factor (compared to the 16 percent who claimed it as a supporting factor in the British study). In sum, then, around half of all Christians in the US (compared to Finney's 27 percent in the UK) are influenced by their spouse or partner in coming to faith—a very significant finding of our study.

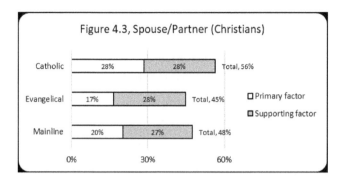

Figure 4.3, Spouse/Partner (Christians)

The differences between males and females in relation to the importance of spouse or partner influence is noteworthy, with females influencing males to become Christian far more than the reverse. Among Mainline Protestants and Catholics, males describe female partners as the primary factor about twice as often as females claim male partners (Figure 4.4). The asymmetry is less pronounced among Evangelicals (19 percent of males say female partners are the primary influence and the reverse is true for 13 percent of females). We wondered whether the differences between Evangelical males and other Christian males at this point might be related to Evangelical attitudes toward gender roles, especially Evangelical views on male authority within the household.

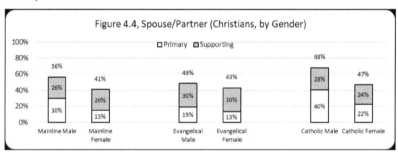

Figure 4.4, Spouse/Partner (Christians, by Gender)

Two-thirds of all Catholic males cite their spouse or partner as influential and just under half of all Catholic females. That is quite remarkable, and Finney found similar data, speculating upon reflection that this "might be because the Catholic church has paid more attention to the help and support of the family than other groups and emphasized the importance attached to bringing up children in the Catholic faith."[2] Our data suggest that this is apparently still the case in the US where Catholic identity remains relatively strong within families, at least in relation to the influence of

2. Finney, *Finding Faith Today*, 39.

spouse or partner. Interestingly, parental influence within Catholicism is actually lower than in other Christian traditions (see below under "Parents").

Age differences are an important factor when it comes to the influence from spouses or partners. Persons in the 25 to 44 age range are much more likely than persons in other age ranges to claim a spouse or partner as the primary factor.

Figure 4.5, Percentage of age group claiming spouse or partner as primary factor in coming to faith (Christians)			
18–24	25–44	45–64	65+
15%	27%	19%	14%

Digging into the particularities of our respondents, we learned that being able to share the same (or parallel) journey of faith together was valued most highly by about a third of those Christians claiming spouse or partner as a primary or supporting factor. Respondents spoke of deciding things together, of mutuality, of sharing important conversations, and of "working through this" together, all of which make the journey easier or more satisfying.

> This is something that we did together. We started the journey together. When either of us felt anything or needed to learn more we were there for each other.

> We are both committed to the church and to our faith. We have the same spiritual goals, and are in line with each other, so it makes the journey that much easier.

> Being with someone with the same beliefs and understanding I can talk to him I can ask questions without worrying that he will judge me.

> I think sharing our faith makes our marriage stronger.

For another third, the accent fell more strongly on the support, love, and acceptance of the spouse or partner, even if no mention was made of a shared journey.

> My spouse was unconditionally loving and accepting of my personhood.

> He was supportive, although ultimately didn't choose to be a part of the church at this particular moment in time. . . . However, I feel the best thing to do is to let him come around on his own.

She supported me completely and did not judge my choice.

For yet another third, the focus was more on ways the partner helped the process along by leading the way, usually as one who was already a Christian. At times, this help came in the form of engaging in conversation or helping the other partner come to knowledge or clarity about the faith without judgment or pressure. In most cases, it had to do with modeling the faith in important ways.

> *She has faith like Jesus mentioned we should have, like a child. She believes and knows she does. She isn't always the best at pushing to pray, or going to church, but she knows what she believes. I struggled for a long time, looking for answers. She's a model for me to just believe.*

> *He lives his religion every day and is such a caring, wonderfully patient man.*

> *She was leaps and bound ahead of me with her spiritual walk— what an incredible example!*

> *She was there to answer questions that I was too embarrassed to ask in the group setting. She was knowledgeable and kind with her words.*

> *He was the one who started us going to church. We talked about finding a church for several years, but my husband made it a priority for us to go, and we did and haven't stopped since.*

> *He helped me understand scripture and those things I struggled with. He prayed with and for me.*

Other responses do not fit neatly in any category, such as a few who mentioned marriage or relational problems that had an influence on their faith commitment as an attempt to save their relationship. A couple of other surprising responses cited the partner's influence precisely because he or she was not supportive, and instead overly skeptical and judgmental. This had the adverse effect of shoring up the individual's resolve to make a new faith commitment.

Their own children

Children can be a critically important factor in the process of making a new faith commitment, and children are either the primary or a supporting factor for one in three Christians (Figure 4.6).

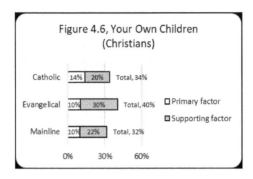

Figure 4.6, Your Own Children (Christians)

This is especially true for females, 13 percent of whom claim that their children were a primary factor (Figure 4.7).[3] For Catholics, this is matched by males who make a similar claim, though the percentage drops to 8 percent of Evangelical males and only 3 percent of Mainline Protestant males. Males and females compare with each other a bit more equally in each tradition when we combine children as both a primary factor and a supporting factor. The exception is Evangelicals, where there is more imbalance. Half of Evangelical females cite children as a primary or supporting factor compared to less than a third of the males. For all groups, the greatest number by far of persons claiming children as a primary or supporting factor fall in the 25 to 44 age bracket, which should not be surprising given that is the age group starting families or thinking seriously about how their children will be raised.

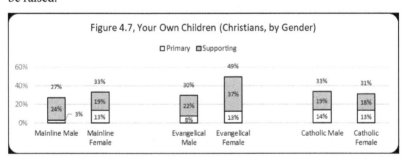

Figure 4.7, Your Own Children (Christians, by Gender)

About two-thirds of those who listed their children as a primary or supporting factor in coming to faith stressed that when starting a family it was important to them that their children be raised in the context of the church and with Christian faith and values. For many, this meant being a good role model and influence, or being the kind of parent the children deserved.

3. Finney found that 3 percent of men and 13 percent of women said this was a main factor; and 12 percent of men and 30 percent of women said it was either a primary or a supporting factor; ibid., 40.

We were talking about starting a family. I wanted us to make decisions on how we would raise our children, and we needed to agree on religion. I decided it was time to explore my faith so we could make decisions.

Not attending church didn't seem like such a big issue until I realized that I didn't want my own children growing up without even a frame of reference in regards to God. Not to mention that I then also realized how much I wanted them to experience God for themselves in a very real and personal way.

I wanted to serve as a spiritual role model for my children the way that my parents were for me as a child.

I realized that if I didn't show them that Christianity was important to me, it wouldn't be important to them.

In the other third of the cases where persons listed their children as a factor, this was because their children were involved in church already. The children got their parents to go to church, demonstrated an influential excitement about the church, or in some way supported their parents in the process.

My child was excited on fire for God. It is inspiring.

We baptized our children into the church and started their education by taking them to Sunday School. As they were members of the church and were receiving education, I wanted that for myself as well.

The baptism of our child forced me to grapple with a profession of faith and come to a better understanding of that profession and my own faith.

My daughter gave me books to read and would encourage me with scripture and pray with me and for me.

A last subset of persons, though small in number, found the very process of giving birth or having and raising children something of a profound miracle and sacrament, or a vehicle for God's voice to be heard. Infant baptisms were also named by several persons as significant experiences of welcome by the church and a time for parents to reflect on the importance of faith in their own lives.

Parents

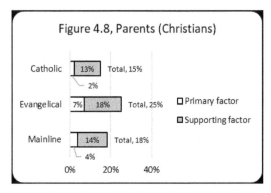

Parents are a primary influence for 4 percent of Mainline Protestants and 2 percent of Catholics, while 7 percent of Evangelicals cite this factor as primary.[4] Differences between males and females are negligible, but, as one might expect, the percentage is slightly higher for younger persons.

When we combine those who list parents as a primary factor with those who list them as a supporting factor, Evangelicals still outnumber Mainline Protestants and Catholics, demonstrating the importance of coming from a Christian home for Evangelicals. Given that Mainline Protestants and Catholics have lower retention rates than Evangelicals—and thus produce more persons who have left or are inactive in the religion of their parents—we would expect to see that parents and family have less importance for them than other influences.[5]

Other family members

As Figure 4.9 shows, around 3 percent of all Christians making a new faith commitment identify other family members as the main factor leading to their commitment. That number rises considerably when we add those who claim other family members as a supporting factor, though the differences by Christian tradition are pronounced. As with those who cite parents, there are no appreciable differences by gender for those who cite other family members.

Among our study participants, a third did not identify a particular person, though those most often singled out were siblings (22 percent), parents-in-law (14 percent), aunts and uncles (11 percent), cousins (9

4. In Finney's study, 6 percent said parents were the main factor and 12 percent said they were a supporting factor; ibid., 42.

5. Pew, "America's Changing Religious Landscape," 39.

percent), and grandparents (6 percent). About half of those choosing other family members claimed they were role models, exemplars, or those who had paved the way for them through their own faith commitment:

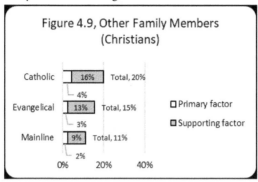

My husband's family was greatly influential because they showed me what a Christian family looked like and how they acted. They encouraged me, talked to me about what I was reading in the Word, took me to church, and really cared for me as if I was their own daughter. They showed me the love of Christ.

I have an aunt that has always supported me throughout my life despite its twists and turns. She is very religious. She not only goes to church, but practices outside without judgment and with a great deal of humility.

My maternal grandparents were two of the most godly people I've known. They influenced me primarily by how their faith helped them through several crises in their lives.

The other half cited other family member as encouraging them or lending some sort of support during the process of coming to faith.

Family members encouraged me and were so happy I found a church. They have attended services with me and other programs at the church. They always ask me about the church and what we are doing. My family's engagement and interest encouraged me to keep attending and to stay active.

Other family members who were also Christ-followers, encouraged me to read my Bible, to pray, and to live in a God-honoring way through example and positive reinforcement.

FRIENDS AND OTHER INFLUENTIAL INDIVIDUALS

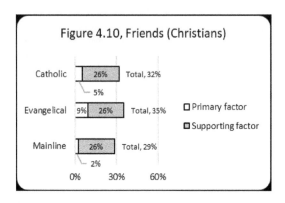

Figure 4.10, Friends (Christians)

The influence of friends is yet another important factor in coming to faith for Christians—almost as much as parents and other family members combined. Friends are a primary factor for 2 percent of Mainline Protestants, 5 percent of Catholics, and 9 percent of Evangelicals. When primary and supporting factors are combined, friends are a factor for around one-third of all Christians. Given that Evangelicals place a high premium on evangelizing other persons, it is not surprising that the influence of friends is especially high in that tradition.

While there is not a tremendous difference between males and females where the influence of friends is concerned, age is an exceptionally important variable. Almost one in four persons in the 18 to 24 age bracket cite friends as a primary or supporting influence (Figure 4.11). That then drops to 4 percent in later years.

Figure 4.11, Percentage of age group claiming friends as the primary factor in coming to faith (Christians)			
18–24	25–44	45–64	65+
22%	4%	4%	9%

Other persons who do not fall in the category of clergy, family, or friends should not be left out of the story. Almost a quarter of Evangelicals and Catholics claim other persons are a primary or supporting factor in coming to faith, though that is less true for Mainline Protestants (Figure 4.12).

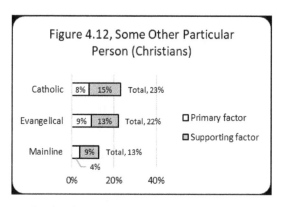

Figure 4.12, Some Other Particular Person (Christians)

Catholic — 8% | 15% | Total, 23%
Evangelical — 9% | 13% | Total, 22%
Mainline — 9% | Total, 13% — 4%

☐ Primary factor
☐ Supporting factor

0%   20%   40%

Over two-thirds of the Christians in our study claimed that friends and other persons who were neither clergy nor family members provided encouragement, dialogue, perspective, and support in the process of coming to faith. In several cases, this was directly related to support while experiencing adversity, pain, and struggle. It was especially interesting to hear the number of persons who affirmed that their friends did not force Christianity on them, but gently provided a witness and invitation.

> *They provided dialogue and invited me to Christian-based activities that enhanced my interest.*

> *I've been blessed to have friends at work and at church to discuss spiritual matters and to fellowship and support each other.*

> *They encouraged me and shared the truth that they knew.*

> *My friends were the ones who led me to Jesus, the ones who supported me in my times of pain and struggles and never left my side in time of need.*

The other third of the respondents focused their remarks more on the way friends served as role models or exemplars of faith.

> *My friends are a testament of faith.*
> *I had a couple of friends who had found Christ and I saw the resounding change in them.*

> *Examples of energetic and committed Catholic practice, while remaining normal!*

> *One friend in particular was very outspoken about her faith. She lives it everyday, but she is not pushy.*

Only a quarter of all persons who claimed friends or other persons as important referenced just one person as the important influence. For most, it was the support and solidarity found within a community of friends who were Christians that was most important. As Finney wrote twenty-five years ago, "*For most people the corporate life of the church is a vital element in the process of becoming a Christian and for about a quarter it is the vital factor.* Forms of evangelism which fail to recognize this are doomed."[6]

CHURCHLY AND OTHER RELIGIOUS ACTIVITIES

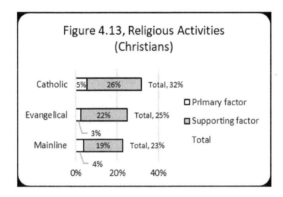

Figure 4.13, Religious Activities (Christians)

While a small percentage of Christians identify religious activities as the primary factor in their experience of coming to faith (far fewer than Buddhists or Jews, for example), a little over a quarter say it is either a primary or supporting factor (Figure 4.13). Age is a significant variable here. Nine percent of Christians age 18 to 24 say these activities are the primary factor in coming to faith, while that is true for only 2 to 3 percent of those over 24. Since persons surveyed could choose the congregation itself as a factor (see below, where it is treated under its own heading), some important religious activity can be assumed to show up there as well. Indeed, there is considerable overlap among this category, the congregation, Christian friends, and the minister.

Christians in our study who identified this factor as important named classes, groups, Bible studies, camps, retreats, worship services, outreach programs, and ministries of all types. Half of all those who chose this factor, whether primary or supporting, did so because of the way the activities provided opportunities for growth, education, and transformation.

6. Finney, *Finding Faith Today*, 43. Italics in the original.

The retreat was wonderful, and then we built off that with local community service projects, etc. that allowed me to see our faith in action and bond with God and the other men in the group. At that time, the liturgy of the Catholic Church was very appealing to me as well.

Seeing how the Orthodox worship, in the Liturgy specifically, was very moving for me. I saw in it a truth and a beauty I had never seen in other forms of Christianity. I was also very drawn to the history of the Church, the influence of the Saints of the past was very present in the Church today.

My wife and I attended a small group that changed our lives, saved our marriage and led us to a fantastic church.

The first Ladies Retreat I went to with my daughter sponsored by [my church] showed more love, forgiveness, joy, desire to learn more. (I had never felt worthy to attend such an event before.)

The small group studies helped me to study the Word even deeper and I got a sense of fellowship from my church family.

A little over a quarter of those who selected religious activities mentioned their importance as providing means of involvement, inclusion, belonging, fellowship, and community building.

Yes, activities were very important. We immediately got our children involved in the children's choir—which occurred on Wednesday nights. It was at this time we found a community of parents and still interact with them outside of church. This foundation gave the kids and the parents are stronger sense of community. We immediately joined a neighborhood group from our church and began hosting in our home to get more involved. All of this gave us a stronger foundation outside of only attending Sunday services.

I was surrounded by people who lived their faith. I was no longer isolated . . .

I engaged in small groups, outreach activities, and volunteering in order to connect with others in my congregation. It was important for me to have these connections and to get to know others in my church to keep me connected and feel needed and wanted.

Lastly, 15 percent of those who selected religious activities cited their importance for providing channels of service and outreach.

I was participating in various volunteer events and attending various lectures within the church. What I took away from all is that this was the life that I needed—focus more on service and appreciating others and their thoughts/situations.

Volunteering and helping those less fortunate than myself is the very reason I was looking for a commitment to a church and is very important.

A volunteer organization that is loosely affiliated with my parish serves our homeless downtown neighbors. I have always had a desire to serve the poor and the marginalized. Serving our homeless neighbors at this organization made me feel God's presence in a very real way.

THE CONGREGATION

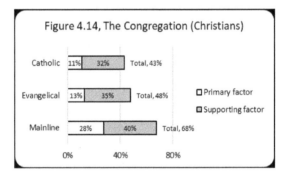

Figure 4.14, The Congregation (Christians)

The congregation is among the top three factors most frequently selected by Christians making a new faith commitment—the other two being the minister and the spouse or partner. Though the congregation is predominant for persons of all Christian traditions, it is especially so for Mainline Protestants with 21 percent of males and 32 percent of females identifying the congregation as the primary factor and a remarkable 61 percent of males and 70 percent of females claiming it as a primary or supporting factor (Figure 4.15). Congregations are important in other Christian traditions as well, and, again, slightly more so for females than for males.

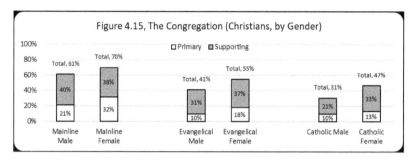

Figure 4.15, The Congregation (Christians, by Gender)

Figure 4.16 shows the growing importance of the congregation in the process of coming to faith as persons grow older. By contrast, friends and spouses or partners tend to be slightly more important at a younger age.

Figure 4.16, Percentage of age group claiming a congregation as the primary factor in coming to faith			
18–24	25–44	45–64	65+
7%	15%	26%	26%

Three-quarters of the persons who chose the congregation as an important factor in their faith commitment described the church with terms like *warm, welcoming, inclusive, accepting, non-judgmental, accepting, supportive, loving, friendly, safe, comfortable, feels like home, inviting, like-minded, generous, kind.* The most frequently mentioned of these (at 39%) was the word *welcome.*

The other quarter who chose the congregation as either primary or supporting mentioned features of the congregation such as it being alive or dynamic, spiritually formative, right or orthodox in its teachings and practices, supportive in its programs, or exemplary in its outreach and service in the wider community.

> *The progressiveness of our Catholic community and their true modern connection to what is really happening in our community and what our community needs.*
>
> *My cathedral community (especially the choir) and Jesuit high school were places rooted in faith that stressed loving community and allowed me to ask questions. I was able to grow and develop spiritually in these environments, leading me eventually to pursue initiation into Christian community through baptism.*
>
> *My campus church practiced discipleship intensely, and I have much to thank them for that.*

While it was not a place of blooming social activity for me, its rigor in Bible study and fighting sin has heavily contributed to my spiritual survival today.

The congregation had a strong focus on outreach and this was important to me

This new church is very involved in the local community through participation with a local shelter as well as participating as a soup drive church amongst many local denominational churches in our town to help feed the homeless and needy. The congregation is a nice mix of people of different age groups, ethnicities and many younger parents with children my boys' age and provided a nice environment to feel a part of.

This congregation doesn't have a lot of money, power or prestige. They are who they are and come without judgement. I like to say there is nothing sexy about them; they are real and sometimes it is awkward but so beautiful. They do outreach and have a meal program every week. I liked that there was action behind this church.

Missions oriented, open to all people, leading in community events impacting on lives of those who live here.

When asked what was most important about the congregation or faith community they now attend, almost a third of Roman Catholics and Orthodox say the worship, and close to another third say the welcome they experienced from the community. By contrast, about half of Evangelicals identify the preaching and teaching at their church to be the most important feature. Mainline Protestant responses are spread more equally across the features of worship, preaching, and welcome. But Mainline Protestants are almost three times as likely (9 percent) as Catholics (3 percent) or Evangelicals (4 percent) to lift up the social outreach and ministry of the church as the primary feature (Figure 4.17).

For those who chose to write in their own answers rather than select from among the five options provided, several Evangelicals identified the presence of the Holy Spirit, Jesus, or God in the church and worship. Evangelicals also suggested the importance of the church being doctrinally or biblically sound, and they cited Bible studies, youth groups, and children's programs in particular. Catholics who wrote in their own answers mentioned the sacraments or the Mass. Mainline Protestants often mentioned inclusivity, diversity, and the music or arts.

Figure 4.17, What *is the single most import*ant feature of the church you now attend? (Christians)					
	The welcome	The clergy's preaching & teaching	Worship	Educational programs	Social outreach/ ministry	Other (write in)
Catholic	31%	24%	32%	2%	3%	8%
Evangelical	20%	48%	19%	0%	4%	9%
Mainline	29%	30%	21%	5%	9%	7%

When persons were asked to list all features they found important (in other words, more than just one primary feature), and when we combine those answers with the most important feature mentioned above, we get the results displayed in Figure 4.18 (the total for each group will exceed 100 percent since they could choose more than one). Differences between Christian traditions are less sharp in this picture—for example, the welcome was consistently rated as important by about three-quarters of all Christians. However, some of the distinctives remain recognizable. It is worth noting that we also found little difference by age group in the responses to this question with one exception: 18- to 24-year-olds are more likely to lift up worship as the primary feature of their community (28 percent of their cohort as compared to 21 percent of other age cohorts) and to play down the importance of the educational programs of their community (7 percent of their cohort as compared to 14 percent of other age cohorts).

Figure 4.18, What *are the most important* features of the church you now attend? (Christians)					
	The welcome	The clergy's preaching & teaching	Worship	Educational programs	Social outreach/ ministry	Other (write in)
Catholic	73%	59%	70%	34%	38%	13%
Evangelical	73%	84%	74%	33%	40%	17%
Mainline	77%	81%	69%	35%	53%	16%

Choosing a Congregation

We asked Christians how they chose the church of which they are now a part (Figure 4.19). This question, though related to the previous one about the most important features of their congregation, has a different cast to it. One-third of all Catholics and Orthodox cite geographical proximity, which affirms the continuing relevance of the parish model of those traditions. A parish is a defined territory within a larger area of jurisdiction, and a church, along with its "parish minister," is established as caring for that territory. Persons in that locality thus automatically belong to that particular parish. In more recent times, and especially within Protestantism, people are more likely to travel to a church they like, sometimes as a result of "church shop-ping." They might, therefore, travel past multiple other churches on the way. But Catholics and Orthodox are much more likely to attend their parish church rather than travel outside their neighborhood or local community.

After geographical proximity, the second most frequently cited reason for choice of congregation for Catholics is that it is the church of their family or a church to which a family member invited them (18 percent). The third most frequently mentioned reason for Catholics is a prior affiliation or relationship (12 percent). Another 10 percent of Catholics choose their congregation on the basis of its welcome or inclusion, and 9 percent report having gone "church shopping," with the decision hinging on specific qualities they liked or with which they were most comfortable.

Seventeen percent of Evangelicals attribute their choice of congregation to family connections, 13 percent to church shopping, 12 percent to prior relationship or affiliation, and 11 percent to being invited by friends or other persons with whom they had contact. Interestingly, 9 percent of Evangelicals claim that God specifically directed them, an option that barely registers for Catholics or Mainline Protestants. Eight percent of Evangelicals say they were most attentive to the beliefs and teachings of the church, usually focused on how "biblical" the church is. Only 7 percent claim that their decision was due to proximity.

The number one reason Mainline Protestants choose their congregation (19 percent) is as the result of a process of "church shopping," research, or searching on the internet, while another 15 percent say they had a prior relationship or affiliation. Thirteen percent claim geographical proximity.

Figure 4.19, How did you choose which church to go to? (Christians)			
	Catholic	Evangelical	Mainline
Proximity	33%	7%	13%
Church shopping	9%	13%	14%
Prior relationship or affiliation	12%	12%	15%
Family	18%	17%	11%
Friends or others	5%	13%	11%
Church's welcome/inclusion	10%	8%	11%
Minister	7%	8%	6%
God led them	1%	9%	1%
Advertising/TV/Internet	1%	0%	2%
Research/Internet search	1%	3%	4%
Random, fate, or it chose them	1%	1%	4%
Some other feature of church	3%	8%	8%

How Easy or Difficult to Start Attending?

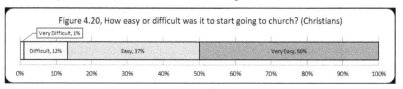

Figure 4.20, How easy or difficult was it to start going to church? (Christians)

Over one-third (37 percent) of new or recommitted Christians find it easy to begin going to church and another 50 percent find it "very easy." There are no appreciable differences by Christian tradition on this question, moreover (Figure 4.20). There are, however, slight differences based on whether persons had already been occasional churchgoers prior to making their commitment. Ninety-two percent of occasional churchgoers find it easy or very easy to attend church regularly after their commitment, while that is true for 85 percent of those who had not attended church much. That difference is not tremendous, and, in fact, it is a much smaller difference than Finney's survey turned up in England twenty-five years ago. Finney found that 83 percent of those who had previously been occasional churchgoers claimed regular church attendance was "very easy" or "quite easy" while that number dropped to only 68 percent for those who had never attended church.[7]

7. Ibid., 75.

Slightly more males (90 percent) than females (86 percent) find it easy to start attending church. That is not a wide margin of difference, but more females than males cited family obligations and self-confidence or shyness as issues in attending. It must be remembered, of course, that our survey was deliberately directed to those who had already become part of a faith community, so we do not know how many found churchgoing so difficult that they gave up. Congregations should never underestimate how difficult it can be to make churchgoing a regular practice, and how intimidating church culture can be for those who are not accustomed to it.

DREAMS AND VISIONS

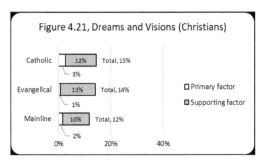

Figure 4.21, Dreams and Visions (Christians)

We asked about dreams and visions, just as Bishop Finney had done, so that we could compare the US situation three decades later. He asked the question because other studies showed as much as 62 percent of the total population had experienced something "strange" (spiritually speaking) happen to them.[8] We found that while only around 2 percent of all Christians claim a dream or vision as the primary factor in coming to faith, quite a few more (about 12 percent) claim it as either a primary or supporting factor.

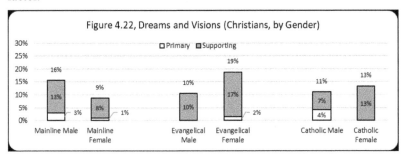

Figure 4.22, Dreams and Visions (Christians, by Gender)

8. Ibid., 49.

Women in Evangelical and Catholic traditions are more likely than men to cite the importance of this factor, but the reverse is true for Mainline Protestants (Figure 4.22). Across all traditions, those age 18 to 24 are more likely to select dreams and visions than those 25 and older (see Figure 4.23).

Figure 4.23, Percentage of age group claiming a dream or vision as the primary factor in coming to faith (Christians)			
18–24	25–44	45–64	65+
7%	15%	26%	26%

While the number selecting dreams and visions as an important factor is relatively small, the accounts are often vivid. For some, the dreams or visions are important because they are a form of communication or calling.

I had dreams about the world ending and not knowing God. This also told me that I had better get my life straightened out.

God speaks to me in dreams and visions. As well, I feel God's loving embrace and sense of communion and wholeness in time of contemplation.

Most felt reassured, directed, or motivated by their dreams or visions.

They did not come from my own imagination, nor could I ever have dreamed or seen all the things I've seen. My moments, that I normally keep to myself, I believe to be something much more than myself, I believe them to be a sign, instructions to something I haven't quite figured out yet. Having seen all the powerful things in my dreams, it's hard to think of them as anything other than something great and powerful. They allow me to know that God loves me, otherwise why would he show them to me.

When I feel like I am facing the dark alone, my maternal grandmother visits me. She talks to me about always believing and taking the right path. My grandmother died in [. . .] and she was the greatest influence in life. She taught me all about faith and the right path.

For others, the dreams or visions helped them in some other way.

I saw myself before God, naked and finally was able to accept me for me as God already did.

My deceased father came to me in a dream. He hugged me and told me he was sorry that he should have been a better father. This caused me to do a lot of thinking . . . It gave me a new perspective.

We asked a slightly different question to our participants about whether they had ever had, at any time in their life, any out-of-the-ordinary experiences they would describe as religious in some way. About six in ten Christians say they have had such experiences (with no significant variation related to one's Christian tradition), though for the most part these were not perceived by them as factors influencing their new faith commitment. The experiences were remarkable and strengthening, but they did not necessarily lead to conversion or recommitment.

A MINISTER

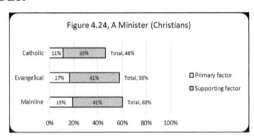

Figure 4.24, A Minister (Christians)

Among the many factors in coming to faith, few are more important for Christians than the minister, priest, or pastor. Anywhere between 11 to 19 percent of Christians (depending on tradition) say the minister was the primary factor for them (Figure 4.24), so this factor ranks right up there with the congregation and spouse or partner as among the top three factors in our study. If we combine those who chose the minister as the primary factor with those who chose the minister as a supporting factor, the number rises to about half of all Catholics and around 60 percent of all Protestants. We did not find enormous differences by gender, but there is some variation by age, however slight, with the percentage of those citing the importance of the minister rising as persons get older (Figure 4.25).

Figure 4.25, Percentage of age group claiming a minister as the primary factor in coming to faith (Christians)			
18–24	25–44	45–64	65+
13%	15%	17%	24%

Ministers are significant for the process of coming to faith in multiple ways. They provide a role model for faith, they preach and teach, they are agents of welcome and hospitality, they provide care and counseling, and they shape the life, worship, and outreach of the congregation. While all of these were mentioned throughout the responses we received, Figure 4.26

provides a bit more detail about which features of the minister are the most important as a factor in the process of coming to faith.

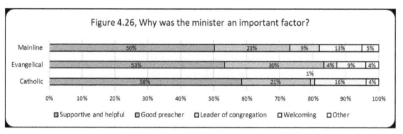

Figure 4.26, Why was the minister an important factor?

Supportive, helpful, caring

Half or more of the Christians in our study claimed the minister was supportive, affirming, influential, caring, and helpful. Often this support was educational, answering questions and clearing up misunderstandings. But ministers were also spoken of as spiritual guides and companions. Several persons in our study remarked about how helpful it was that they could relate to the minister, sometimes because of similar background or experiences. Of those who identified the minister as an important factor, 16 percent of Evangelicals, 15 percent of Mainline Protestants, and 8 percent of Catholics highlighted the fact that their minister went out of the way to make time for them. Often this support and care was in the context of a pastoral presence such as hospital visits or weddings, or during bereavement. The minister's own personal example, holiness, and spirituality were cited regularly as important, and we cannot underestimate their function as role models for people who are journeying toward faith. Other words that came up frequently were *wise, caring, encouraging, credible,* and *compassionate.*

> *He spoke to me and slowly guided me on the path to joining the Catholic Church. Little by little revealing the truth of the scripture.*

> *The Pastoral Associate at our parish . . . is the kindest most genuine person I had ever met. She took us into the parish family and guided us through each step. She still serves as my spiritual guide.*

> *He was patient with me and gently guided me in my spiritual quest.*

> *I liked him and felt comfortable talking to him, and his no pressure way of Christ.*

> *Because she's the most gifted/awesome Pastor there is. I've never felt the oh wow, I want to learn more or wonder about this part of scripture. She makes things so clear and understanding. Never*

been so close to a Pastor before in my entire life. I saw how God was working in her life and now I want to be just like her.

My priest affirmed God's love for me, even when I doubted God could love me.

He was down to earth and was easy to talk to and relate to. It made listening to his homilies that much more interesting.

He came immediately to the hospital and was very caring when my daughter was gravely ill.

Preaching

The next most important quality Christians mention in describing their ministers is their ability to preach. We know that this is especially important for Evangelicals, 30 percent of whom claim the preaching was most important for them. But preaching is also important for 23 percent of Mainline Protestants and 21 percent of Catholics. Persons tend to be attracted to preaching that is explanatory and biblical but also engaging, accessible, practical, and relevant.

My pastor taught the word of God in a way that I wanted to have a close walk with God.

He spoke of the Word so easily and made me understand it comfortably.

I found the father at the Cathedral open-minded, intelligent, charismatic and his sermons are practical, inspirational and full of love.
His preaching of the Scripture was clear and bold, yet humble. I had never heard any of these things before, but I didn't feel like an idiot for not knowing. The sermons were accessible to me.

Because she and her sermons were intelligent, sensitive, informative, and practical. I learned something new and or useful every time. It was an unexpected experience.

The way she spoke it made me feel as if maybe my life wasn't over, like I might still matter to someone if I would just stop running from him.

The way in which her sermons teach is very inclusive to many per-spectives and situations. You can feel the love she has for everyone in the congregation.

Welcoming and non-judgmental

Closely related to the other two reasons for selecting the minister as important is the quality of welcome and hospitality. Sixteen percent of the Catholics, 13 percent of the Mainline Protestants, and 9 percent of Evangelicals mentioned specifically how much they appreciate the minister being accepting, welcoming, and hospitable. It is especially impressive how often this was linked to being nonjudgmental.

Finding gay-friendly priests was very important to me. Being accepted in church with my partner was very important.

The pastors at [. . .] are so welcoming and make you feel as if you have been part of the family all along. It is unbelievable the love you feel there.

He did not talk down or make me feel bad for my mistakes I had made, he made me just know I was human and belonged.

Made me feel at home right away—welcomed me, learned my name, encouraged me to do more and get more involved; also helped me discern my calling.

His openness and acceptance of all people regardless of race, creed, color, etc.

She totally engaged me in conversation and freely accepted me.

Leadership

Among those Christians who selected the minister as a primary or supporting factor, 9 percent of Mainline Protestants, 4 percent of Evangelicals and 1 percent of Catholics mentioned as important the leadership of the minister within the life of the congregation. When the pastor sets a tone of openness, inclusion, and welcome, and displays a love for and dedication to the people in the congregation—as well as to those who are visitors—this can be extraordinarily significant for how people find faith. For that reason, the minister's leadership qualities can easily overlap with other qualities such as support, care, and welcome.

> *He was a very understanding and down to earth leader of his congregation.*

> *Our Pastor is totally dedicated to her congregation. She has enthusiasm and is extremely open to ideas and is always willing to try new ways to teach scripture. She makes going to Church fun and rewarding. Her door and her time is always open and she is never judgmental.*

> *She made me feel challenged and leads the congregation to care for one another.*

> *I found a minister who I really connected with, who cared about her congregation and was sincere in her teaching.*

SCRIPTURE

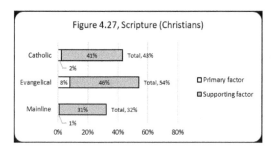

Figure 4.27, Scripture (Christians)

The number of Christians for whom Scripture is the primary factor in coming to faith depends greatly on the tradition in which that happens. Eight percent of Evangelicals say Scripture is primary as compared with only 2 percent of Catholics and 1 percent of Mainline Protestants. To be sure, we expected to see some of these differences, given the role the Bible plays in Evangelical identity, theology, and practice. Well over half of all Evangelicals identify Scripture as either a primary or supporting factor while that is true for 43 percent of Catholics and only a third of Mainline Protestants. Persons age 18 to 24, moreover, are three times as likely as persons 25 and older to identify Scripture as an important factor in their faith commitment.

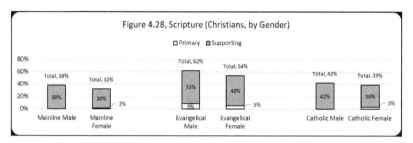

Figure 4.28, Scripture (Christians, by Gender)

Almost half of the Christians in our study who selected Scripture spoke about the Bible as providing new direction, inspiration, change, or guidance in their lives.

> *The Bible became more real to me and verses that had seemed boring before now became alive and active.*

> *I read every day and highlighted every word and page. I felt comfort and guidance when reading. I wanted to be better and help others. I was able to turn my anger over when reading how I should behave.*

> *Scripture was important because I needed guidance in my life. Scripture helps provide me with answers to things going on in my life.*

Many persons spoke about the Bible as an authority or foundation for their faith, often with dispassionate, matter-of-fact language.

> *As I read the Bible and was taught the Scripture I realized it was true and I wanted to live my life according to God's Word.*

> *I began reading the Bible immediately after my conversion, and have read it through many times since. The Bible is my authoritative rule of faith and conduct. Through the Bible, God reveals His plans and purposes for our lives.*

> *Scripture was and is important because it provided answers to all the questions I had about my faith and still have. Researching and studying scripture continues to open my eyes and mind.*

Others emphasized Scripture as alive and spoke of a dynamic relationship with Scripture that was more than just gaining new information.

> *It is the foundation for my growth in following Our Lord and Savior, Jesus Christ. The Bible is my living connection to Him and shows me ways He can use me to help others in this world!*

I've always read scripture, but this time it seemed to really come alive. I talked to my friend about the scripture readings and then we would talk about how they applied to today's everyday life.

It touched my heart and soul.

Several spoke of the convicting power of Scripture.

Scripture points me to Christ and allows me to know God more each and every day. It also encourages, convicts, and points to truth at all times.

Many times I witnessed scripture and it often helped me to realize how lost I was and how much I needed a relationship with Christ.

Every time I read my bible I knew I was guilty of being not close in my relationship with God.

For a number of respondents, the Bible revealed something to them.

I prayed for a very specific answer and found it in the first scripture I read upon opening the Bible at random.

I had never read the gospel. It helped me to breakdown preconceived notions about organized religion and church going people.

As I read and began to apply its teachings, I soon discovered its divinity. It helped me to understand God's nature and his desire for us; His love and faithfulness.

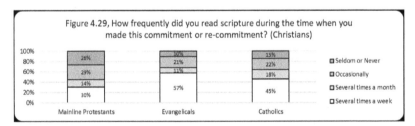

Figure 4.29, How frequently did you read scripture during the time when you made this commitment or re-commitment? (Christians)

In order to assess the extent to which Scripture might have been important to persons during the time they were making their new commitment, we asked how frequently they read Scripture and how helpful they found it. Again we found that Scripture is much more important to Evangelicals than to Mainline Protestants or Catholics, as Figures 4.29 and 4.30 demonstrate. Evangelicals in our study had read Scripture more often than Catholics and far more often than Mainline Protestants. Of those who had read it several times each week, an average of 98 percent found it very helpful or at least somewhat helpful (Figure 4.30).

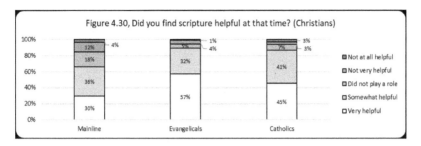

Figure 4.30, Did you find scripture helpful at that time? (Christians)

TELEVISION OR RADIO PROGRAMS

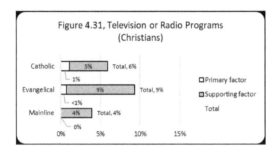

Figure 4.31, Television or Radio Programs (Christians)

A very small number of Christians cite television or radio programs as the primary factor leading to their faith commitment. Nine percent of Evangelicals and 5 percent of Catholics find these media to be at least a supporting factor. Since most religious programming in the US is either Evangelical or Catholic in origin, it is perhaps to be expected that persons coming to faith in those two traditions are more likely to be touched by that programming. What may be more important for the purposes of this study, however, is the question of whether non-Christians as a whole are reached by Christian television and radio programming, or whether those media instead have the tendency to "preach to the converted." Of course, our study secured its participants in the context of churches, so we did not look for (nor do we know the numbers of) those who make Christian faith commitments mediated wholly through television or the radio without any subsequent church participation.

Figure 4.32, "Participation in Electronic and Offline Religious Activities"[N]	
New media	%
Saw religion shared online	46
Shared own faith online	20
Old media	

Watched religious television	23
Listened to religious talk radio	20
Listened to Christian rock	19
Offline participation	
Shared faith in real-life setting	40
A. Pew, "Participation in Electronic and Offline Religious Activities."	

We do know, however, that television and radio are far less important for the communication of faith than newer online media. According to a 2014 Pew Research Center study, one in five persons in the US share their religious faith online in any given week. That points to a shift in the influence of media on faith, since that number is about the same as the number of those who access religious talk radio, religious TV programs, or Christian rock music combined.[9] Within a given week, almost half of all adults in the US are exposed to someone else sharing their religious faith online.

The Pew study found that white Evangelicals and black Protestants are far more likely than other Christian groups to report watching a religious television program, listening to religious talk radio, or sharing their faith online. The report also revealed that television and radio (what the report referred to as "old media") were viewed primarily by persons over fifty while newer media had greater appeal to those under thirty. These data are confirmed by the results of our study, where two-thirds of the small number of Christians who selected television or radio were over fifty years old.

Many for whom radio or television motivated their conversion or commitment described the shows in the words of one 73-year-old, who said, "It spoke to me. It was relevant to me." Or in the words of a 51-year-old: "It was a form of media that God used to capture my attention to His presence." A few Evangelicals mentioned Joel Osteen as motivating them to look for a Christian church. As one person said, "I recall seeing a number of 'TV Evangelists' asking for money and promising miracles. I recall scandals that involved well know preachers and illicit affairs. I found all this very distasteful, but those very concerns allowed me to form hard questions about faith and practice." Others mentioned Oprah, Krista Tippett's *Speaking of Faith* on NPR, Charles Stanley, Kenneth Hagin, Joyce Meyer, Chuck Swindoll, and the 700 Club. Several Catholics mentioned the Roman Catholic Eternal Word Television Network (EWTN).

For a good number of Christians who selected this factor as either primary or supporting, radio and television programming served as a

9. Pew, "Religion and Electronic Media," 1.

confirmation, support, or "fuel" that was supplementary to their attendance and participation in church. Others described the programing as
informative.

> *I think Oprah has opened many of us up to ideas that would*
> *have previously been considered unChristian, even heretical. Her*
> *championing of people like Eckhart Tolle, Michael Beckwith, and*
> *Maya Angelou made these ideas more mainstream.*

> *My commute to work took 30 minutes and I became sick of music*
> *on the radio. I found a Christian talk show that I listened to every*
> *morning and another on the way home. I listened to the repeats,*
> *I loved it all. What a gift and how far reaching Christian radio*
> *can be.*

> *My [aunt] told me about Joel Osteen. I never really was interested*
> *in watching tv evangelists but I did because she said he was really*
> *good. I started watching one evening just by chance. I was shocked*
> *at how good he was, and how I could understand his message so*
> *clearly. So many times during my life I have not understood what*
> *the preacher was trying to preach. Watching Joel Osteen really*
> *touched me and I still watch him as often as I can.*

> *I had watched the Visual Bible on television, which helped me*
> *understand the life of Jesus Christ.*

> *Radio programs/podcasts helped me by answering questions I*
> *had. And a lot of the time a program would come up and an-*
> *swer a question or a thought I previously had before the program,*
> *whether right before or a week before.*

LITERATURE, DRAMA, AND MUSIC

Only 2 to 4 percent of Christians claim that literature, drama, and music are the primary factor in their faith commitment, though 13 to 18 percent say they are supporting factors. Persons cited older classics like
Augustine's *Confessions*, the writings of C. S. Lewis, or John Bunyan's *The
Pilgrim's Progress*. But some also mentioned more recent popular books
such as Lee Strobel's *The Case for Christ*, Rick Warren's *The Purpose Driven
Life*, or William Young's *The Shack*. Some of these books opened up new
truths while others provided context and background for understanding
Christianity or the Bible for those unfamiliar with either. For some making
a new faith commitment, the books were inspirational or devotional, while

for others the influence was described in more intellectual terms. Several persons mentioned movies, including *Son of God*, *Chariots of Fire*, *The Mission*, *Sound of Music*, and *God is Not Dead*.

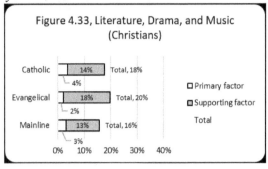

Figure 4.33, Literature, Drama, and Music (Christians)

Almost half of those who selected this category focused on music as the most important factor in their faith commitment:

It was like therapy. At times, the songs seemed to be selected just for me to heal my soul.

The music of Catholicism is profound and liturgically complementary.

I joined the choir at Church and was introduced to music I had never heard before. It just struck a chord and I really could hear it speaking to me. Music touches my soul and especially when it sings God's praises.

I can very much relate to Christian Rock music. It speaks to me and helps me to stay focused on God's word.

The music is inspiring, uplifting, and yet meditative. Not a show, not a concert, but a genuine spiritual experience.

The church choir's music touched me both intellectually and emotionally. It made we want to praise God in that way and maybe help others praise God through music as well.

EVANGELISTIC EVENTS

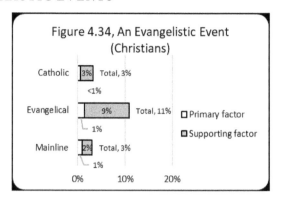

Only 1 percent of Christians cite evangelistic events as the primary factor in coming to faith. For the persons in our study, these included such things as revival meetings or crusades, but just as often persons mentioned conferences or retreats. While 11 percent of Evangelicals say evangelistic events are either a primary or supporting factor, just 3 percent of Mainline Protestants and Catholics do so.

Though few in number, persons in our study citing evangelistic events highlighted the confidence, inspiration, or power they received from them. Some found in them information they did not previously have or a specific calling or opportunity to make a decision that was compelling and highly significant. Baptisms, worship services, the Mass, and the Lord's Supper are perhaps not typically considered "evangelistic events," and they were not described as such under this heading by any respondents. But it is important to note that Christian rituals were mentioned with some frequency elsewhere in the study as influential in the process of coming to faith. They were every bit as "evangelistic" as the revivals and crusades more typically understood as such.

OTHER FACTORS

A small percentage (7 percent) of our study participants could not choose one of the fourteen options we provided as a primary factor in their coming to faith. For many of those persons, it was just impossible to settle on one as more important than others. Others identified the primary factor as their own personal desire, awakening, self-awareness, or internal longing (we saw that with persons of other religious faiths as well). But there were a few other intriguing answers supplied as "write-ins."

Among Catholics:

- School

- Pope Francis

- The beautiful peace and quiet sense of worthiness I feel, while standing in a cathedral

Among Evangelical Protestants:

- Spiritual activity in my home

- Volunteering with elderly/children

- Bad circumstances

- Videos on YouTube

Among Mainline Protestants

- A post on Facebook

- The overwhelming beauty of nature and the sense of Him being close by.

- Al-Anon

- AA

- Loneliness and sorrow

OBSTACLES?

One of the things we wanted to know is whether persons coming to faith found any of their religion's teachings, practices, persons, or institutions to be an obstacle in making their new commitment. A little over half of Roman Catholic respondents claimed there were indeed obstacles, while 39 percent of Mainline Protestants and 32 percent of Evangelicals said there were. The responses are highly significant for our study, and the differences between the Christian traditions are worth exploring in more detail.

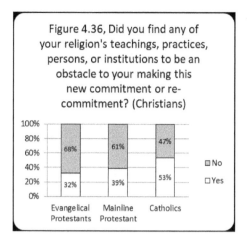

Figure 4.36, Did you find any of your religion's teachings, practices, persons, or institutions to be an obstacle to your making this new commitment or re-commitment? (Christians)

Evangelicals

Just over a third of Evangelicals who encountered obstacles mentioned specific theological or ethical questions. The most common were:

- the challenge of reconciling science with faith, or evolution with creation;

- their church's negative position on homosexuality or marriage equality; and

- difficulties with the Bible or with an exalted view of the authority of Scripture they had encountered.

> *I feel like many Christians put God in a box and are only interested in believing the parts of the Bible that suit them. And I don't like naive people that don't believe in science and proven fact.*

> *I have an education in sciences and was confused by some who insist the world is 6000 years old. As it says in Psalm 90:4, "For a thousand years in thy sight are but as yesterday when it is past, and as a watch in the night." I see no conflict, yet conflict in theology exists. My answer to those who conflict with my beliefs is "God isn't that small."*

> *The only obstacle I struggle with is the issue with same sex marriage. I have friends who are gay and some are married with children and I love them dearly. This is my only source of conflict, but I believe that is between God and the individual.*

For several Evangelicals, the challenge had to do with their early experiences, training, or teaching (Catholicism was frequently singled out for criticism), or with the inflexibility or irrelevance of the faith they had encountered. They listed questions about beliefs pertaining to hell and the devil, the doctrines of predestination and total depravity, the exclusivism of Christianity, the Trinity, tithing, rebaptism, and some of the places in Hebrew and Christian Scripture where God is portrayed as not especially loving or compassionate.

Another third of Evangelicals said they experienced Christians as inconsistent, hypocritical, overly judgmental, or holding them back in some way. Ministers and family members were singled out most often in this regard. As one woman put it,

> *I was raised in a church that focused on worshiping God out of fear rather than love. This was something that I knew that I was not looking for this time.*

Another female protested,

> *Many times when expressing frustration or doubt over a situation I would hear "God has it" or "God is in control," which only made me feel like a defenseless pawn in a large chess game. The blind faith of some I find irritating because my more urgent questions get dismissed as questions not to be asked.*

At times these obstacles pertained to ordinary human imperfections that persons coming to faith simply had to learn to accept so that they could move forward. More often, however, the obstacles were irreconcilable (and continued to be irreconcilable) with what they had now come to understand as authentic Christian faith.

Mainline Protestants

Like Evangelicals, Mainline Protestants also mentioned particular theological or ethical questions and challenges. But whereas only about a third of Evangelicals cited problems here, just over half of Mainline Protestants did, and a much greater number mentioned disagreements with traditional Christian stances on homosexuality or gay marriage. In most cases, they found those obstacles in other Christian groups, which is precisely why they ended up turning to one of the Mainline denominations. Mainline Christians frequently cited obstacles they found in their previous experiences with Catholicism and Evangelicalism, and in about equal numbers. While they cited problematic attitudes related to homosexuality in both of those traditions, they also identified obstacles related to the treatment of women.

They pointed to problems with Catholic stances on human sexuality, marriage, and divorce and with Evangelical views on the Bible, salvation, guilt, hell, and the exclusiveness of Christ.

> *One of the reasons I was able to make a new faith commitment was because I found a non-creedal, covenant-based church. Accepting that it was possible for a church to be non-creedal, and yet still to profess beliefs that fit within the broad umbrella of Christianity, was itself in some sense a turning point for me.*

> *I don't actually believe in the factual nature of what I say in the Nicene Creed. This gave me pause but didn't keep me from fully making a commitment.*

> *I find much of the scripture as useful metaphor, not to be taken literally. It's easy to get overly focused on minutiae and lose the overall perspective of what is trying to be conveyed in stories or parables.*

Not all Mainline Protestants found it easy to adjust to the open or progressive theologies of the tradition within which they were making their new commitment.

> *I struggled with how much theological freedom my new denomination offered. I wasn't used to being asked my opinion when I asked about whether certain activities were permitted.*

> *For the Episcopal Church, I find it frustrating that they have virtually no doctrinal statements and try to see all sides & both sides forever, never arriving at any conclusion.*

> *The Religious Society of Friends is a pacifist faith group. I was not raised to believe in nonviolence, or as we put it, to remove the occasion for all war. I grew up believing that war was a terrible thing, but a necessary evil. That was a challenge to me, but I've made great progress since then.*

Some cited other Christians and clergy as an obstacle because of their hypocrisy and inconsistency, but fewer Mainline Protestants (10 percent) fell in this category than Evangelicals (33 percent). Most of the other 40 percent of Mainline Protestants listed a range of obstacles associated with the churches they had experienced in the past, especially with a perceived lack of inclusion and acceptance (which was mentioned most frequently). A good number also mentioned institutional politics or a preoccupation with institutional maintenance and an off-putting level of commitment that was expected of them (including financial commitment). A few also mentioned challenges with the boring or irrelevant character of Mainline worship.

> *I had a bad view of organized religion. I found them to be exclusive like a country club if you were not like them.*

> *Acceptance was a major factor in finding and joining a Church.*

> *The only thing that truly kept me back was my old church. They could find ways to make you feel as if you didn't belong, that this was their religion, their church and you, really I, was nothing, that I shouldn't be there.*

Catholics

Like many Christians, some Catholics reported challenges with traditional Christian beliefs such as the Trinity or the fate of non-Christians. But those did not surface much in their answers to this question. Yet Catholics outnumbered Protestants in identifying obstacles. Far more often than Protestants, Roman Catholics cited a litany of church practices and ethical positions they experienced as roadblocks. Many of these remain problematic, even after their new faith commitment. But while some said they have reconciled themselves to those teachings and practices, most said they simply disregard or continue to oppose them. Several described themselves as not feeling the need to agree with all Catholic teachings in order to remain Catholic.

By far, the most difficult teaching of the church for those becoming Catholic pertains to homosexuality and gay marriage. After that, the church's positions most frequently mentioned as obstacles (in order of frequency) are birth control, gender roles and women's ordination, marriage and divorce, abortion, the hierarchical organization of the church and clergy, veneration of Mary and the saints, closed communion to non-Catholics, and recent sex scandals along with their cover-up.

> *Most of the politics of the Catholic Church turned me away at first. I still get really annoyed at the archaic thoughts of some of the clergy. However, once I realized that the church is really not about the clergy and really about the community and the people I came around to the idea of joining and staying as a Catholic.*

> *I think the Catholic church is very backwards about the role of women in the church, about same-sex marriage and love, about*

birth control, and about trying so hard to 'cover up' the 'problem' of abuse that has emerged in the last decade or so.

There were stances with the church I didn't agree with and I was having a hard time understanding how do you move forward in a religion that you don't agree with 100%. Can you call yourself a catholic if you don't agree with big portions of their "rules?"

Remaining Obstacles?

We asked whether there are any teachings, practices, persons, or institutions that continue to prove difficult. While the number responding affirmatively to this question went down, the difference was slight. For some persons, the obstacles they encountered were in churches or traditions that they subsequently left. For most others, those obstacles remain, and they have simply decided to live with them, to continue to study and think about them, or to keep working through the issues as they move along the journey of faith. As one Catholic woman put it, "It's a process I grow into daily . . . it's easier now." Resources in working through these issues include prayer, trusting God, participating in study groups, and talking with ministers and friends. Several Catholics specifically mentioned Pope Francis as helping, and as making it easier to be Catholic without feeling the need to follow all the teachings of the church.

WHAT WAS MOST APPEALING?

When persons were asked if they found any of Christianity's teachings, practices, persons, or institutions particularly appealing, we found an incredible diversity of answers, though several common threads that illustrate the distinctives of each Christian tradition.

Catholics

Catholics spoke most frequently of loving Catholicism itself—the long history of the church, its traditions, worship, and teachings, and the experience of being part of a truly global family and community. As one man answered, "The consistency of the Catholic Liturgy, I find beautiful and it gives me a sense of peace and safety." Indeed, several persons used the word "consistency" to emphasize the commonality of faith, practice, and liturgy shared by Catholics from parish to parish and nation to nation. The celebration of Eucharist, or Mass, was frequently mentioned appreciatively.

Another feature of Catholicism lifted up with regularity was the church's emphasis on social justice, good works, mercy, and the importance of loving and serving others. As one young attorney put it, "the Church's teachings on helping the less fortunate and on being humble are appealing and stand in stark contrast to millionaire pastors in megachurches with mansions which I find appalling." Again, Pope Francis was singled out as an inspiration, and others expressed appreciation for opportunities to volunteer in their parishes.

As one might expect, several persons identified particular individuals and ministers for whom they were appreciative and whose teachings or outreach and care were both attractive and appealing. Beyond that, other features of the Catholic tradition that persons found appealing were devotion to Mary and the veneration of saints, prayer, the rosary, and particular Catholic authors or historical figures.

> I find the Catholic emphasis on good works particularly appealing. Faith is important, of course, but as St. James said, faith without works is dead.

> The commitment to charity and human suffering. I am a big fan of Pope Francis.

> The intervention of the saints and the Blessed Mother, praying the Rosary.

> I love the way the Mass is structured and that no matter where you are in the world if you are in a Catholic Church you will hear the same readings and same gospel. It feels like a big community, not just a single church.

> I deeply enjoy the beauty and respectfulness of the liturgy.

> I find the sacrament of reconciliation to be extremely gratifying, knowing (and learning to trust) that God really has forgiven me for my past misdoings.

> I had always been troubled by many Protestants' reliance on the Bible as the literal truth; the Bible contradicts itself. I take great comfort in what I see as a more intellectual approach in the Catholic Church that allows us to read the Bible within the context of its history and of our understanding of it over time.

Evangelicals

One out of five Evangelicals spoke about the appeal of Christ as their savior and about their relationship with Christ. While some expressed this in the devotional language of love for Christ (and Christ's love for them), others emphasized the importance of Christ's teachings as appealing. Another one-fifth of the responses focused on salvation, forgiveness, or grace. And while these responses tended to focus on personal experience, many had the cast of doctrinal assertions or beliefs.

One out of five Evangelicals lifted up Scripture as appealing, consistent with what we have already seen in this chapter. They love studying the Bible and meditating upon it. They are drawn to particular stories from Scripture, and they are passionate about preaching that is biblical. They are also drawn to ministers and churches that are biblically grounded. Yet another fifth of Evangelicals focused on their congregation or community, and the fellowship and acceptance they have found there. This response overlaps with a sizeable group of responses that highlighted the pastor or pastoral staff.

> *All of God's Word is appealing. I have made it my life-long commitment to study and to know it. For in doing so I know the Lord more accurately so I can serve Him more faithfully!*

> *I found all of the teachings appealing. I wanted to learn everything I could about Jesus!*

> *It is not about a religion but about a relationship with Jesus.*

> *The Gospel of grace. The free salvation only by the sacrifice of Christ in the cross.*

> *Our pastor is great at presenting the true Word and teaching.*

> *The pastor at my church have such powerful and relevant messages every week. They motivated me and made me want to continue to attend and learn more about God.*

Mainline Protestants

Just under a third of Mainline Protestants found the inclusiveness, welcome, and acceptance of their congregations to be most appealing.

> *Christian love and inclusive community. Social ministry and outreach programs to help the poor and vulnerable in our community.*

I love the sacramental and liturgical nature of the Episcopal church. I also love the fact that they are inclusive, respect woman and treat them with equality, and have a very spiritual—but still realistic—view of human sexuality.

I LOVE the UCC's views, beliefs, and values . . . open and affirming, value women, accepting of all just as they are, God is still speaking.

Yes, church is inclusive of all people (race, sexual orientation, all are welcome). It's a diverse community. Focus is on leading a loving and caring life and helping others rather than judging others.

Another quarter of Mainline Protestants focused on the congregation's worship format or liturgy, the preaching style, the music, and the support and care of the clergy.

I have a connection with the pastor and the congregation.

I like that the service starts on time and ends in an hour. I like that it is predictable and the same service at every Anglican/Episcopal church in the world. I love the music, liturgy, and rituals. I think the church service is very beautiful.

Those ministers who could apply Biblical teachings to the current world and times.

Traditional hymns and rituals maintain the sanctity of worship. Mission work of the church is an example of putting faith into practice.

Fifteen percent talked about forgiveness, salvation, or Christian teachings (often the freedom found in the Mainline approach to Christian teachings).

I found the practice of involvement in church decisions very positive. I also found the church's teaching of understanding rather than judgement very important.

I like how Methodism seems to be less about man-made rules and more about God. In Methodism, women can be pastors, there are no rules about not eating meat on Fridays or giving something up for Lent. There is more emphasis on following God's ways.

I like that Quakerism relies on the individual to seek God and to discern what God means to them. I like that we take [. . .] Jesus's commandments to love God and each other seriously and put that into practice. I like the fact that Quakers are not as concerned about the mythology of Christianity and have gone to the roots of Jesus's ministry of loving one another and serving those less fortunate.

The Golden Rule of do unto others as you would have them do unto you. Love God. Live with guidance from the Bible. Serve God and my fellows.

Yes, I found the Episcopal Church's emphasis on God's infinite love and benevolence and compassion refreshing and a source of hope.

Summary

It is striking how thoroughly the distinctives of the major traditions within Christianity come through in all these responses—both those that identify obstacles and those that highlight what is appealing. For those who find faith as Christians, the unique family characteristics of a particular tradition within Christianity often make all the difference. For the most part, these distinctives are more than shallow consumer preferences, as if persons were choosing furniture from a warehouse of options. The distinctives run deep, and shape not only the decisions and commitments of those who find faith but the very nature of faith itself.

5

Christians: Is There a Change?

TRYING TO DETERMINE WHAT changes, if any, take place in the lives of persons who have recently made a faith commitment is an important, but challenging, aspect of the Finding Faith Today study. If the journey of faith is one that takes place over time for most people, we might not expect to see immediate major shifts in attitudes, conduct, social views, or ethical commitments. On the other hand, if the commitment is more than a superficial club membership, we should expect that new Christians would report some changes in convictions and behaviors. The changes we looked at rely on self-reporting, of course, but we can at least gauge how those persons understood what this commitment means in their lives. Our study inquired about those changes from a variety of perspectives—including spirituality and self-perception; religious behavior such as prayer, Scripture reading, and church attendance; personal moral behavior; and stances on important social issues. Is a new commitment to faith life-changing and, if so, how?

CHURCH ATTENDANCE

As Figure 5.1 shows, prior to their new commitment, less than 40 percent of persons making a new faith commitment had been attending church at least once per month (the line on the chart refers to that threshold as "regular attendance").

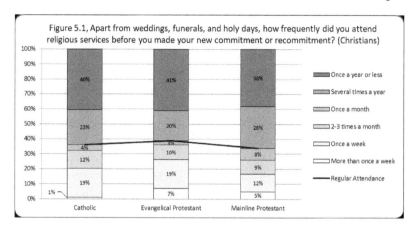

Figure 5.1, Apart from weddings, funerals, and holy days, how frequently did you attend religious services before you made your new commitment or recommitment? (Christians)

The changes in churchgoing reported after a new faith commitment are striking (Figure 5.2):

- 17 percent of Mainline Protestants went to church once or more per week prior to making their new faith commitment; that increased to 75 percent afterwards.

- 22 percent of Roman Catholics went to church once or more per week prior to making their new faith commitment; attendance increased to 87 percent afterwards.

- 29 percent of Evangelicals went to church once or more per week prior to making their new faith commitment; that increased to 90 percent afterwards, with almost half attending more than once per week.

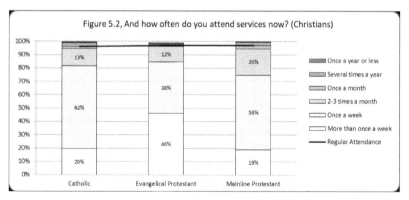

Figure 5.2, And how often do you attend services now? (Christians)

Some persons were unaffected in their church attendance, including no more than 3 percent who were non-attenders and remained so. We also saw a small minority who had been attending regularly and for whom this new commitment, while an important next step on their journey, was not one that substantively affected their churchgoing. But for the vast majority, the step of making a new and public faith commitment makes a large difference in their way of life, especially when one considers the pressures on time in US culture and how precious the weekend is for those who try to find time for rest, recreation, and catching up on household chores. Then too, employees in the US work longer hours and with a longer work week than those in other industrialized nations, are more likely to work full-time, and are more likely to work on weekends (one-third of the US workforce now works on weekends).[1]

Because there is a well-documented gender gap in US church attendance, we wanted to see if that held true for the subjects of our study. We know from other research that the typical US congregation is about 60 percent female in composition and that women are more likely than men to say religion is "very important in their lives" (59 percent vs. 47 percent).[2] Women are also more likely than men to attend religious services at least once per week (40 percent vs. 31 percent). The data from our study, however, demonstrate that a new faith commitment changes that gender gap substantially (not to mention that it doubles the nationwide attendance rate for Christians more generally). Among Protestants, far more males than females report attending church at least once per week: 89 percent vs 82 percent for Evangelicals and 79 percent vs 73 percent for Mainline Protestants (Figure 5.3). For Roman Catholics, by contrast, females (82 percent) are still more likely than males (79 percent) to attend at least once per week. Those differences are even more pronounced when we isolate those who attend more than once per week, as Figure 5.3 illustrates.

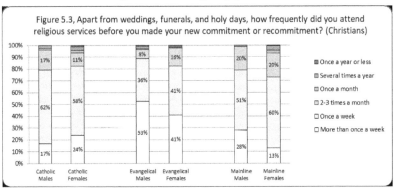

Figure 5.3, Apart from weddings, funerals, and holy days, how frequently did you attend religious services before you made your new commitment or recommitment? (Christians)

1. Ingraham, "Nearly One Third."
2. Pew, "America's Changing Religious Landscape," 50.

OTHER FORMS OF INVOLVEMENT

In addition to asking about church attendance, we asked persons about other ways they are involved in religious groups, fellowships, or studies. We found a wide range of responses. First, we asked about their overall involvement in the life and activities of their church (Figure 5.4). Protestants are the most active, with 84 percent of Evangelicals and 82 percent of Mainline Protestants claiming to be somewhat or very involved. By contrast, 67 percent of Catholics are somewhat or very involved. Only 21 percent of Catholics say they are "very active," or about half the number of Protestants.

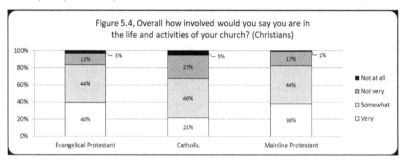

Figure 5.4, Overall how involved would you say you are in the life and activities of your church? (Christians)

As Figure 5.5 shows, 43 percent of Catholics, 53 percent of Mainline Protestants, and 73 percent of Evangelicals report weekly activity in groups of one kind or another. Much of this involvement is related to education, formation, and discipleship such as Bible and book studies, prayer circles, catechism classes, youth groups, RCIA for Catholics, Sunday school, etc. But persons in the study also report a host of other sorts of groups including groups designed for socializing, meals, and fellowship; counseling and recovery groups; volunteer or mission groups involved in charitable, evangelistic, or social justice outreach; and administrative groups such as church boards and committees.

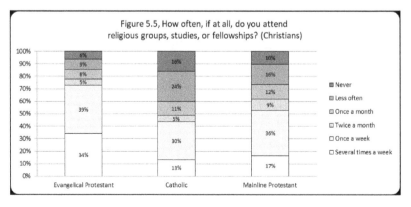

Figure 5.5, How often, if at all, do you attend religious groups, studies, or fellowships? (Christians)

It is significant that one-third of Roman Catholics and one quarter of Mainline Protestants are not finding means of support, involvement, and growth beyond Sunday worship. Most of those who are not very involved, moreover, are not happy with their level of involvement (Figure 5.6).

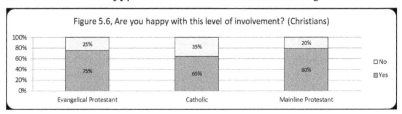

Figure 5.6, Are you happy with this level of involvement? (Christians)

About a quarter of those who say they are not happy with their level of involvement cite time restraints as the major issue, usually because of family or work obligations. Another 15 to 20 percent indicate that there are restraints such as distance to the church, health limitations, or financial burdens that prevented them from being involved. Another 15 percent (but of Catholics and Evangelicals only) mention challenges with integration. In some cases, they are still searching for their place or purpose in becoming involved. In other cases, they lack confidence or are shy and introverted.

I have more to give and I am still searching for my right fit.

I want to feel more connected with more people. It will just take time to get to know folks.

I have a hard time fitting in groups.

I'd like to be more involved and have been increasing my involvement but it's a challenge because I'm introverted so "getting out there" and doing things is a challenge for me.

A small minority of persons identify limitations with the church itself that pose challenges for their own involvement.

I would like to be more involved in church activities such as being a communion minister or usher but classes are seldom offered.

Need our kids in a kids Sunday School program and weekly kids Bible program. Current church doesn't offer it. We may be moving soon, so we're holding back on getting too involved since we may soon need a different church.

I feel like I am too busy with home/family life. Also lack of knowledge about other small groups available.

I'd like to be more involved but most of the groups are for people under 18 or over 30.

I don't really know how to build connection in the church.

I would love to be more involved, I just haven't found a way to serve in which I can be useful and effective.

MULTIPLE RELIGIOUS BELONGING

We asked the persons in our study if they currently participate in religious services or activities from any other religion in order to assess the extent of multiple religious belonging for new or recommitted Christians. There are large theological differences among Christian traditions about the possibility, for example, of being both a Buddhist and a Christian (to name only one configuration), and this possibility often comes down to how one understands the exclusivity of the person and work of Christ, the nature of the church, and the character of salvation. There are also differences among Christians in how they understand what exactly is going on in other religious traditions—whether, that is, they are in competition with one another or whether, by contrast, they might be complementary in some ways.

Only about 2 percent of Roman Catholics said yes to that question, though that is doubled if one counts attending a Protestant worship service as multiple religious belonging, since several Catholics identified that as, for them, participating in "another religion." Several mentioned reading books with teachings from other faith traditions or practicing yoga and meditation, though in a Christian context.

About 3 percent of Evangelicals said yes to this question, with a few mentioning participation in Buddhist practices and traditions and a few mentioning Jewish customs and holidays. As with Catholics, though now in reverse, a few identified their participation in Catholic services as participating in another religion.

Just over 8 percent of Mainline Protestants claimed to participate currently in other religious traditions—the vast majority claiming Buddhist meditation, mindfulness, and instruction, or Jewish practices, classes, and holidays. Several others mentioned participating in interfaith events, Hindu, Bahá'í, Unitarian Universalist, or Native American practices, or social and charitable activities. No Orthodox Christians claimed participation in other religious traditions, though, again, the sample size is too small to make generalizations.

READING SCRIPTURE

Recall that only 1 percent of Mainline Protestants, 2 percent of Catholics, and 8 percent of Evangelicals cite Scripture as the primary factor in their recent faith commitment. Far more claim Scripture to be either a primary or supporting factor, and when asked if they read Scripture at the time they were making their commitment, 30 percent of Mainline Protestants, 45 percent of Catholics, and 57 percent of Evangelicals say they read several times a week.

We asked how often they read Scripture privately now in order to see if things had changed. Roman Catholics report that they now read Scripture less each week than during the time they were making their commitment, dropping from 57 percent originally to 35 percent (as we will see in chapter 6, this is typical of Jewish converts as well). We found that for Protestants, regular Scripture reading increased slightly, even though Scripture is not nearly as important to Mainline Protestants as it is to Evangelicals. As Figure 5.7 demonstrates, Evangelical Protestants are twice as likely as their Mainline counterparts to read Scripture several times a week. Almost a quarter of Mainline Protestants who had made a new faith commitment now seldom or never read Scripture privately.

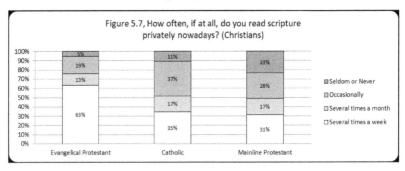

Figure 5.7, How often, if at all, do you read scripture privately nowadays? (Christians)

In all cases, the percentage of those who now read the Bible "seldom or never" went down (from 10 percent to 5 percent for Evangelicals, from 15 percent to 11 percent for Catholics, and from 26 to 23 percent for Mainline Protestants). When asked further how important Scripture is now to their faith, we find a fairly similar picture. Ninety-five percent of Evangelicals, 88 percent of Catholics, and 82 percent of Mainline Protestants say Scripture is "very" or "somewhat" important (Figure 5.8).

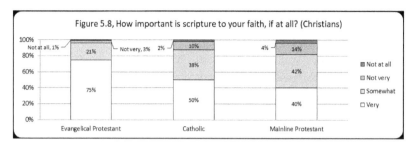

Figure 5.8, How important is scripture to your faith, if at all? (Christians)

GOD

When asked whether they had thought about God much prior to making their faith commitment, 40 percent of Evangelicals and almost half (48 percent) of all other Christian respondents say they had done so a great deal (Figure 5.9). Evangelicals, it must be remembered, are more likely to experience a sudden conversion, and that likely accounts for more of them not having given God much thought prior to their commitment. For those whose experience of faith is more gradual, God may be on their minds for some time.

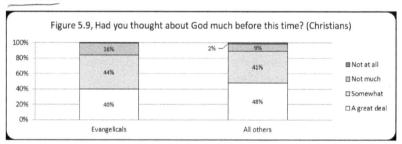

Figure 5.9, Had you thought about God much before this time? (Christians)

This difference between Evangelicals and other Christians also registers when we asked persons in the study how they would have described God before making their new faith commitment and how they would describe God now (Figure 5.10). Over two-thirds (68 percent) of Evangelicals claim their view of God has changed substantially, with another 12 percent reporting some growth and alteration in their understanding of and relationship with God. This is a significant contrast to Catholics and Mainline Protestants, for whom far fewer (45 percent of Catholics and 51 percent of Mainline Protestants) report substantive change in their perceptions of God. This, again, could be due to the higher numbers of "gradualists" among the latter in contrast to Evangelicals.

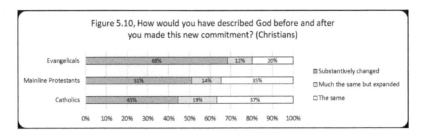

Figure 5.10, How would you have described God before and after you made this new commitment? (Christians)

When one's image of God did change, for most persons in the study that meant their image of God moved from an image of God as distant, impersonal, mysterious, or aloof to an image of God as present, revealed, personal, and caring. Similarly, while a good number reported understanding God prior to their commitment in classical terms such as creator, all-knowing, or all-powerful, and while those qualities did not get displaced altogether, they were not as foregrounded now. Instead, God's character as present, listening, and loving was more prominent. For Evangelicals, God as savior was especially conspicuous.

For quite a number of persons, the differences in their view of God before and after were even starker. God had been viewed as harsh, vengeful, shaming, judging, stern, or even unloving; but now God was perceived as the complete opposite. Often those who reported this kind of change cited their own life experiences at the time (abuse, addiction, loss, guilt) as shaping their negative views of God.

What was perhaps most interesting about the responses to this set of questions was the enthusiasm in the answers. For the vast majority, these were not just rote answers to a questionnaire or interview. They often took the form of a testimony with exclamation marks, and the responses were self-involving rather than abstract. At times, this produced what may appear to be exaggerations, but after reading and hearing hundreds and hundreds of different responses, the sincerity and authenticity of the responses was impressive.

CHANGES THAT FINDING FAITH HAS MADE

In addition to hearing from persons in our study about changes to their church attendance, Scripture reading, or images of God, we also asked them to rate the amount of change they think has taken place in their life in relation to a variety of measures on a scale of 0–5. We suggested six types of change based on those that have shown up in other studies of religious conversion: (1) beliefs, (2) actions and lifestyle, (3) spiritual practices, (4) relations with others, (5) happiness, and (6) hopefulness.

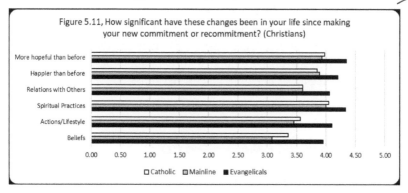

Figure 5.11, How significant have these changes been in your life since making your new commitment or recommitment? (Christians)

As can readily be seen from Figure 5.11, Evangelicals, considerably more than persons from other Christian traditions, think of themselves as having changed more by every measure. At the same time, changes in spiritual practices are identified by the largest number of persons from across all Christians traditions. For Mainline Christians, finding faith turns out to be far less about changes in beliefs than it is about other types of changes.

We also considered age as a variable. As Figure 5.12 shows, there is little difference by age, except for those in the 18 to 24 age category, who report considerably more change in their lives across the board. Of course, it could be that younger persons tend to over-inflate the changes being made in their lives. But surely it is not a stretch to believe that young people are inclined to make significant changes as a result of coming to faith, or that older persons might be a bit more established in their thinking or practices.

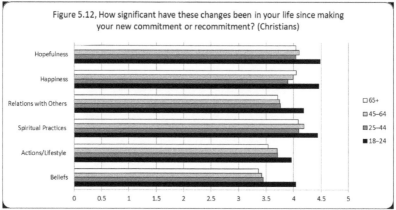

Figure 5.12, How significant have these changes been in your life since making your new commitment or recommitment? (Christians)

While it was helpful to get responses from our participants to our questions about change, we also wanted to hear directly from them, using their own words and categories. We asked them the open question, "What is the main difference that becoming a Christian (or a more committed Christian) has made in your life?" Just under 2 percent of Christians said there was no change, but the vast majority of responses were generally quite positive, with a great variety in the ways people describe the change (Figure 5.13). Since persons often responded with multiple descriptions of the change, the percentages in Figure 5.13 exceed 100%.

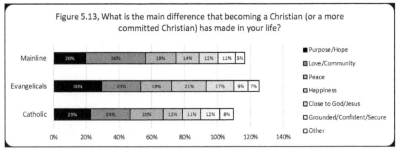

Figure 5.13, What is the main difference that becoming a Christian (or a more committed Christian) has made in your life?

Purpose, Meaning, and Hope

One of the largest groups of responses (30 percent of Evangelicals, 23 percent of Catholics, and 20 percent of Mainline Protestants) is related to a greater sense of purpose, direction, meaning, fulfilment, and hope. Twice as many Evangelicals as other Christians describe the change in their lives using the language of hope. But while research shows that Evangelicals do indeed tend to believe more strongly in heaven, the kind of hope they accentuate was rarely described in otherworldly or afterlife terms for all our Christian respondents, Evangelicals included. Instead, persons tend to talk about hope as purpose, meaning, and direction for themselves, the world, and the future.

I feel more complete than I did before.

Has given me a foundation and purpose for being on this earth.

I feel a greater purpose and greater connection to the world as a whole.

I feel a real sense of life again and hope for the future.

I wake up and go to bed with a smile on my face, hope in my heart and a song on my lips!

Being a Christian has given me a life in the sense of assurance of God's concern for me and hope through knowing my life has meaning.

*I now have hope. I have trust in what the Lord has set for me and
I am excited about the future.*

It has increased my hopefulness—in humanity, in myself, in good.

I strongly believe that I am going to Heaven.

Love and Relationships

The second of the two largest groups of responses center on growth in their
love for others and an improvement in the quality of their relationships.
Over a third of all Mainline Protestants describe their lives now as being
more loving, understanding, compassionate, accepting, and caring while
being less self-centered and judgmental. At times, this is also described as
a greater sense of belonging in community or of being involved in social
outreach. Several Mainline Protestants described the change in relation to
being a better spouse, partner, or parent. This is significantly more than the
24 percent of Evangelicals and Catholics who describe the change similarly,
though we should not downplay the importance of this type of change for
those groups as well, since it is the most frequently mentioned for Catholics
and the second most frequently mentioned for Evangelicals. Throughout
the entire study, we have seen that Mainline Protestants tend to accentuate
the importance of community and congregation by describing their faith
in more social and less individualistic terms, and this tendency bears itself
out here. Still, one finds an impressive focus on love from all Christians as
central to the change that faith has made in their lives.

I am more patient and respectful to others in the world.

*I think less about myself and more about others. I serve others as
much as possible.*

*I think more about the consequences of my day-to-day actions. I'm
more generous, compassionate, thoughtful, and I feel like I have a
larger view of the world, the universe.*

*I believe I am more thoughtful and considerate of others and have
a more loving and understanding relationship with my family.*

I do not judge people.

*I feel more accepted by people, and feel better about my life. I try to
serve and help others much more than I did previously.*

I have become more tolerant of differences and a bit kinder and more thoughtful of others in the process.

I try to be more accepting and forgiving of others.

It has brought a greater sense of community into my life that I did not have before.

Peace

Constituting the third largest group of responses overall (and with little difference among the Christian traditions), about one in five Christians describe themselves as having a greater sense of peace, comfort, and contentedness, with less fear, worry, anxiety, and stress.

I am calmer and have more peace in all I do: work, play, social, family.

I feel more at peace with myself.

I have more peace knowing I can trust in God to lead me through tough times.

It has relieved so much stress knowing that God has a purpose for me and is there at all times. I have become happier seeing the glory in small things.

I am more relaxed—more certain that God is with me.

Less anxiety because I leave worries and my life in his hands.

Happiness

One of the places we saw significant differences among the three major Christian traditions is when it comes to identifying change in terms of happiness or joy. Twelve percent of Catholics say they are happier, 14 percent of Mainline Protestants, and 21 percent of Evangelicals. It is difficult to explain exactly why Evangelicals report being so much happier than others, though many of their answers have a greater tendency to relate their happiness to a release of guilt and a greater sense of trust in God with less self-reliance. They are more likely to describe themselves as recipients of grace and as no longer being under the law. The following are representative of all Christian responses in the study focusing on happiness and joy.

Much happier, relaxed, and more positive.

I am an overall happier person. Since my official commitment, I have had multiple friends tell me that I am in a seemly much better mood/attitude.

I feel like a more joyful person.

I am not so hard on myself and I am more open to the positives in life.

I feel happier now that I am a Christian. I had a lot of bitterness in my heart and I was very depressed. I was able to let go of the bitterness with the help of my pastor's teachings and with Scripture. My depression is much better now. I often turn to the Bible when I feel down.

I feel like a weight has been lifted off of me.

Closer to God

About one in ten Mainline Protestants and Catholics describe the change in their lives as related to their having a closer relationship with God or Jesus. An even higher percentage of Evangelicals do so, indeed almost twice as many. This proximity to God was often described in terms of "not being alone," though God's presence was also described as bringing guidance, comfort, and peace.

More cognizant of God's presence in my life and of the value of each day.

The closeness I feel with God. Knowing I have a safe place to go for peace and comfort.

I no longer feel like I am losing control of my life. God is in control.

I am more conscience of God's presence in my life. I am happier and not so stressed. I am more thankful for a lot more now.

I feel grounded and connected to the divine Presence of God that sustains me and gives me purpose and hope and peace.

Grounded, Secure, and Confident

Lastly, about one in ten of all respondents described themselves as more grounded in their faith, or more secure, balanced, and confident because of their trust in God.

> *Many burdens seem to have been lifted off of my shoulders. My life seems to be grounded and strengthened by my faith.*

> *It gives me a strong center from which to act in a loving and just manner. It also helps me engage in social ministry.*

> *I have become more self-assured.*

> *I am more confident. I know that when I trust God, things will work out.*

> *I feel I am more grounded since finding a church home.*

> *It has centered me and made me realize what is important in life.*

SOCIAL ISSUES

Is finding faith associated with any significant changes in views on social issues for Christians? We have already seen in this study that what it means to be a Christian can vary greatly by theological tradition, and that is no less true when it comes to social issues. We asked about eight pressing, contemporary social issues, and our question to study participants was, "How have your attitudes and positions on the following social issues changed, if at all, since making your new commitment or recommitment?"

We especially wanted to look for where changes were occurring, so changes of more than 5 percent are reflected by darker shading in the chart below. But we also have here a good indicator of Christian positions more generally on these social issues within each tradition. The data represented here, then, imply some level of correlation between finding faith and the change new or recommitted Christians perceived in themselves. Comparison of these data with those from other faith traditions can be found in Appendix C and throughout the remainder of the book.

Figure 5.14, How have your attitudes and positions on the following social issues changed, if at all, since making your new commitment or recommitment?"	Already opposed, became more opposed	Already opposed, remain just as opposed	Now become opposed	No opinion/ Don't know	Now became supportive	Already supported, stayed just as supportive	Already supportive, became more supportive
Right to an Abortion							
Evangelicals	24%	35%	14%	14%	1%	11%	1%
Mainline	3%	18%	5%	19%	2%	49%	3%
Catholics	19%	27%	17%	18%	2%	17%	1%
Gay Marriage							
Evangelicals	22%	31%	9%	15%	4%	16%	3%
Mainline	3%	10%	2%	13%	10%	43%	19%
Catholics	12%	18%	5%	23%	1%	34%	7%
Gun Control							
Evangelicals	8%	21%	2%	24%	8%	29%	8%
Mainline	6%	20%	1%	21%	4%	38%	10%
Catholics	5%	20%	3%	28%	3%	34%	7%
War							
Evangelicals	10%	21%	6%	39%	2%	20%	1%
Mainline	11%	41%	5%	26%	2%	13%	2%
Catholics	15%	38%	6%	30%	1%	10%	1%
Women's Equality							
Evangelicals	1%	4%	1%	21%	3%	55%	15%
Mainline	0%	0%	0%	7%	2%	68%	22%
Catholics	1%	2%	1%	13%	4%	66%	14%
Racial Justice							
Evangelicals	3%	5%	0%	18%	5%	53%	17%
Mainline	0%	1%	2%	10%	3%	61%	24%
Catholics	1%	3%	1%	10%	3%	67%	14%
Economic Justice for the Poor							
Evangelicals	2%	5%	0%	24%	11%	40%	18%
Mainline	0%	1%	1%	12%	6%	44%	36%
Catholics	2%	1%	1%	17%	5%	46%	29%
Care for the Natural Environment							
Evangelicals	2%	3%	0%	20%	9%	49%	17%
Mainline	0%	0%	0%	12%	4%	58%	25%
Catholics	1%	2%	0%	15%	5%	56%	21%

Reproductive Rights

Since making their new faith commitment, a significant number of Catholics (17 percent) and Evangelicals (14 percent) became newly opposed to women having a right to an abortion. That represents the highest percentage of change to a new position, whether in opposition or in support, of any social issue we measured. An additional 19 percent of Catholics and 24 percent of Evangelicals were already opposed but became even more opposed since making their new commitment. We did not see as much change for Mainline Protestants, half of whom were already supportive of the right to an abortion. A small percentage (5 percent) became newly opposed.

Gay Marriage

The situation is similar in some respects when it comes to the question of same-sex marriage, though with more complexity when it comes to Catholics. While one in ten Mainline Protestants became newly supportive of same-sex marriage since making a new faith commitment, Evangelicals are the mirror opposite with about one in ten who became newly opposed. Slightly over half of Evangelicals were already opposed to same-sex marriage, including 22 percent who became more opposed. By contrast, almost two-thirds of Mainline Protestants were already supportive, including 19 percent who strengthened their support.

The situation is a bit different for Catholics than for Evangelicals or Mainline Protestants. Forty-one percent were already supportive of same-sex marriage (including 7 percent who became more supportive) as compared to only 30 percent of Catholics who were opposed (including 12 percent who became more opposed). A small percentage (5 percent) of Catholics became newly opposed to same-sex marriage, while hardly any became newly supportive. Clearly on this social issue Catholics cannot be painted with the same brush as Protestants.

Gun Control

About a quarter of all respondents have no opinion or don't know what they think about gun control. This could be because they have not formulated a position or found the issue too complex. Or perhaps it was less important to them than other social issues. But we saw this same level of complexity in the other religious groups we studied. Overall, we saw little change among new Christians on this issue, though most of the change moves in the direction of support for gun control. At 8 percent, Evangelicals are the largest group of those who became newly supportive. For the most part, Mainline Protestants and Catholics were already supportive or became even more supportive. In the time since we gathered the data for this study, there have been several mass shootings in the US followed by new momentum for more robust gun control legislation, so it may be that persons would have stronger opinions on the subject than we saw in our participants at the time.

War

It's hard to imagine anyone being supportive of war as a blanket assertion, and this could be why we saw such a large number of persons reply that they don't have an opinion or don't know (39 percent of Evangelicals, 30 percent of Catholics, and 26 percent of Mainline Protestants). We asked simply about their view on "war," rather than any specific military intervention, so that may have left the question a bit murky. At the time of the survey, a protracted "War on Terror" was still being waged in Afghanistan. Evangelicals in our study were the most supportive of war, and that parallels other studies that have shown Evangelicals (or at least white Evangelicals) as having more support than other religious groups for military action.[3] However, very few persons from any Christian tradition became even more supportive of war than they already were since making their new faith commitment. Just over half of all Mainline Protestants and Catholics are either already opposed to war or became even more opposed. About the same number in all three Christian traditions (5 to 6 percent) became newly opposed.

Women's Equality

Only 2 percent of Evangelicals and Catholics became newly opposed or more opposed to women's equality after finding faith (though "women's equality" surely means different things to different people). Most Mainline Protestants (90 percent) were already supportive or became even more supportive of women's equality (indeed, only two of 331 Mainline Protestants were opposed). Eighty percent of Catholics and 70 percent of Evangelicals were also already supportive or became more supportive of women's equality. Only 7 percent of Mainline Protestants do not have an opinion on the subject, and it is clear that support for women's equality is overwhelming

3. As in the case of the war in Iraq. See Pew, "Different Faiths," and Gallup, "Support for War."

among that group of Christians. It is astonishing that, by contrast, 21 percent of Evangelicals have not formulated an opinion on the subject, and
neither have 13 percent of Catholics.

Racial Justice

The responses to the question of racial justice were almost the same as the
responses to women's equality in all Christian traditions. Again, it is impossible to know from our study what exactly respondents might think racial
justice entails in their context. Only a very few persons in all three traditions
were not as supportive of racial justice as they were of women's equality.
Indeed, only one Evangelical (out of 262) had become newly opposed to
racial justice since finding faith. Five percent of Evangelicals, by contrast,
became newly supportive. At the same time, we saw slightly greater opposition to racial justice (8 percent) than to women's equality (6 percent) among
Evangelicals.

Economic Justice for the Poor

Compared to other Christians, Evangelicals report a considerably higher
percentage of those who already opposed economic justice for the poor (5
percent) or who became more opposed (2 percent) after making a new faith
commitment. But only one person reported becoming newly opposed after
finding faith. In fact, 11 percent of Evangelicals became newly supportive of economic justice for the poor, which is a significant change for this
group. Mainline Protestants and Catholics were already solidly supportive
of economic justice. Still, it will no doubt come as a concern to many that
24 percent of Evangelicals and 17 percent of Catholics in the study have no
opinion on the matter or just don't know.

Care for the Natural Environment

The last social issue we asked about had to do with care for the natural environment, where we found the highest levels of support among all Christians. Seventy-nine percent of Mainline Protestants were already supportive
or became more supportive, and an additional 6 percent became newly
supportive. For Catholics, that was 74 percent with an additional 5 percent
newly supportive; and for Evangelicals, it was 59 percent with an additional
11 percent newly supportive. Though it is true that Evangelicals were less

supportive overall, we also saw the largest growth in persons becoming newly supportive among Evangelicals. It is safe to say that Christians across the theological spectrum are increasingly grasping the significance of environmental concerns as an important part of what it means to be a Christian.

CONCLUSION

By way of conclusion, it may be helpful to put into larger perspective the difference finding faith as a Christian makes to the social issues discussed above. First, it is important to recognize that these are reports about one's "attitudes" or "positions." We do not know the extent to which these attitudes translate into actions. But of course the gap between professed beliefs and actions besets most human beings. At the same time, knowing that a position has changed since finding faith is an important part of understanding the wider significance of faith in the world. Secondly, it is important to recall that we were the ones who asked about these changes. For the most part, stances on social issues were not the starting place for Christians when asked to describe in their own words the kinds of changes that had come with their newfound faith. That is not always the case, and as we saw in chapter 2, about two-thirds of Mainline Protestants and a little over half of all Catholics (only about a third of Evangelicals) identify what it means to be a Christian as primarily a matter of actions and lifestyle, which often explicitly includes social action, inclusivity, peacemaking, and justice-seeking.

Lastly, while we asked about changes in relation to social issues we did not ask about changes in private personal morality—behaviors such as smoking, gambling, alcohol or substance abuse, lying, sexual morality, etc. But producing a list of personal moral issues for a project such as this is fraught with challenges. Whose list of what behaviors should we use? Some Christians think that the use of contraception is immoral and for others it hardly registers as a moral conundrum. Indeed, it would be immoral *not* to use contraception. Others think Christians should never use profanity, while others use it all the time. Also, ethical customs and mores change considerably over time. Fifty years ago, dancing and cinema-going were prohibited by some Evangelical groups in the US, but that has changed considerably. We chose not to go down the road of designing a survey that tried to capture changes in personal morality, though in hindsight perhaps an open-ended question allowing respondents to indicate what they thought had changed in their morality would have been helpful.

6

Judaism

As of 2014, about 70 percent of the US population identified as Christian, and that is one of the reasons this study has given so much attention to Christianity and the three major traditions within it. Other religious faiths account for under 6 percent of the remaining population, with an additional 23 percent unaffiliated, (atheist, agnostic, or nothing in particular).[1] While adherents of these other religions are a much smaller percentage of the US population, we were very interested to learn how persons come to faith in those traditions (to the extent the language of "faith" is even applicable), using as many of the same categories and questions with them as we did with the Christian participants in the study. In this way, we were able to get a fairly good comparative sense of the different paths one is likely to take in adopting a religious tradition in the US, the primary factors that shape religious conversion and renewal, and the most important changes associated with that new commitment. At the same time, not all of the questions in our study transfer easily across all faith traditions.

Jews make up the largest percentage of non-Christian religious adherents in the US at 1.9 percent of the total population.[2] We look at Judaism in this chapter, and though the sample size is much smaller than our Christian population in the study, we were able to draw some solid conclusions about how persons commit to Judaism—whether for the first time as converts (as in most of the cases we looked at) or when activating and formalizing a commitment to the faith into which they were born.

---

1. Pew, "America's Changing Religious Landscape," 50.
2. Ibid., 4.

WHO PARTICIPATED IN THE STUDY?

Fifty-nine Jewish adults participated in the study, and among those the median age was 39, considerably younger than the median age of religious, or "observant" Jewish adults in the United States, which is 52.[3] As can be seen from Figure 6.1, the 30 to 49-year-old age group is represented much higher in our study than the US national average,[4] and that may tell us something about the age when persons are more likely to make a new commitment of this sort.

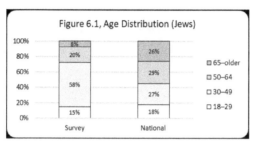

Figure 6.1, Age Distribution (Jews)

Eighty-three percent of the Jewish persons in our study graduated with a bachelors or graduate degree. This is a considerably higher average educational attainment than the national average among Jews (60 percent), which is itself much higher than that of the US general public (28 percent).[5] Readers may recall that 76 percent of the Christians in our study had a college or graduate degree, confirming an overall trend among respondents in our study toward having exceptionally high levels of education.

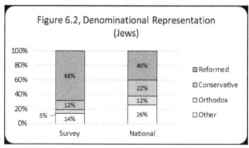

Figure 6.2, Denominational Representation (Jews)

As with Christians, we saw some differences among Jewish denominations, though for the most part I will not be stressing those the way I did

3. Pew, "A Portrait of Jewish Americans," 39. Unless otherwise noted, figures in this chapter will refer to religious Jews only. Non-religious, secular, or cultural Jews make up 22 percent of the total Jewish population in the US (7), and the median age of that group is 43.

4. Ibid.

5. Ibid., 42.

with Christians since the overall numbers are not large enough to allow for that kind of close comparison. Figure 6.2 illustrates the percentage of Jews in each of the major US denominational groupings. Reform Jews are over-represented in our study, and that will make a few differences in the interpretation of the data as we move along.

HOW DID JEWS SIGNAL THEIR FAITH?

We asked the Jews in our study how they signaled their new faith commitment or recommitment. Seventy-seven percent report going to the mikveh, a ritual of immersion in water for the purposes of initiation or conversion, similar to Christian baptism, which derives from this Jewish practice. Just over a quarter of the Reform Jews added membership (sometimes in combination with mikveh, and sometimes as the sole way of signaling). Other responses included: study and classes usually for up to a year, faithful participation and attendance in the community, an essay exam, a meeting with a rabbinical court (beit din), studying for bat mitzvah or bar mitzvah, and a conversion ceremony in Temple after the mikveh. Only a couple of persons mentioned ceremonial brit milah, or bris (circumcision). In addition to mikveh, Orthodox Jews also reported daily prayers, keeping Jewish dietary laws, and keeping Sabbath laws.

WHAT DOES IT MEAN TO BE JEWISH?

Half of all Jews in our study focused their answers to the question of what it means to be Jewish on the importance of being a people, a community, a worldwide family. Most often, that focus included an emphasis on Jewish heritage, culture, holidays, and identity. Jews are an historical people, we heard from many—a people who have "survived" and who share an identity across millennia.

> *It is being a part of a people that have struggled throughout history but they persevered and did some pretty incredible things along the way. They are a people that values deeds over decrees. They value education. Most of all, they are a tribe and what binds us together are the faith and traditions they have passed down over the years.*

> *Being Jewish means that you are a part of an ancient religion that you can mold into your own.*

> To belong to the community of Jews world-wide, and celebrate
> such belonging by participation in Jewish holidays and rituals.

> It means being a part of an amazingly rich history of a people who
> have been beaten down over & over only to rise up, time & again.
> That built a very community-based faith.

Another 50 percent of Jewish respondents (and these percentages will
overlap somewhat, since some responses had multiple parts) said that to
be Jewish is to live and act in a particular way, guided by Torah and Jewish
values, keeping the commandments, exercising compassion, doing social
justice, or acting in a way that seeks *tikkun olam* ("repair of the world").

> To be Jewish is to use your spiritual life, as well as your secular life,
> to repair the world (tikkun olam).

> Being Jewish means owning your history, being resilient and re-
> sourceful, and caring about the world. Being Jewish means being
> compassionate, seeking knowledge, and improving the world we
> live in.

> To me being Jewish is living a life guided by the Torah.

> For me it is about family, and a platform in which to raise my
> children. I believe the background of the Jewish faith is its sense of
> morality which leads to raising responsible and good people that
> respect and appreciate the community and people around them.

> In part it is a responsibility to make the world a better place. So-
> cial justice is very important to me.

A little over a third of all responses focused on education, seeking knowledge, studying Torah, asking questions, and engaging in lively
thought, contemplation, and ideas. A few people mentioned Jewish beliefs
and their importance, but that was not where the accent fell for the most
part. Rather, the emphasis was on the life of the mind more than believing
certain things.

> Being Jewish to me is the ability to be able to have questions about
> religion and have it be O.K. to have questions. It is the unbroken
> chain from Abraham to today that connects every one of us. It is
> passing the torch to the next generation making sure they under-
> stand the triumphs and the tribulations that we have suffered over
> the years. It is the link to the past that strengthens our future.

> There is a poem that has a line to the effect of, "I am Jewish be-
> cause it demands of me no abdication of the mind." And that is

huge for me . . . Being Jewish is being a part of an age old history, and weaving ourselves and the modern world into it as it changes and moves into the future. There are so many different ways to be Jewish.

To take on a burden not only of law but of thought, contemplation and wrestling with ideas.

About 10 percent of all responses cited Jewish practices, both at home and at synagogue. These could range from worship and prayer to dietary practices and clothing. It is difficult to isolate this as a fourth distinct answer to the question of what it means to be Jewish since several of the responses here overlap with the first set of responses focused on Jewish heritage and identity, as well as the second set of responses, which were focused on a Jewish lifestyle and way of acting in the world. Still, it is worth highlighting the emphasis some persons placed on practices as distinctive to Jewish identity.

It means participation in worship and education. It means maintaining room in the home for Jewish thought and practices.

I think it is an active belief in God, but also a daily practice. I don't necessarily think it's about going to temple each day, but how you live your life and carry yourself. It is about how you maintain your relationships, how you make special all that you have in your life and, in doing so, you honor God.

For me, it means that my husband can raise our daughter in the Jewish faith, and this makes me very happy (because it makes him happy). Additionally, it makes me feel even more included in my husband's family—I really enjoy the Jewish traditions involving family gatherings/dinners.

WERE THEY NEW TO JUDAISM?

Most people (82 percent) making a new Jewish faith commitment were those converting from outside Judaism. The other 18 percent were already Jewish, but for the most part uncommitted and looking to make a new start or to activate the faith into which they were born. This is a very different situation from Christianity, where we saw that as many as two-thirds of Mainline Protestants and Catholics (and even 44 percent of Evangelicals) think of themselves as nominally Christians prior to making their new faith commitment.

When we look more closely at those who were new to Judaism, we find that a little over half (56 percent) had no religious background, including a few who claim to have been atheists (5 percent) or agnostics (5 percent). Thirty percent converted from Christianity, 7 percent from Buddhism, and the remaining 7 percent from some other religion.

COMING TO FAITH—A GRADUAL OR SUDDEN EXPERIENCE?

Committing to Jewish faith takes time for most persons. Eighty-six percent of the Jews in our study said that coming to faith is a gradual process. Indeed, the median time is five years, considerably longer than the median of three years for Christians. But several responses point to a process that may span decades. The average length of time for persons in our study was ten years; no one said it took less than a year (Figure 6.3).

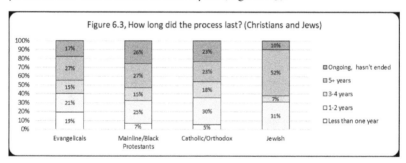

Figure 6.3, How long did the process last? (Christians and Jews)

Judaism is, in many ways, a stark contrast to a tradition such as Evangelicalism, where we find persons resolutely seeking the conversion of others and where that conversion can often happen right on the spot or in a moment of time. Jews typically understand that conversion is about changing one's entire life, practices, and social identity, and that can range from daily practices including what one eats and what one wears to the way one conceives of time, through Sabbath practices and the annual calendar. In Jewish tradition, a rabbi is supposed to turn away a potential convert three times, reminding that person that Jews are a persecuted and oppressed people, before allowing him or her to begin the process of conversion. Persons who seek to convert to Judaism must study, prepare themselves, and prove themselves over a period of time. The individual may also need to be approved by a rabbinical council (beit din), a three-person Jewish court made up of rabbis or other persons knowledgeable about Jewish law (though that is not always required in Reform Judaism). The council asks questions of candidates for conversion and seeks to ascertain the authenticity of the resolution to convert and knowledge about Judaism. Different rabbis may have different expectations that would not untypically include a long course on Judaism, regular meetings with the rabbi, a year of observing major Jewish holidays, and regular attendance at synagogue across a year.

For the most part, education and instruction is central to becoming Jewish. Eighty-three percent of the Jews in our study received some sort of instructional class when making their new commitment. That number is 79 percent for Reform Jews, while 100 percent of Conservative and Reconstructionist Jews (though their numbers were few in our study) said they received instruction. The vast majority of all Jews (96 percent) found the classes helpful.

THE JOURNEY

If we ask *why* persons decide to make this new declaration or commitment within the Jewish faith, we find answers that are significantly different from what we saw with Christians.

Figure 6.4, Why did you decide to make this commitment or recommitment? (Jews)	
Reason	Percent
To formalize, or it just felt right	37%
The Family	24%
Teachings, Beliefs, Tradition	24%
Need, Loss, Illness, Death	6%
Congregation, Minister, Others	2%
Experience of God	2%
Needed a Change	2%
Other	4%

The most frequently mentioned (37 percent) set of responses were those that described this decision as the natural or organic thing to do at the time, the next step in their journey, or arising from a desire to formalize or make official and public what had been happening in their lives. While Evangelicals also identified this reason frequently, their descriptions had more to do with testifying to an inner experience or relationship with God. Jewish respondents, by contrast, focused more on the practical and sociocultural dimensions of being incorporated into a religion or community.

In my heart I had always felt Jewish, this was just my way of aligning my heart with my deeds.

I was living life according to Jewish beliefs and wanted to make my commitment official.

I had been regularly attending synagogue services with my wife for over 35 years and decided to formalize my commitment.

Several reasons, but foremost was that I was an active member of the Jewish community and wanted to identify more concretely with the community. It was not a religious conversion for me as much as a tribal conversion.

It was required by our temple for my children to be able to continue in Hebrew school past Kindergarten age.

One-quarter of all Jewish responses focused on the importance of taking this step for family reasons—whether because they wanted to raise their children in a Jewish household, for the sake of a partner or spouse, or to maintain unity in the wider family. This was also a frequent response, it will be recalled, for Roman Catholics in our study.

I married a Jewish woman and wanted our family to have a single religious identity.

I met my now husband and he is Jewish, I was interested in his faith and slowly I began to realize that Judaism is something I would like to pursue. So I started studying and reading about it.

My kids were now old enough for Religious School and I was determined to raise them in the Jewish faith, as I was.

When my husband and I married in 1989, we decided to have a Jewish home and raise any children Jewish. I remained an active "Jew by choice" until I decided to make it truly official by going to the mikveh.

Another quarter of the responses to the question of why persons made this new commitment emphasized the teachings, practices, values, or traditions of Judaism itself. By contrast, only 5 to 6 percent of Christians answered similarly with respect to Christianity. In fact, a little more than a third of the Jewish responses in this category explicitly contrasted Judaism with Christianity, with which they had become disenchanted or disconnected in some way. In Judaism, they said, they found a religion that answered their questions better, encouraged them to ask questions, or gave them a framework of living that they found uplifting and fulfilling.

Though I was born Christian, I had not practiced an organized religion nor believed in aspects of Christianity for many years. I have always believed in G-d. I find in Judaism a religion that allows healthy dialog and discussion of beliefs and customs, especially as related to contemporary life. This was missing in my upbringing as a Christian.

I was raised a Christian and nobody could answer questions I had. I started studying Judaism and the answers were there.

Judaism meets my spiritual needs and allows me to practice my faith in my own way by integrating Jewish belief and practice into my daily life.

Lifelong admiration for Judaism, the Jewish People, a personal lifelong relationship with one Creator, and a critical, personal rejection of the tenets of Christianity.

Only 2 percent of the responses identified the congregation or minister as the primary reason for their decision, whereas those were among the top responses to the question of "why?" for Christians. Likewise, only a very few Jewish persons mentioned other reasons that appeared with frequency among Christians such as a loss, need, illness, death, or as a direct response to a call from or experience of the divine.

Important Incidents Along the Way

We asked those who experienced coming to faith as a gradual process whether there were any particularly important incidents during their journey. Most said yes, and their answers parallel some of the reasons cited above. The most frequently mentioned (one-fourth of all responses) were synagogue-related events or rituals. This may counterbalance, to some degree, the lack of reference to congregations as one of the main reasons for coming to faith. While the congregation may not have been a primary reason for converting or recommitting oneself, clearly the activities in a congregation proved important during the process.

So, for example, attending a bat mitzvah service of a close friend's daughter awakened the fullness of Jewish spiritual experience for one person. For another, it was her own daughter's bat mitzvah that was important. Attending a Jewish wedding was a key incident for another person. Celebration of Jewish holidays (both in synagogue and at home) was meaningful for many persons as they journeyed toward Jewish faith.

Reading and study were mentioned by 18 percent of Jewish respondents. Persons mentioned conversion classes, reading books on Judaism, or studying with a rabbi. Another 18 percent of the responses focused on the importance of family, and in particular the influence of Jewish spouses, partners, fiancées, or children. So, for example, one man said, "I started to make this commitment when I was married and wanting to grow spiritually with my wife and her family."

State of Mind

We asked what their state of mind was at the time they made their new commitment. Christian responses to this question were divided about equally between states of mind that could reasonably be considered negative or undesirable, on one hand, and more settled, positive, or fulfilled states of mind, on the other hand. By contrast, the Jews in our study possessed far more positive states of mind at the time (58 percent). Responses fell into the following three broad types:

Negatively tending responses

- 8 percent recovering from trauma or grief
- 10 percent depressed, sad, or anxious
- 3 percent apathetic, unfulfilled

Questing or open responses

- 21 percent questioning, inquisitive, reflective, searching, or open

Neutral or positively tending responses

- 38 percent content, blessed, calm, and happy (a few mentioned excited and eager)
- 15 percent focused, clear, certain, determined
- 5 percent normal, nothing stands out

Prayer and Consciousness of God

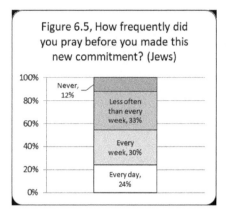

Figure 6.5, How frequently did you pray before you made this new commitment? (Jews)

Forty-three percent of Jews prayed daily or weekly prior to making their new faith commitment (Figure 6.5). That is about the same as we found with Evangelicals, but less than Mainline Protestants and Catholics. Again, this difference comes back to the fact that most Jews making a faith commitment do not come from Jewish or other religious backgrounds. In that way they are more like Evangelicals, among whom greater numbers turn to Christianity from no religious background.

Drawn in by Others or Active Seekers?

Those finding faith in the Jewish tradition, like most Christians, very much consider themselves active seekers in the process—more than eight out of ten (Figure 6.6). Persons are much less likely (at about a third of the total) to describe themselves as having been drawn in by others without actively seeking.

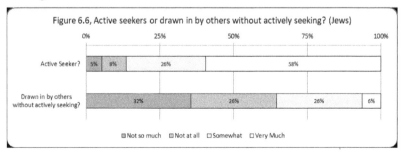

Figure 6.6, Active seekers or drawn in by others without actively seeking? (Jews)

Religious or Spiritual?

A solid majority of Jews described themselves as "both spiritual and religious." Orthodox Jews had no problem referring to themselves simply as "religious," but since they are under-represented in the survey, the percentages for all Jews combined for that answer are lower than they might have been otherwise.

Figure 6.7, "Religious" or "Spiritual"? (Jews)				
"Religious"	"Spiritual but not Religious"	"Both Spiritual and Religious"	"Neither Spiritual nor Religious"	"Don't know"
12%	20%	59%	2%	7%

FACTORS LEADING TO FAITH

One of the most important parts of a study like this is asking persons to identify the primary factor, as well as any supporting factors, in their recent commitment. As we did with the Christian population, we first asked persons to identify the main factor among fourteen possibilities that led to their commitment. Secondly, we gave them the opportunity to identify as many "supporting factors" as they wished from among those same possibilities. We also invited the respondents to write in their own choice if it was not listed. The results are as follows (Figure 6.8):

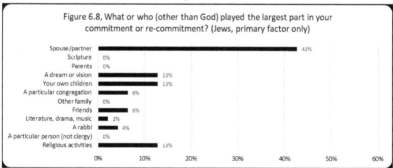

Figure 6.8, What or who (other than God) played the largest part in your commitment or re-commitment? (Jews, primary factor only)

We were not surprised to see the prominence of spouse/partner and children, especially given what our respondents had already said about their reasons for making this new faith commitment and about what was going on in their lives at the time. Religious activities and rituals are clearly also important for Jews coming to faith. But the prominence of dreams and visions stood out as surprising. When we asked persons to list all factors that were important alongside the primary factor, we get a fuller picture (Figure 6.9). Now the congregation, rabbi, and Scripture gain in importance, even though the factors already identified as primary remain prominent.

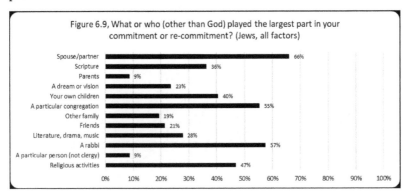

Figure 6.9, What or who (other than God) played the largest part in your commitment or re-commitment? (Jews, all factors)

The Family

Spouse or Partner

There is no more significant factor in coming to faith for Jews than family members. This is particularly true in relation to one's spouse, partner, or fiancé, a significant factor for two-thirds of respondents and the primary factor for 43 percent. There is, moreover, little difference in the percentages between males and females at this point.

Almost half of those who signaled the importance of the spouse, partner, or fiancé accented the support and help they experienced, often by accepting whatever decision they made without pressuring the individual.

> He too did not put any pressure on me. I knew this was MY decision.

> He was very supportive and helpful.

> I wanted and needed his support because his love matters in my life. He is not religious, but has fully supported my conversion, and having our children be Jewish as well.

> My partner who is now my spouse was extremely supportive and attended classes with me.

> He was very helpful answering any questions I had.

My spouse is secular, and he did not convert with me. However he supported me completely and continues to do so.

Very happy I was converting and very supportive although not at all pressuring.

For another third of those who selected the spouse, partner, or fiancé (and for many of those mentioned above), it was important to have a Jewish home and family and to be able to share a life together shaped by a common faith.

I want to be more spiritually connected to my wife, children and my extended family.

We are starting a life together and I wanted to make sure we were "on the same page" when it came to our home life, our potential children and family. As my conversion study went on it became a point of strength in our relationship and became more and more important to me.

Connecting through culture and history is as important as identifying with a common religious understanding for me and my spouse. Our identities and how we communicate with each other and our families are shaped by the ways we incorporate Jewish learning and debate in our lives.

He is my life partner and part of committing to the faith includes a commitment to living life in the faith.

Lastly, there were those who talked about their partners helping the process along by leading the way, engaging in dialogue and debate, answering questions, or modeling Jewish faith in a way that was inviting.

My wife is Jewish and her family and community made me see what I had been missing in my life.

Prior to beginning my relationship with my significant other, I was religiously unaffiliated. He became the most important person in my conversion process because it is through experiences with him and his family that I experienced Judaism and decided that it was the place for me.

Had I not met my wife, I am not sure if/when I would have discovered Judaism and the community she grew up in. This community really opened my eyes to what the possibilities are for a group of people to come together and believe in a life choice and practice.

Their own children

Forty percent of Jews making a new faith commitment cite children as an important factor (13 percent claim children as the primary factor). This is as true for males as for females, moreover. In one case, children were identified because they helped in guiding the person to faith. But that was not the case for the overwhelming majority, who were more concerned to raise their children in a Jewish home, rooted in Jewish traditions and heritage. Thus, the desire to be able to answer questions about Judaism, celebrate its rituals and holidays as a family, and model its values and practices led persons to undertake the process of conversion or to make a public commitment to Jewish faith.

> *I want my children to have a Jewish upbringing just like me. I want them to know the stories and the holidays and to be proud of their heritage. I want them to learn Hebrew so that they will feel comfortable in any synagogue that they walk into.*

> *I had decided when I became pregnant that I would raise my child in the Jewish faith (my husband's faith) and after our son was born I began to feel it was important for me to share Judaism with my child. I realized that in picking the Jewish faith for him, I had begun the process of my conversion.*

> *I want my children to grow up feeling as if they are a part if something. Judaism is a big part if my identity and I want to share that with them.*

> *I had committed them [children] and raised them Jewish. Whether they follow through or not, I can't say, but I feel I gave them a solid foundation.*

> *I wanted to have a united family and I thought a good step in providing this was to share the same religion.*

Parents and other family members

While parents and family were not a primary factor for any of the Jews in our study, parents were a supporting factor for 9 percent and other family members were a supporting factor for 19 percent. In one case, parents were cited because they had enrolled the individual in private Jewish religious school at an early age. In other cases, coming to faith was, at least in part, out of respect for their parents' desire that they become Jewish. Family members were important as supportive and welcoming and as role models who showed the way a Jewish family lives.

Friends and other persons in particular

Just under a third of Jewish persons who find faith say that friends or other persons (not related as family members) were a primary or a supporting factor. These friends often introduced them to Jewish life, practices, and holidays, or functioned as guides when they were seeking support and answers. As one individual put it, "My friend answered any question I had about Judaism as well as sharing her own spiritual journey and experiences with me. However, she never evangelized or tried to convince me to convert. She simply guided me in whatever direction I chose to go. Her non-judgmental attitude and willingness to share her thoughts and experiences with me led me to realize that Judaism was a welcoming and diverse faith that I could call home."

Religious Activities

When asked about whether religious activities had an influence on their journey toward faith, almost half of all Jews claim they are a primary or supporting factor (this includes 13 percent who identify such practices as the primary factor). For many Jews, these activities are more than just instrumental in acquiring some private or internal "faith." The practices *are* the faith, the essence of the religion itself. They enact one's devotion to God, bring transformation, and constitute one's relationships and inclusion within a community. The range of activities is truly impressive. Persons in our study mentioned activities such as Shabbat or prayer services, holidays, dinners, weddings, rituals within the home, committees, classes, book clubs, community outreach programs, and concerts.

> *I attended weekend classes and religious services regularly. Learning more about Judaism and experiencing in a community was key to my gradual conversion process. Weekly progress and feedback. I also had regular one-on-one meetings with my rabbi where regularly explored my conversion progress.*

> *The ceremony and ritual inherent to observant Jewish life really struck a chord with me. I absolutely warmed to the practice of having physical activities to enhance and deepen everything from holidays to daily life, making each moment holy.*

All of the times I went to synagogues and lived and breathed Judaism. That was very important in my steady interest in Judaism.

Attending Shabbat services and taking part in prayer and ritual has made me feel connected to every other Jew in the world who is saying these prayers and performing these rituals. It has made me realize that I'm not simply joining a faith tradition, instead I am becoming a part of a community that has existed for thousands of years.

I had never really practiced or observed religious holidays or rituals in my life before my conversion and these became very important to me through the conversion process. My husband to be had not previously been observant before my conversion (however he was Jewish) and this became important for both of us.

The Congregation

While the congregation is a primary factor for only 6 percent of those making a new commitment to faith in the Jewish tradition, it is a primary or supporting factor for 55 percent. Over half of those who mentioned the importance of the congregation named the welcome, inclusion, warmth, and acceptance they experience within a Jewish community:

I feel at home in our congregation.

I felt very accepted and my congregation puts great emphasis on social justice.

The congregants were welcoming and supportive of me during my conversion process. Upon the completion of my conversion, the community was extremely warm and complimentary of my accomplishment.

The congregation I was involved with during conversion is a small but close community of kind people. During my formal conversion ceremony, I was welcomed like a member of the family, so to speak, with warmth and love.

They are a welcoming and open minded community.

For others it was the experience of community formation and nurture that was central in the conversion process. As one retiree put it, "The congregation provided the opportunity to pray together, whatever that means. I found a greater depth in a spiritual experience with other people rather than a solitary one." The rabbi or ministerial staff were, for many persons, an important feature of the synagogue in their process of coming to faith, though the influence of clergy is discussed more fully below under "the rabbi."

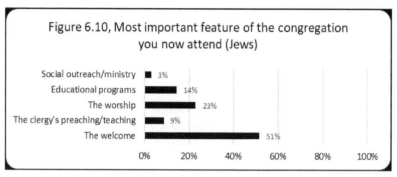

Figure 6.10, Most important feature of the congregation you now attend (Jews)

Figure 6.10 illustrates the most important features of the congregation according to all Jewish respondents, not just those who chose the congregation as one of the most important factors in their coming to faith. Half affirmed the importance of the welcome they experienced.

When persons were asked to list all features they found important (they could identify several) and when we add those answers along with the single feature they identified as most important above, we get the results displayed in Figure 6.11. The vast majority of all Jewish respondents mentioned the welcome (91 percent) while the other four features were claimed as important by about half of the respondents as well.

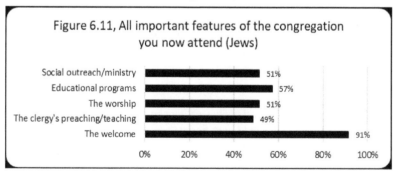

Figure 6.11, All important features of the congregation you now attend (Jews)

Choosing a Congregation

We asked how persons chose their congregation, a question closely related to the previous one about what was most important about their congregation. While some particular feature of the congregation was primary for a quarter of all Jewish respondents, the proximity of the congregation was most important for 21 percent and the welcome they received was most important for 17 percent (Figure 6.12).

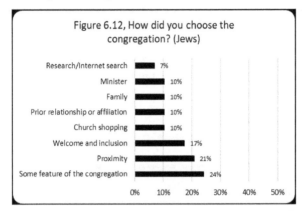

Figure 6.12, How did you choose the congregation? (Jews)

When Jews who had recently started attending services after making their commitment were asked how easy or difficult they found it to start attending, 21 percent said "very easy" (as compared to 50 percent of Christians), 50 percent said "easy," and 29 percent said "difficult."

Dreams and Visions

The number of Jews who identified dreams and visions as an important factor in coming to faith surprised us. Thirteen percent of all Jewish respondents identified them as primary and another 10 percent said they were a supportive factor—a total of one-fourth of all respondents. All of them were female. The dreams and visions described by our participants had less of a supernatural cast to them and were remarkably consistent from person to person, focusing on a desire to be Jewish and on what that might look like if they went through with the conversion.

It helped me feel like all of my searching had a purpose and at the end of my search I would come back to where my soul is at home. I had a glimpse of what would be if I chose to do what was necessary to get there.

Because in my dream I knew it was really possible to become what I wanted to become in real life, I knew that I could become Jewish because it was so real to me in my dream.

Because for the first time I felt a strong sense of belonging, not just to the present congregation, but to a much larger network of people. I understood the services, the whole religion just made sense to me. It was like finally seeing the light, what it all means.

My vision was to live a Jewish life; it was important to me to be able to practice Judaism.

When our Jewish participants were asked whether they had ever had, at any time in their life, any out-of-the-ordinary experiences they would describe as religious in some way, 38 percent said yes, which is considerably lower than the 59 percent of Christians who said yes. And yet only about 12 percent of Christians claimed dreams or visions as a primary or supporting factor in their coming to faith compared to about twice that for Jews.

The Rabbi

While the rabbi was only mentioned by 4 percent of Jewish participants as the primary factor in their coming to faith, that number rises to 57 percent when combined with those who saw the rabbi as a supporting factor. That is considerably higher than we saw for Catholics at 46 percent but about the same as we saw with Protestants at 58 to 60 percent. As was mentioned at the beginning of this chapter, the road to Jewish conversion requires knowledge and a proven commitment to Jewish observances over an extended period of time (usually at least a year). For that reason, the rabbi has a crucial role in walking persons through the process and ultimately even deciding on whether the candidate stands ready to undergo conversion. Bearing all that in mind, several common themes surfaced in the descriptions we heard from those talking about the importance of their rabbi.

Over half of those mentioning the rabbi spoke of his or her being accessible, relatable, "real," and down to earth; persons frequently spoke of having made a "connection" to their rabbi. These qualities in a rabbi were typically also connected to feeling supported, welcomed, and guided. Candidates for conversion naturally have many questions, so having a rabbi who is patient and shows genuine interest in and care for the person is vital.

The Rabbi was the person who was to walk me through my conversion, step by step, and tell me when he thought I was ready for conversion.

The Rabbi was very easy to talk to, as I had many questions.

Rabbi [. . .] was thoughtful, encouraging, and inquisitive. He asked questions which enabled me to reflect and make a positive decision.

She did not put pressure of any kind of me, but offered support and encouragement.

The rabbi met with me and my wife, answered questions, suggested books, and confirmed that Judaism was open to people like us.

Following on these qualities, the other most frequently mentioned characteristics were the rabbi's abilities as a teacher, knowledge of the Jewish faith, openness to questions, and ability to guide, explain things, and offer counsel.

The Rabbi that did my conversion with me I felt I have a real connection to. He explained things to me spiritually that just made sense like nothing else before. He was a Rabbi that I felt I could look up to, but also study with, and he could help me with mine and my family's spiritual growth.

He is a remarkable teacher of the highest intellectual caliber. He looks Scripture contradictions in the eye.

Incredibly educated, willing to talk and argue any time, passionate believer.

My sponsoring rabbi and instructing rabbi for my Introduction to Judaism class were instrumental to my Jewish formation. My sponsoring rabbi presided over my first Jewish Shabbat service; the way he presents his services and the requirements he understood of me to take for my conversion process were directly in line with the pathway I wanted to take in becoming Jewish.

Scripture

A little over one-third of Jews identified Scripture as a supporting factor in their faith commitment, though no one claimed it as the primary factor. New converts spoke frequently about their love of studying Scripture within the Jewish tradition. At the time they were making their faith commitment, a little over half of all Jewish respondents (and not just those who chose Scripture as an important factor) read Scripture at least several times a month, including 12 percent who read it several times each week.

For about one-fourth, Scripture played no role at that time, but for half it was somewhat helpful and for 22 percent very helpful. As we will see later in this chapter, however, Scripture reading became less frequent after conversion or recommitment.

I love the stories from the Torah, the Midrashim, relating how each Torah portion for the week during Shabbat, helps to enrich our lives today. My sponsoring rabbi was incredible and engaging during services and I found myself hanging on every word during his Torah readings in his warm, charismatic manner.

Learning the Torah gave me insight on the Jewish faith.

Listening to and learning about the Oral and Written Torah is something I never encountered before. The midrash told during services are engaging and I personally find value in the lessons they teach and the window to our beliefs and customs.

Saw the possibilities of how Scripture can remove you from the mundane.

The Torah is the foundation and as the saying goes "turn it, and turn it, for everything is in it." It is a teaching book and a guide to life and shows how both we and our ancestors experience joy and sorrow, faith and doubt, etc.

Literature, drama, and music

A little over one-fourth of persons making a Jewish faith commitment found literature, drama, and music to be at least a supporting factor in making that commitment. They talked about understanding Jewish faith as more than something interior and spiritual (in a narrow sense) but fully cultural, historical, and material. Several mentioned their love of Jewish music and the arts from which they drew inspiration and strength. Jewish books and stories also helped them in building a Jewish identity while on the path of conversion.

OBSTACLES?

When persons coming to faith as Jews were asked if they found any of their religion's teachings, practices, persons, or institutions to be an obstacle in making their new commitment, a slight majority (56 percent) said no. But that still leaves a good number who found difficulties and challenges. Some of those obstacles pertained to Jewish observances, practices, and rituals— for example, fasting or Sabbath observance. As one person put it, "I'm not a ritual person." For another, it was the prohibition against tattoos (given the extent of their own). Learning Hebrew can be a challenge. In some

instances, Reform Jews mentioned challenges with outward Jewish observances as their reasons for not becoming Orthodox, and several mentioned
their annoyance at how some ultra-Orthodox Jews do not consider them
to be fully Jewish. Zionism, how to think of the State of Israel, and Israeli
treatment of Palestinians were of concern to several persons. Some found
challenges around how to tell Christian friends and family members about
their decision to convert.

For the most part, persons found ways to adapt to those challenges,
work around them, or live with the tensions, though some remain. The tat-
tooed individual has decided to wear sweaters to temple, even in the sum-
mer. New converts have found ways to tell persons about their decision, if
they think that really matters. For some, adapting to dietary laws or learning
Hebrew will be a longer process. Others still wrestle with the strictness of
some Jewish communities or rabbis.

WHAT WAS MOST APPEALING?

When persons were asked if they found any of Judaism's teachings, practices,
persons, or institutions particularly appealing, we heard great enthusiasm
for their faith tradition along with a remarkable breadth of answers, many
of them confirming or reiterating what has already been said in this chapter.
Again, the rabbis were often singled out as especially helpful, down to earth,
and supportive. Several cited the Jewish love for learning, the value of dis-
sent and asking questions, and the reputation of Jews as "a people of the
book." The Torah itself was appealing as was the tradition of interpretation
around it. A large number of persons mentioned the holidays (especially
the High Holidays), Jewish traditions, the Shabbat dinner at home, prayers,
and "unplugging" for a day of rest. Jewish music and its zest for life was
accentuated.

There is a sense of social responsibility and commitment to human
rights in Judaism that we found highlighted in many of the answers to this
question. Several expressed an appreciation for a focus on "now" rather
than on the afterlife, as they put it, or the focus on right actions rather than
right doctrine. The historical development and adaptability of Judaism to
changing times was lifted up in some instances. Reform Jews emphasized
the appeal of their own particular tradition, its openness to personal interpretation, and its inclusivity, especially with respect to sexual orientation
and the roles of women.

IS THERE A CHANGE?

In an attempt to grasp what changes come with finding faith in the Jewish tradition, we asked about religious practices, spirituality, and self-perception; about attendance at religious services; and about stances on important social issues.

Attendance at services

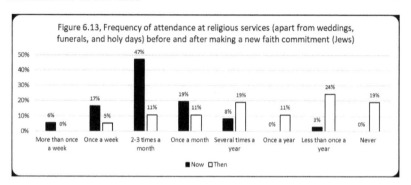

Figure 6.13, Frequency of attendance at religious services (apart from weddings, funerals, and holy days) before and after making a new faith commitment (Jews)

As Figure 6.13 shows, about 27 percent of persons making a new Jewish faith commitment had been attending religious services once per month or more prior to making that commitment. But that number rises to almost 90 percent afterwards, a remarkable shift representing a considerable set of changes in lifestyle and priorities.

Other Forms of Involvement

When asked about their overall involvement in the life and activities of their synagogue (Figure 6.14), about two-thirds of the Jews in our study claimed to be somewhat or very active. That is about the same as we saw with Roman Catholics, though considerably less than with Protestants (82 to 84 percent). Most Jews (61 percent) are happy with their level of involvement (again, about the same as Catholics at 65 percent), but not as happy as Evangelicals (75 percent) or Mainline Protestants (80 percent). Clearly those with higher levels of religious involvement are at the same time happier with those levels of involvement. There are, of course, a variety of reasons as to why persons are not as involved as they would like to be. Some of those relate to family caregiving, work responsibilities, or geographical distance from the synagogue. Other reasons cited have more to do with uncertainties about how to get involved, nervousness about how to step into new social situations, or how to find belonging.

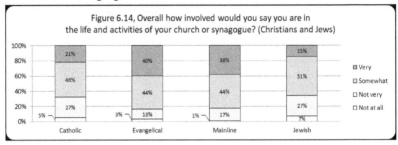

Figure 6.14, Overall how involved would you say you are in the life and activities of your church or synagogue? (Christians and Jews)

If we examine activity in religious groups, studies, or fellowships (Figure 6.15), we get a similar picture, with 31 percent of Jews reporting weekly activity of some kind (as compared to 43 percent of Catholics, 53 percent of Mainline Protestants, and 73 percent of Evangelicals). Torah study and adult education classes were frequently mentioned as well as a host of other educational workshops, book groups, Talmud study, and Hebrew language classes. In addition, persons mentioned family or children's groups and events, friendship groups, women's groups, social functions, young professionals networking groups, celebrations, and social gatherings. Opportunities for volunteer work or social or political action events were also mentioned by a few persons.

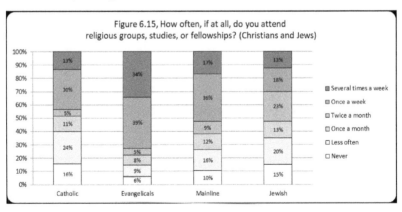

Figure 6.15, How often, if at all, do you attend religious groups, studies, or fellowships? (Christians and Jews)

Multiple Religious Belonging

Only a very few Jews in our study reported participation in religious services or activities from other religions. A small percentage mentioned practicing Buddhist meditation from time to time or giving gifts to family at Christmas, but little more than that.

Reading Scripture

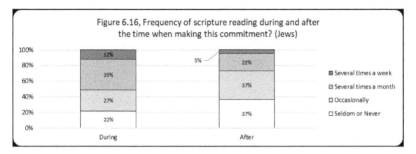

Figure 6.16, Frequency of scripture reading during and after the time when making this commitment? (Jews)

As mentioned earlier, no Jews cited Scripture as the primary factor in their recent faith commitment, though around one-third claimed it to be a supporting factor. Figure 6.16 shows the frequency of Scripture reading during the time they were making their new faith commitment and after making their new faith commitment. Scripture has an important role for Jews during the extended period of study and formation prior to conversion, but the drop-off in frequency points to a lessening of that role afterwards. When asked now about the importance of Scripture to their faith, moreover, only 17 percent of Jews find it very important, a stark contrast to the 40 to 75 percent of Christians who still find it very important (Figure 6.17).

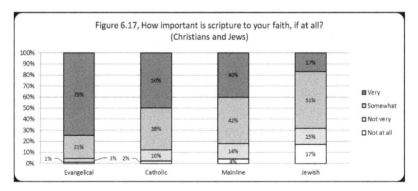

Figure 6.17, How important is scripture to your faith, if at all? (Christians and Jews)

God

When asked whether they had thought about God much prior to making their faith commitment, about half all Jewish respondents said they had done so a great deal and another fourth said they had done so "somewhat." When we asked specifically about whether and, if so, how, their views of God had changed, we found that for about one-third not much had changed. For another third, how they viewed God had changed substantially, and for the other third, their views were much the same but had expanded, or at least they possessed an increased openness and tolerance to other views. Again, there are significant differences here from Christians, for whom we saw more substantive change reported (68 percent of Evangelicals, 51 percent of Mainline Protestants, and 45 percent of Catholics).

Changes that finding faith has made

As we did with Christian populations, we asked our Jewish participants to rate the significance of six types of change that are often associated with religious conversions: (1) beliefs, (2) actions and lifestyle, (3) spiritual practices, (4) relations with others, (5) happiness, and (6) hopefulness. Figure 6.18 illustrates their self-understanding in relation to each and in comparison with Christian responses.

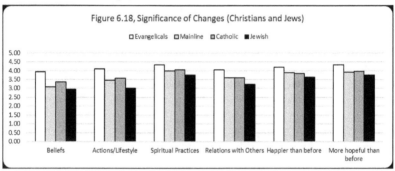

Jewish persons rated spiritual practices and hopefulness as having changed most significantly in their lives (happiness was also rated highly), though the extent of all changes was considered to be lower by Jews than by Christians for every measure. Of course, it could be that Christians tend to over-inflate the changes made in their lives or that Jews tend to underestimate the changes. But if we accept an equivalency in self-reporting, then it appears that coming to faith as a Jew has slightly less impact in these six areas.

While understanding these various changes is important, we also wanted to hear directly from our Jewish participants about how they understood the changes in their lives, using their own words and categories. We asked them the open question, "What is the main difference that becoming a Jew (or a more committed Jew) has made in your life?" The responses were overwhelmingly positive, with several common threads uniting them. Around 40 percent of the responses expressed how grounded, confident, and secure they now were. As one man in his mid-forties put it, "Judaism has given me a different framework upon which to see the world." And as a young woman said, "I feel like it has provided my household with a more solid foundation. My spirituality has never really been as strong as it is now and I find it very comforting for me. I have never had faith until this point and I feel like I have gained something for the better." Persons spoke of now feeling part of something bigger than them and possessing more knowledge and guidance.

For 30 percent (and these figures may overlap with one another since some persons mentioned multiple changes in their lives), the changes had more to do with their experience of community and connection, and a growing love for others. One new convert put it this way: "It's made me very content and enveloped me in a feeling of community." Another said, "A sense of belonging to a community that feels a bit like home. I have less a sense of wandering and a more focused sense of purpose."

A significant number of people spoke about changes in their family relationships bringing more connection, centering, continuity, and unity. The home is, as we have seen, a very special place for the practice of Jewish faith, and that was signaled consistently in the responses from our participants.

Social Issues

Lastly, we also asked our Jewish participants in the study about any changes in their attitudes or positions on social issues. We did not see an incredible amount of change, though it was quite a contrast to compare Jewish and Christian attitudes on social issues. The great majority of Jews were already solidly supportive of the right to abortion, gay marriage, women's equality, racial justice, care for the natural environment, and (to a lesser extent) economic justice for the poor. But even with the latter, it is here that we saw the greatest change with 12 percent now becoming supportive.

Figure 6.19, How have your attitudes and positions on the following social issues changed, if at all, since making your new commitment or recommitment?" (Jews)	Already opposed, became more opposed	Already opposed, remain just as opposed	Now become opposed	No opinion/Don't know	Now became supportive	Already supported, stayed just as supportive	Already supportive, became more supportive
Right to an Abortion	0%	0%	0%	8%	0%	88%	4%
Gay Marriage	0%	0%	0%	4%	0%	84%	12%
Gun Control	0%	4%	0%	12%	4%	52%	28%
War	8%	36%	0%	24%	8%	24%	0%
Women's Equality	0%	0%	0%	0%	0%	92%	8%
Racial Justice	0%	0%	0%	0%	4%	76%	20%
Economic Justice for the Poor	0%	0%	0%	4%	12%	64%	20%
Care for the Natural Environment	0%	0%	0%	0%	8%	76%	16%

Attitudes toward war were certainly the most complex among these issues, but war is, of course, a complicated topic for most humans, and there are a number of variables that perennially complicate the matter. The relationship of Judaism to conflict in the Middle East is certainly one of those complicating variables. It was on the subject of war that we saw the largest number (24 percent) who didn't know or had no opinion on the subject, perhaps reflecting an associated ambivalence. Interestingly, while 8 percent had become supportive of war after making their new faith commitment, no one had become opposed, even if some who were already opposed had become more opposed.

CONCLUSION

Becoming Jewish is far more than adopting a set of beliefs or doctrines, having a religious experience, or taking a membership vow. If anything is clear from the Jewish participants in our study, becoming Jewish is adopting a way of life, a culture, a social identity, and a sense of being a people. For just these reasons, family, tradition, and religious observances are crucial factors in coming to faith as a Jew. But what we saw with the persons in our study was far more than bowing to empty formalities or customs. We found a passion for study and learning. We saw a craving for the space to ask questions, to express doubts, and to grow and seek wisdom without easy answers. We also found a robust desire to heal and "repair the world," to serve others with compassion and justice, and to live out the real-world teachings of Torah. To be sure, "finding faith" is a spiritual journey for those who turn to Judaism, but it is a journey that is material, cultural, social, and practical through and through.

7

Buddhism

WHO PARTICIPATED IN THE STUDY?

BUDDHISM IS THE FOURTH largest religious tradition in the US at 0.7 percent of the population, though just seven years ago it was the third largest (Islam has now surpassed Buddhism as the third largest tradition).[1] Buddhists may be relatively small in number within the US, but they represent an important global connection and impact. The influence of Buddhism exceeds its number of formal adherents given the fact that persons from a variety of religious traditions (especially Christianity and Judaism) also consider themselves to be Buddhists or at least open to and interested in Buddhist philosophy and practices.

Figure 7.1, Age Distribution (Buddhists)

In this study 173 Buddhist adults participated, a robust sample size for which we were grateful. Among those, the median age is 54, much older than the other religious groups we studied. It is also much older than the

1. Pew, "America's Changing Religious Landscape," 4.

median age of Buddhist adults in the US (39).[2] If the participants in our study are a representative population, we conclude that those who convert to Buddhism (as distinct from being born into Buddhist families, for example) tend to be much older than either the general population or the Buddhist population in the US. Three quarters of the Buddhists in our study had graduated with a bachelors or graduate degree. That is comparable to the Christians in our study and a considerably higher educational attainment level than the US national average.[3]

Just as with Christians and Jews, not all Buddhists are the same—far from it. There are many different streams, sects, philosophies, and movements within Buddhism, though it is generally accepted that there are three main traditions: Theravada, Mahayana, and Vajrayana. All were represented in some form in our study, though the Mahayana (including especially Zen) and Vajrayana (or Tibetan Buddhism) traditions were most abundantly represented, with a little over a third of all respondents identifying with some form of Mahayana and another third claiming some form of Vajrayana. A quarter of our Buddhist respondents did not identify any particular tradition, and 5 percent identified themselves with the Theravada tradition. Within the various streams of Buddhism there are impressive differences between sects, though for the most part my analysis in this chapter will not focus on parsing out those differences. Whether Buddhism should even be called a "faith" was a question that came up often in listening to those who participated. It could perhaps better be called a practice, or a philosophy, and several of our respondents preferred some other word, even if they were willing to work with the questions we had for the sake of the larger project.

HOW DID BUDDHISTS SIGNAL THEIR COMMITMENT?

We asked Buddhists in our study how they signaled their new commitment, and just over half (56 percent) mentioned their participation in some ceremony or ritual whereby they "took refuge," took precepts or vows, or received lay or monastic ordination. To "take refuge" refers to more than just adopting a belief or subscribing to membership, but is a ritual enacting a faith, or trusting confidence in the "three jewels" of Buddhism—the Buddha, the Dharma (the Buddha's teachings), and the Sangha (the Buddhist community). In addition to those participating in some formal ceremony or ritual, 28 percent of Buddhists claimed that they received membership in a community as their way of signaling their new commitment. There were

2. Ibid., 50.
3. Ibid., 42.

those who cited both. About 10 percent talked about having simply taken up Buddhist practice, especially meditation.

WHAT DOES IT MEAN TO BE BUDDHIST?

We asked what it means to be a Buddhist, and several consistent themes emerged. These themes are not watertight or independent, and often they were explicitly linked together by respondents. A few persons bristled at the very question because it implied to them an "identity" that, at the core of Buddhist teaching, is rejected or understood as impermanent. To ask or answer the question, therefore, would already miss the point! A few replied with a "koan," a type of riddle or paradox that Zen Buddhists sometimes use to demonstrate the limits of linear thinking and logical arguments. So, for example, in response to the question, "What does it mean to be a Buddhist?" one Buddhist answered, "Because the oak tree grows in the courtyard." Another said, "it means nothing and, of course, everything."

One of the most recurring themes we heard from Buddhist respondents was that of practice, action, or a way of living in relation to others. They wanted to emphasize that Buddhism is not solely or even primarily a belief system. Among the most frequently named characteristics of a Buddhist life were compassion, acceptance, kindness, and love; living in harmony with others and all creation; lessening the suffering of others; letting go of attachments; not judging others or harming others; and seeking enlightenment both for oneself and for others. For some, those practices were focused more on study and meditation. But these were not understood as irrelevant to the former; rather, they were intimately connected. As one artist (and practitioner of Tibetan Buddhism) put it, to be a Buddhist means "practicing meditation and acting with presence, mindfulness, wisdom, compassion." Some other responses to the question include:

> It means you see life as beauty and your job is to show others through your practice the beauty and joy of a life of kindness and non judgement and love of all living things. But do not preach this only show it by your own actions.

> To make generosity, compassion and loving-kindness an important practice in your everyday life. To integrate compassion and wisdom to each decision made. To love and support others on their spiritual path and even support those on no spiritual path, as long as they are not harming themselves or others.

It means you are endeavoring to live your life with compassion and clarity and peace, as much as possible, compassion for all sentient beings.

To be a Buddhist is to practice compassion, let go of attachments, live in the present, be gentle with self and others.

To refrain from harming others. To train your mind to find its true nature. To act compassionately towards all beings and regard all beings as having been your mother and worthy of your kindness and regard. "The teachings of the Buddha are not something to believe, they are something to do." That is how I live. Kindness and compassion in action.

Closely related to the above is a second theme that surfaced regularly—Buddhism as a way of being in the world. This certainly includes practices and actions, but the accent here is on being rather than doing—for example, a mindfulness as one goes through life, living in the present, following a middle way of moderation between extremes, living simply and intentionally, or seeking enlightenment.

To be one who aspires to awakening.

To be simple, happy and less focused on a separate self and all the suffering that doing/being otherwise brings.

To be a Zen Buddhist (the only one I really know about) just means to practice living in the moment with clarity, and making a commitment to save all beings.

It means to look within and not without.

To be committed to the path of waking up to reality, the truth of the way things are; and to align the way you live, your actions and interactions, in accord with that.

Connected closely to descriptions of Buddhism as a way of living or being were answers that accentuated a new understanding, awareness, or knowledge. This was often described in terms of a realization or awareness (for example, that the source of suffering is clinging to self); an embrace of change, interdependence, and impermanence; being awake to the way things are; and seeing with clarity. Being a Buddhist was also described in terms of training, mindfulness, and a commitment to study and practice.

To be committed to the path of waking up to reality, the truth of the way things are; and to align the way you live, your actions and interactions, in accord with that.

To be Awake.

It means you understand the ego is a fabrication and that the true nature of reality is infinite interdependence. This leads to a realization of great profundity and bliss becomes one's normal state of being.

To accept the four noble truths. To believe that you are the agent of your own suffering. To recognize that ego is not the truth. To see life as energy.

Lastly, a good number of new Buddhists described what it means to be a Buddhist with explicit reference to the Buddha, his teachings, and his path, often with the language of "to follow." These references overlap considerably with the previously mentioned themes, but the explicit references to the Buddha and his path warrant our highlighting them as a unique theme so that the connections to him do not get lost.

To follow the path that the Buddha and the sincere followers since have laid out. To truly internalize the mind-set and live the life of a Buddha.

To practice the way of Buddha

To follow the teachings of the Buddha, in an attempt to ease suffering through the 8 Fold Path.

To be a Buddhist is to acknowledge Gautama's attainment and to do my best to emulate him appropriately.

WERE THEY BUDDHISTS BEFORE THIS NEW COMMITMENT?

The great majority (89 percent) of those who make a new Buddhist commitment are relatively new to Buddhism. This is similar to Judaism, as we saw in chapter 6, where most making a new commitment are converts. But, again, it is quite different from Christianity, where up to two-thirds of Mainline Protestants and Catholics and 44 percent of Evangelicals think of themselves as nominally Christians prior to making their new faith commitment. Just under a quarter (22 percent) of those persons who were not Buddhist prior to the time of making this new commitment had no prior religious affiliation. A little over a quarter (27 percent) were Christians previously (a few still are), and the remainder described themselves as agnostic (17 percent), atheist (8 percent), Jewish (6 percent)—though mostly secular), or some other religious group.

COMING TO FAITH—A GRADUAL OR SUDDEN EXPERIENCE?

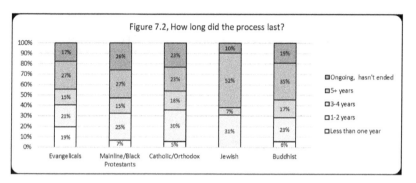

Figure 7.2, How long did the process last?

Seventy-nine percent of the persons becoming Buddhist in the US claim that it was a gradual process, while the remainder see it as more sudden and datable. The median length of time for those coming to faith gradually is three years, the same as for Christians. And, of course, as with other religious traditions, a good percentage claim the journey is ongoing. Seventy percent of the Buddhists in our study received some sort of instructional class when making their new commitment, and a remarkable 100 percent of those taking the classes found them helpful.

THE JOURNEY

When asked *why* they decided to make this new commitment as a Buddhist, participants in our study responded in ways that are considerably different from Jews or Christians (Figure 7.3). For the most part, Buddhists take the step of commitment either (a) because they found value in the practices or were convinced by the teachings and path of Buddhism (42 percent) or (b) because they wanted to take the next step in their journey or to formalize that commitment publicly, or because they saw it is as the natural, sensible, or right thing to do (39 percent). Of the remaining 19 percent, answers focus primarily on the value of community and the importance of a particular sangha or teacher (7 percent), or as a way of healing from physical and emotional wounds or attaining sobriety (4 percent). There are very few references from Buddhists to doing it for family reasons such as we saw with Jews and Catholics.

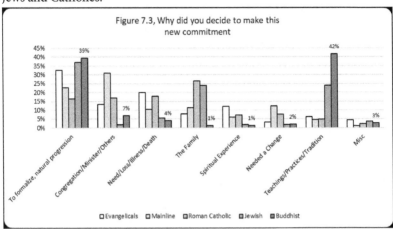

Figure 7.3, Why did you decide to make this new commitment

As noted above, the attraction to the Buddhist tradition and path—to its teachings, truths, and practices—was exceptionally strong as a reason for making this commitment. Buddhists described the teachings as true, clear, and concrete, as making intellectual and practical sense, and as speaking to the heart. Making a public commitment served to align persons with those teachings and to express the changes they had experienced since they had begun to walk the Buddhist path.

> Zen was the first philosophy to give me concrete instruction in clearing out my mental "clutter."

> I could feel the truth of the practices. I could see the effects they were having in my life. I felt a deep heart connection to my teacher who helped put in perspective some profound experiences of the ineffable I had prior to our meeting.

> Positive results I was enjoying from the practice.

> I found Buddhist teachings important for my spiritual well-being, especially because they emphasize serving others.

> The Buddha is my teacher. To him, his teachings, and his community I look for guidance. Buddhism, in all of its messiness, contradictions, and simplicity, makes utter sense to me.

Those who said they made a public commitment as a way of formalizing what was already happening in their lives often wanted to confirm to their community their commitment or to take the next step on their own journey. Others described the reason as simply "following their heart" or "I just knew that I had to do it." For some, then, it was less a decision as it was the continuation of a path they had already begun.

> *It felt like a natural progression. Once I started studying this particular tradition of Buddhism it felt like yes, this is what I've believed most of my life. It spoke to what I had already been observing, understanding, and contemplating. Making the formal ceremony with my teacher felt natural.*

> *To further my understanding of Buddhism and practice with other like-minded individuals.*

> *It was a natural expression of my whole being. It expressed a commitment to the community of what I already felt in my life.*

> *After substantial study, I decided to make this commitment to allow more in-depth participation and study.*

> *To confirm publicly and in the traditional way to myself and others that I was committed to this sangha (faith community)*

Along the Way

When Buddhists were asked whether there were any particularly important incidents during their journey, most said yes, and by far the most frequently mentioned set of responses (a little over half) were those that focused on reading, study, meditation, trainings, courses, retreats, or travel. The second most frequent response (about a quarter of the total) referenced some sort of loss, bereavement, illness, or breakup in relationship. Participating in a Buddhist community was named explicitly by just under 10 percent as contributing to their faith commitment.

State of Mind

We asked what their state of mind was at the time they made their new commitment, just as we did for others in the study. As with Christians, Buddhist responses were divided about equally between states of mind that could reasonably be considered negative or undesirable, on one hand, and more settled, positive, and fulfilled states of mind, on the other hand. However, there was a much larger percentage of Buddhists (27 percent) who were in a searching, open, and questing state of mind than for either Christians (19 percent) or Jews (21 percent). Responses from Buddhists fell largely into three groups:

Negatively tending responses

- 3 percent recovering from trauma or grief
- 32 percent depressed, sad, confused, or anxious
- 3 percent apathetic, unfulfilled

Questing or open responses

- 27 percent questioning, inquisitive, reflective, searching, or open

Neutral or positively tending responses

- 26 percent content, blessed, calm, and happy (several said eager or excited)
- 5 percent focused, clear, certain, determined
- 4 percent normal, nothing stands out

Drawn in by Others or Active Seekers?

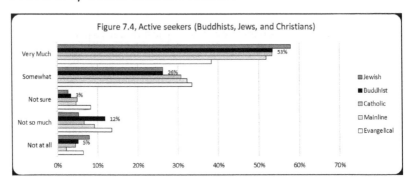

Figure 7.4, Active seekers (Buddhists, Jews, and Christians)

Compared to Christians and Jews, Buddhists are, on the whole, persons who actively seek Buddhism rather than being drawn in by others. Buddhism has traditionally been a missionary faith across the centuries, but it is not especially known for having a strong evangelistic or missionary profile in the US, especially compared with Christianity. Figures 7.4 and 7.5 illustrate the differences among the religious traditions at this point. While Jews have the largest number of those who report actively seeking, 74 percent of Buddhists say they were not drawn in by others (Figure 7.5), considerably more than any other group in our study.

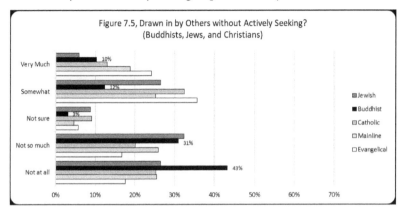

Religious or Spiritual?

Buddhists are pretty evenly split between describing themselves as "spiritual but not religious" and "both spiritual and religious." Interestingly, those in the Vajrayana tradition are much less likely (25 percent) to prefer "spiritual but not religious" and more likely (68 percent) to prefer "both spiritual and religious," which may tell us something about the slightly more explicitly religious nature of that form of Buddhism relative to other forms.

Figure 7.6, "Religious" or "Spiritual"?					
	"Religious"	"Spiritual but not Religious"	"Both Spiritual and Religious"	"Neither Spiritual nor Religious"	"Don't know"
Evangelical	16%	26%	48%	2%	8%
Mainline	14%	15%	63%	0%	8%
Catholic	25%	7%	61%	2%	5%
Jewish	12%	20%	59%	2%	7%
Buddhist	3%	47%	42%	3%	5%

FACTORS LEADING TO FAITH

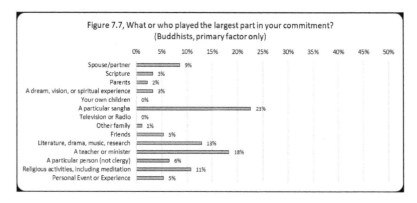

Figure 7.7, What or who played the largest part in your commitment? (Buddhists, primary factor only)

One of the most intriguing parts of our study is learning what persons identify as the primary and supporting factors in coming to faith (again, recognizing the complexity of the word *faith* for Buddhists). As we did with others, we asked Buddhists first to identify the main factor among fourteen possibilities that led to their commitment. But at their suggestion we added a fifteenth category: "a personal event or experience," and indeed it attracted several responses. In hindsight, it might have been helpful to have had this as an option for all respondents, but our study of Buddhists came too late in the overall project. Secondly, we gave Buddhists the opportunity to identify as many "supporting factors" as they wished from among those same possibilities. We also invited them to write in their own choice if it was not listed. The results are as shown in Figure 7.7.

The Buddhist sangha (community) as well as Buddhist teachers, literature, and meditation practices stand out as especially prominent factors for Buddhists, and often each of these shows up in the context of other responses as well. When we add supporting factors to the primary factor, we get the fuller picture shown in Figure 7.8.

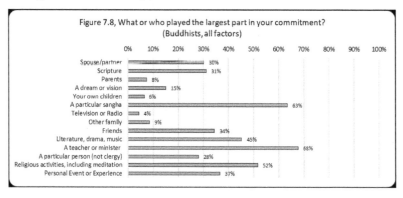

Figure 7.8, What or who played the largest part in your commitment? (Buddhists, all factors)

The Sangha (Buddhist Community)

At 23 percent, the particular Buddhist sangha to which one belongs (referred to as "church" by a few persons) is the most frequently mentioned factor as primary in taking up Buddhism. Sixty-three percent of Buddhists claim it to be a primary or supporting factor, which is the second highest among all Buddhist responses (exceeded only by the teacher, monk, or priest at 68 percent). The sangha was of great importance to new Buddhists as a community of persons engaging in the practices of Buddhism and seeking to understand its teachings together. To make a new commitment to Buddhism is, for many Buddhists, also to commit and to align oneself with a sangha. It is, after all, one of the three "jewels" in which Buddhists take refuge. We heard a strong sense in many of the responses that persons understood the sangha to be a global communion in and through which they are connected to Buddhists worldwide.

All the Buddhism sects I attended were very welcoming, but this one made me feel right at home from the first day.

The community that I ultimately joined is a group of very grounded, very human people. I am very averse to piousness and new age/holy-roller types. These people were very grounded and committed to practice. They were willing to be real with themselves and with each other, and with me.

There are a group of perhaps ten people in the sangha who have been going through the process with me. They are sources of support, discussion and insight.

The sangha truly felt like my spiritual family. I made connections and friends instantly and wanted to stay and be with them! The type of people—including young, smart people and kind, wise older generations also being a part of this community was a good sign for me.

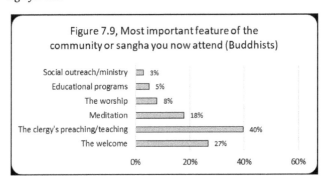

Figure 7.9, Most important feature of the community or sangha you now attend (Buddhists)

Social outreach/ministry	3%
Educational programs	5%
The worship	8%
Meditation	18%
The clergy's preaching/teaching	40%
The welcome	27%

While the welcome of the particular sangha was ranked most important by 27 percent of the Buddhists in our study, 40 percent claimed the
most important feature was the teaching they found there (Figure 7.9). That
stands in marked contrast to Judaism, where the welcome was primary for
51 percent while the teaching and preaching were primary for only 9 percent. It is not far off from Christian descriptions of their churches where the
preaching and teaching is primary for 23 percent of Catholics, 30 percent of
Mainline Protestants, and 49 percent of Evangelicals. Eighteen percent of
Buddhists cited meditation practice as the single most important feature of
their sangha, certainly a unique feature of Buddhist community life.

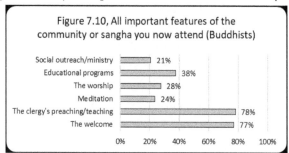

Figure 7.10, All important features of the
community or sangha you now attend (Buddhists)

Social outreach/ministry	21%
Educational programs	38%
The worship	28%
Meditation	24%
The clergy's preaching/teaching	78%
The welcome	77%

When Buddhists were asked to list all of the features of their sangha
that they found important (they could identify more than one, so the total
will exceed 100 percent) and when we add those answers to the single feature they identified as most important above, we get the results displayed in
Figure 7.10. Interestingly, while the teaching is mentioned as important by
over three-quarters of Buddhist respondents, the welcome they experienced
now rises in importance and is mentioned by three-quarters as well.

Choosing a Sangha

When asked how they chose the particular sangha in which they participate, Buddhists most frequently cited proximity, and several noted that in
their location there really aren't that many choices for Buddhists (Figure
7.11). There is also a lot of Internet searching, and many were attracted by
a particular teacher or were looking for a community within a particular
Buddhist tradition (for example, a Zen meditation center).

When Buddhists who had recently started attending were asked how
easy or difficult they found it to start, 83 percent said "easy" or "very easy" (as
compared to 71 percent of Jews and 87 percent of Christians). Only 17 percent say "difficult" or "very difficult" (as compared to 29 percent of Jews and
12 percent of Christians). Clearly, attending meetings or sitting meditation

within the Buddhist tradition is not perceived as a difficult practice to take up, though again we must remember that our study only captures the responses of those who have made a commitment to Buddhist practice.

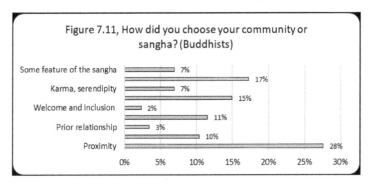

Figure 7.11, How did you choose your community or sangha? (Buddhists)

A Teacher

The second most frequently mentioned primary factor (18 percent of all Buddhist respondents) in making a new Buddhist commitment is the teacher, sensei, master, or lama by whom they were taught. The percentage rises to 68 percent (and becomes the number one response overall) when combined with those who see their teacher as a supporting factor. That is considerably higher than Christians with regard to their pastor or priest, or Jews with regard to their rabbi. In addition to learning Buddhist teachings, one of the reasons the role of the teacher is so central in Buddhism is learning meditation practices, including right posture, breathing, and mindfulness. That is not to say that all Buddhists sit with a teacher regularly. Many of our respondents practice Buddhism from home. But even then, they will typically have some contact with a teacher whether through retreats, special events, or literature. For example, several of the Buddhists in our study referenced Zen Master Thich Nhat Hanh or the Dalai Lama as influential on them, even though they had not all met them personally. A Buddhist teacher guides persons in understanding human experience, transmits Dharma, and hands on a lineage of Buddhism to his or her students. If we can think of following the Buddhist path as similar to learning a skill, such as how to play a musical instrument, we begin to see the importance of the role of the teacher.

> *My Buddhist teacher enabled me to dedicate myself to a specific Buddhist path, and has held me accountable to studying and practicing. Having a spiritual guide who knows me well, he has been about to point out when I'm getting off-track, and to inspire me when I have felt discouraged and disheartened at times. The*

spiritual journey is certainly not linear, at least in my experience, so having someone who can point the way has been invaluable.

My teacher is a living, breathing example of how suffering can be reduced/eliminated.

The Lama or Rinpoche is the lineage relation directly to the Buddha. The teachings are pure this way.

I went to him to understand the nature of my experience. He explained not through words but through his warmth, his presence, his openness, and compassion.

The Buddhist teachers I have met have all studied Buddhist scripture intently, intentionally, and critically. They have asked many of the same questions I have asked and are dedicated to sharing their information with no expectation that they have the "right" answers, only that they are fellow travelers along the path.

Religious Activities

Religious activities can refer to many things within the context of Buddhism, but most of the 11 percent of Buddhists who identify this as the primary factor in their new commitment talk about meditation practice or retreats, rituals, chanting, classes, and "Dharma talks" (which focus on learning Buddhist teachings). Fifty-two percent of Buddhists claim these activities were either a primary or supporting factor. They described the activities as engaging the body and mind, and as centering them and increasing virtues such as patience and compassion.

The Dharma talks during service helped me to understand how the teachings could fit into my life and make me a more calm and reliable source of understanding and compassion. The study class sponsored by the temple and sangha was a very open and inquisitive atmosphere to explore my own understanding and belief.

Attending regular meditation sessions with my sangha as well as quarterly weekend retreats led by a Zen Master helped me to strengthen my practice and become more relaxed and confident in my practice. I also attended regular Zen classes which helped me not only learn more about this spiritual practice that was very foreign to me, but also helped me bond with others following along the same path.

Having retreats, cultural events and class time draw a group of people together in shared experience. Having a community of practitioners allows me to strengthen my practice without directly relying on things/people outside of myself.

The practice of meditation retreats was particularly compelling for me.

Literature and music

Thirteen percent of all persons adopting Buddhism claim that literature and music were primary factors and 45 percent said they were either primary or supporting factors. To put this in perspective, 28 percent of Jews in our study said this factor was primary or supporting and 16 to 20 percent of Christians. As attested to by the participants in our study (and a quick visit to one's local bookstore), Buddhist literature is widespread and popular these days. Indeed, the phrase "nightstand Buddhist" was popularized decades ago to describe persons who are not necessarily converted Buddhists but who enjoy reading Buddhist thought.

The commentaries on the original teachings, particularly those of contemporary Buddhist teachers, help me more easily understand how to apply the teachings to contemporary life.

My first introduction to Zen was through a book on Zen Meditation. I started practicing according to the instructions in the book, then began reading about Buddhism from some other books before I found my first public talk with a Zen master and a sangha with which to practice.

Vocables are an important part of our ceremonies.

The literature really—the scads of books on Tibetan Buddhism are very informative and very helpful.

Bands like Pink Floyd and the Incredible String Band were like elders to me at the time as they seemed to have traversed some of the terrain I was venturing out into. They encouraged and inspired.

No real teachers around, depended on literature for instruction.

Reading books, articles, and listening to Internet recordings and videos informed me of the basics and convinced me to become a Buddhist.

The Family

Spouse or Partner

The spouse or partner is significantly less important as a factor for new Buddhists than for Jews and Christians. For most Buddhists, there is not the social importance that many Jews and Christians attach to raising their children in a Jewish or Christian household. Recall that 66 percent of Jews identify their spouse or partner as an important factor and between 45 to 56 percent of Christians. But only 9 percent of Buddhists list the spouse or partner as the primary factor (with 30 percent claiming spouse or partner as either a primary or supporting factor).

Those who do cite the spouse or partner typically reference that individual's support or influence, or they emphasize the mutuality of their following the Buddhist path.

> We were interested in Buddhism together. I did not want to start being part of an organization my wife was not interested in. This may sound superficial but I did not want to add another thing in my life that was done separate from my family. Especially not religion.

> She supported my decision to become a Buddhist.

> My partner is a dedicated meditator and spiritual person as well, so her presence at the ceremony was a way to support me and my ongoing commitment to practice.

> He became a Buddhist too about the same time and we were able to raise our children in a unified way.

> For support and encouragement—a fellow traveler to share to Path.

Their own children

No Buddhists claim that the primary factor in their commitment was their children—again, a marked contrast with the 13 percent of Jews who did so (40 percent of Jews cited children as either primary or supporting) and the 10 to 14 percent of Christians who did so (32 to 40 percent said children were either a primary or supporting factor). Six percent of Buddhists say their children were a supporting factor—in half the cases because their children supported, inspired, and encouraged them, and in the other half of the cases because they wanted to be able to teach their children well or to possess the composure and calm that Buddhism brought to their lives when dealing with their children's problems.

Parents and other family members

Just 2 percent of Buddhists identify their parents and just 1 percent identify other family members as the primary factor in turning to Buddhism. That percentage climbs slightly to 8 percent for those who claim parents as a primary or supporting factor and 9 percent for those who say the same of other family members. By way of comparison, 29 to 41 percent of Christians claim parents and family were important and 28 percent of Jews. Buddhists in our study who cited this factor said they admire their parents for being supportive as well as for raising them to be open and broad-minded. Other family members were credited with having introduced the persons in our study to Buddhism or supporting them along the way.

Friends and other persons in particular

Eleven percent of Buddhists say that a friend or some other person was their primary influence in adopting Buddhism. That number jumps to an impressive 62 percent who claim other persons as either primary or supporting factors (as compared to 30 percent in the case of Jews and 42 to 57 percent in the case of Christians). This excludes teachers, monks, masters, lamas, or priests, who show up in a separate category, as we will see. Buddhism is clearly a tradition that is transmitted through the influence of other persons, and if we were to add clergy or teachers to this mix, that interpersonal influence becomes even more noteworthy.

Friends or college teachers were important by way of first introducing persons to Buddhism, and some friends served as a motivation to join a Buddhist lineage, to study and meditate, or take formal precepts. They often functioned as "spiritual friends," supporting, encouraging, and providing each other with accountability.

> *My friends within the Sangha are important as they understand the practice and can help me overcome some obstacles. My friends outside the Sangha are equally important as they allow me to "test" my theories of the practice to those who don't understand it.*

> *It is so helpful to have people who are like-minded and willing to walk the path with me! They pick me up when I fall down, and I am able to help them in the same way. I think it would be so*

difficult to walk a different spiritual path [without] anyone else in one's life.

The friends are your Sangha and community where you can share and grow.

Friends in the dharma help keep me on the path.

He taught the university course on Buddhism that I took. He taught me a lot about Buddhist thought and tradition.

Dreams and Visions

Three percent of Buddhists identify dreams and visions as the primary factor in taking up Buddhism, and 15 percent say it was a primary or supporting factor. These dreams and visions are often connected to the Buddhist experience of enlightenment or awakening.

That connection the deep unseen mystery that keeps me questioning, keeps me seeking. I have no need for faith, I have direct experience of my connection to a vast spiritual power.

It showed me that I had been on the wrong path in my life; it was not definitive; it was more like the Buddha's enlightenment; a sudden realization of the truth.

I felt my own spiritual awakening through energetic bodywork.

The vision gave me connection to our ancient ancestors.

When our Buddhist participants were asked whether, at any time in their life, they had ever had any out-of-the-ordinary experiences they would describe as religious in some way, 64 percent say yes, a little higher percentage than the 59 percent of Christians and the 38 percent of Jews who say yes. While some of the responses from Buddhists throughout the study accentuate the rationality of Buddhist practices, teachings, and spirituality, we saw a great deal of openness to mystery among Buddhists on the whole.

Scripture

In the case of Buddhists, it is often important to think of Scripture and other Buddhist literature together. The teachings of the Buddha are the Scriptures of Buddhism, and along with interpretations of those teachings, they are essential for most Buddhists. Just under one-third of all Buddhist respondents identify Scripture as a primary or supporting factor in their faith commitment (including 3 percent who claim it as the primary factor). New adherents of Buddhism spoke powerfully about the practicality of Buddhist Scripture and its ability to bring insight and to expand awareness. At the time they were making their new commitments, a little over half of all Buddhist respondents (and not just those who chose Scripture as an important factor) read Scripture at least several times a month—almost exactly the same as we saw with Jews. By contrast, 68 percent of Evangelicals, 63 percent of Catholics, and only 44 percent of Mainline Protestants read Scripture at least several times a month during the time they were making their new commitment. For only about 15 percent of Buddhists, Scripture played no role at that time, but for 32 percent it was somewhat helpful and for 45 percent, very helpful.

> *Scripture was important for me, as understanding how things come to be as they are helps me understand how to apply them today.*

> *It's more the Zen approach to scripture. Words are no substitute for experience. Words can point to truth but are not truth. Experience trumps scripture. That being said, the Buddhist scriptures provide usable, practical guidelines for living a decent life without getting mired in dogma and theology.*

> *The sutras and the commentaries, both ancient and modern, are a constant source of awakening and expansion of my way of looking at the world, my place in it, and the question of what does and does not constitute faith, for me, in this life.*

> *Reading what the Buddha taught and practiced, and being encouraged to reflect upon its contemporary meaning has helped me clarify what being Buddhist really means, and to discern how I can apply these teachings to my everyday life.*

OBSTACLES?

When asked if they found any of their religion's teaching, practices, persons, or institutions to be an obstacle in making their new commitment, most Buddhists (60 percent) said no, with several emphasizing the breadth and openness within Buddhism, even its compatibility with other religious traditions. The remainder, however, identified a variety of teachings or practices that were hurdles for them.

Several identified the Buddhist teachings on no-self, karma, and, in particular, rebirth, or reincarnation as challenging. In some cases, rituals and chanting were experienced as daunting or too stuck within a particular cultural tradition. As one person put it, "American versions of Buddhism, invariably, spend more time on imitating Asian forms and customs than I am comfortable with." A couple of persons mentioned an enduring misogyny in Buddhism that, while it can surely be found in other religions, is exacerbated by the close, yet hierarchical nature of the teacher-student relationship, which can foster abuse. One mentioned the overwhelming whiteness of meditation centers and the lack of other young adults that made conversion less attractive, at least in the beginning. Finally, several mentioned the difficulty of the "spiritual separation" from their family or friends that occurred as they proceeded down the Buddhist path. Not all relationships fared well under this strain.

For several respondents, some of these obstacles remain after making their new commitment—especially some of the rituals, beliefs (when they are experienced as fixed dogmas), and the hierarchical dimensions of Buddhism. But these new converts have committed themselves to growing, adapting, and bringing changes to their communities.

WHAT WAS MOST APPEALING?

Buddhists were also asked if they found any of their religion's teachings, practices, persons, or institutions particularly appealing. We found an overwhelming positivity and enthusiasm in the responses, most of which focused on a particular teacher, the basic teachings of Buddhism, the practice of meditation, silence, and ritual, or the Buddhist emphasis on a daily non-judgmental and compassionate way of being in the world. Persons especially emphasized the openness and flexibility of Buddhist teachings.

IS THERE A CHANGE?

We wanted to gauge what sort of changes come with adopting Buddhism, and so we asked about changes in religious practices, spirituality, and self-perception; about attendance at religious services; and about stances on important social issues.

Attendance at services

As Figure 7.12 shows, only about 25 percent of persons making a new Buddhist commitment had been attending services or teachings at least once per month prior to making their new commitment. That number rises to 80 percent afterwards, which demonstrates the significant shift that has taken place in their life practices and priorities.

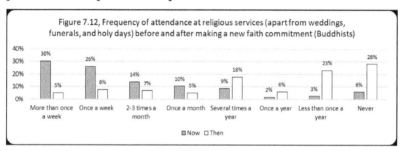

Figure 7.12, Frequency of attendance at religious services (apart from weddings, funerals, and holy days) before and after making a new faith commitment (Buddhists)

Other Forms of Involvement

When we asked about overall involvement in the life and activities of their sangha, temple, or meditation center, we saw the highest rates of involvement of any of the religions studied in this project (Figure 7.13). Forty-six percent of Buddhists claim to be very active and another 33 percent said they are somewhat active. Even with this high percentage, there is still a significant number of Buddhists who are not frequently involved but who practice meditation privately. Unsurprisingly, 87 percent of Buddhists claim to be happy with these high levels of religious involvement.

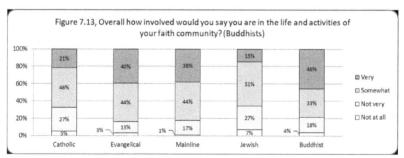

Figure 7.13, Overall how involved would you say you are in the life and activities of your faith community? (Buddhists)

When it comes to groups, studies, and fellowships of various kinds, 59 percent of Buddhists report weekly activity (Figure 7.14), which is higher than Jews (31 percent), Catholics (43 percent), or Mainline Protestants (53 percent)—though Evangelicals remain the most active (73 percent). The vast majority of this activity is related to sitting meditation. Other forms of activity include Dharma study and book studies, retreats, classes, tantric practice, discussion groups, social activities, and opportunities for contemplation.

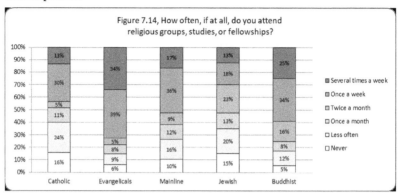

Figure 7.14, How often, if at all, do you attend religious groups, studies, or fellowships?

Multiple Religious Belonging

About one in five Buddhists report participation in religious services or activities of other religions—far more than is the case with Christians or Jews. We heard about participation in Christian churches, Quaker and Unitarian Universalist churches, Jewish synagogues, and yoga. In addition, several were active in interfaith work in their communities.

Reading Scripture

While only 3 percent of Buddhists claim Scripture as the primary factor in their recent commitment (another 28 percent cite it as a supporting factor), 71 percent of Buddhists say that it is very or somewhat important to their faith (Figure 7.15). The frequency of Scripture reading, moreover, was little changed for Buddhists, just slightly increased after their recent commitment.

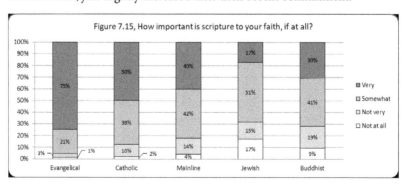

Figure 7.15, How important is scripture to your faith, if at all?

God (or the Divine)

When we asked Buddhists whether they had thought much about God (or the divine) prior to making their commitment, and whether their views had changed, we found first that just under half said that they had thought about God or the divine a great deal and another third said they had done so "somewhat," for a combined 80 percent. That number can be deceiving, however, since less than 5 percent believe in anything like a traditional, external, or personal God or deity(ies).

For about 40 percent, their views had changed substantially since taking up Buddhism, and for another 40 percent their views had not changed much at all. But even those whose views did not change were already atheists, or at least they did not believe in any sort of personal deity—instead more like a universal energy that connects us. For the middle 20 percent, they too largely did not believe in God then or now, but their views on the divine had grown and expanded somewhat.

While the vast majority of Buddhists do not believe in God, that does not mean they do not think about the divine in the sense of a universal, nameless force or energy. The Buddha is not a god for most Buddhists, but is a nature, power, or consciousness within each of us that can be awakened. Some described this Buddha-nature as a spark or light, or source of love. But the word *God*—and, for many, even the notion of "the divine"—does not really fit their experience or their understanding of Buddhist teaching. As a particular Buddhist saying goes, when someone asks, "Who is the Buddha?" the reply is, "Who asks?"

Changes that finding faith has made

As we did with others in the study, we asked our Buddhist participants to rate the significance of six types of change that are often associated with religious conversions: (1) beliefs, (2) actions and lifestyle, (3) spiritual practices, (4) relations with others, (5) happiness, and (6) hopefulness. Figure 7.16 illustrates their self-understanding in relation to each and in comparison with Jewish and Christian responses. Given the Buddhist emphasis on meditation and contemplative practices, one would expect to see significant change reported in that area, and indeed, Buddhists reported the most change in spiritual practices of any religious group. In fact, Buddhists reported significant change in almost every area, second only to Evangelicals. The one exception to this is hopefulness, where Buddhists reported the least amount of change of any group we studied. One certainly does not have to

believe in an afterlife to have hope, but about nine in ten Evangelicals believe in heaven, which may account for some of their exceptionally high
hopefulness.[4] By contrast, just under half of Buddhists believe in heaven
(even fewer Jews do, at 40 percent). We are left wondering why hope was
rated so low by Buddhists, relatively to those from other religious traditions.
Is it related to the absence of a belief in the afterlife?

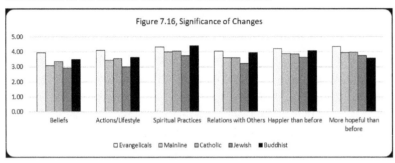

We also asked Buddhist participants to report in their own words and
categories how they understood any significant changes in their lives. We
asked them the open question, "What is the main difference that becoming a Buddhist (or a more committed Buddhist) has made in your life?"
The responses were eager and enthusiastic, around three-quarters of the
time mentioning a change in focus, attitude, outlook, or mindfulness and
connecting that about half the time with an accompanying improvement
in their relations with others. Buddhists consistently referred to themselves
as calm, content, balanced, and grounded; more patient and compassionate
while being less judgmental; more "connected" to themselves and to others;
and more aware or mindful. About 10 percent explicitly named meditation
and mindfulness practice, but it was clear throughout all the responses
that meditation is central in fostering these changes. Another 10 percent
mentioned some change in their understanding or beliefs, and yet another
10 percent stressed the importance of having a community. Typical of the
responses we heard are the following:

> I am happier, more joyful, and more compassionate. I am more
> able to touch my sorrow, grief, or anger when needed without
> lashing out or suffering as much. I have learned how to connect
> deeply with myself and others in ways that are genuine, loving,
> and kind—even when they are difficult.

---

4. Pew, "Belief in Heaven." Note: 88 percent of Evangelicals, 85 percent of Catholics,
and 80 percent of Mainline Protestants believe in heaven.

I am a kinder more mindful of my actions toward others. I try very hard not to judge and accept everyone as they are.

More attentive and relaxed. More accessible to others. Meditation is key.

I am less judgmental, more compassionate. I am more mindful and at peace.

Through meditation I am more aware of my feelings and perceptions. I feel as if I have the tools to increase joy and contentment in my life.

More mindful. Less angry. More compassionate and understanding.

I am a kinder, more compassionate human being and therefore I am happier and more content than I have ever been before in my life.

I no longer kill anything on purpose, even mosquitos! I have great compassion for all beings, including both victims and perpetrators of violence. I believe in reincarnation and believe I am connected to all beings everywhere.

I have a daily practice of mindfulness. That practice has resulted in me being more centered, more calm, more accepting, more open to others.

Trying to live in the moment, appreciating the moment. Not worrying about the future or the past. Enjoying life as you are living it.

Social Issues

Lastly, we asked the Buddhists in our study about any changes in their attitudes or positions on social issues. As with the Jews in our study, Buddhists were, on the whole, already firmly supportive of the right to abortion, same-sex marriage, women's equality, racial justice, care for the natural environment, and economic justice for the poor. Moreover, they grew significantly in their support for most of these. War and gun control were complicated, just as we saw in other religious traditions. We saw very few Buddhists changing positions completely on any issues, and, quite surprisingly, the largest outright change in positions was the 7 percent who were now in support of war (though this came mostly from Buddhists in the Tibetan, or Vajrayana, tradition).

	Already opposed, became more opposed	Already opposed, remain just as opposed	Now become opposed	No opinion/Don't know	Now became supportive	Already supported, stayed just as supportive	Already supportive, became more supportive
Right to an Abortion	0%	2%	2%	12%	2%	76%	7%
Gay Marriage	0%	0%	0%	4%	3%	73%	19%
Gun Control	11%	12%	1%	13%	4%	43%	17%
War	32%	39%	4%	11%	7%	7%	0%
Women's Equality	0%	1%	0%	3%	1%	71%	24%
Racial Justice	0%	1%	0%	3%	0%	67%	30%
Economic Justice for the Poor	0%	0%	0%	4%	2%	56%	38%
Care for the Natural Environment	0%	0%	0%	3%	3%	48%	47%

Figure 7.17, How have your attitudes and positions on the following social issues changed, if at all, since making your new commitment or recommitment?" (Buddhists)

It hardly needs to be said that Buddhists are quite unlike Christians or Jews, and that what it means to be a Buddhist thoroughly shapes how one finds faith in that tradition. Rather than the Buddhist path being one that connects persons to a transcendent deity, calling persons to a morality commanded or empowered by that deity, it is instead a path that awakens new consciousness, mindfulness, and awareness, and that empowers new ways of being present to and connecting with others with patience and compassion. Buddhists are persons who "find faith" through practice, especially the practice of meditation. But, again, that faith is not usually the kind of devotion or spirituality so typical of Western religious traditions, shaped by one's relation to an external transcendence. To have faith—to the extent the word can helpfully be used at all—is to give oneself over, to "take refuge in," the teachings of the Buddha and the community of persons (sangha) who together walk a path toward awakening.

8

Islam

THE PERCENTAGE OF MUSLIMS in the US has grown significantly in the past decade, and is now 1.1 percent of the US population, the third largest religious tradition after Christianity and Judaism. Twenty-three percent of all adult Muslims in the US are converts (by comparison, only 6 percent of Christians are).[1] At the same time, 23 percent of the adults who were raised within Islam no longer identify as Muslim.[2] So Islam is losing about as many persons as it is gaining at present in the US.

A total of fifty Muslims participated in our study, all of them recent converts to Islam. About half of those persons completed the survey and the other half spoke with us in focus groups. Most of the Muslims in our study identified as Sunni (61 percent), the largest Muslim group in the US, at 55 percent of the Muslim population (16 percent identify as Shiite in the US and 14 percent say they are "just Muslim").[3] The remainder of the persons in our study did not identify themselves as belonging to any particular tradition within Islam. Relative to the other groups we have looked at thus far in the book, the smaller number of Muslim participants does not allow us to make the same kind of generalized claims about Muslims. At the same time, we were able to gain in-depth understanding from focus groups that expanded upon what we were able to learn from those who completed a survey, and their stories narrate and provide depth to some of the wider trends we know about coming to faith as a Muslim in the US context.

1. Pew, "The share of Americans," para. 2.
2. Pew, "U.S. Muslims," 119. Twenty-two percent of those have become Christians and 55 percent claim no religious affiliation.
3. Ibid., 8.

The median age of the Muslims in our study is 42, and while that is much lower than the median for the other religious faiths we studied, it is consistent with what we find in the United States more generally. The median age for adult Muslims (the same as for Hindus) is 33, the youngest median age of any religious group in the US.[4] Those who convert to Islam in the US likewise tend to be young, with 26 percent reporting they converted between the ages of 10 to 19 and half during their 20s.[5] Only 4 percent converted after the age of 40.[6]

As to education, three-fourths of our respondents had graduated from college (or gone further), which is significantly higher than the nationwide average for Muslims or the US general public, both at 31 percent.[7]

COMING TO FAITH

As already noted, all of the Muslims in our study are first-time converts to Islam. Three-fourths were previously Christians and the other fourth had no prior religious affiliation. According to a 2017 Pew Research Center study, about half of the Muslim converts in the US were formerly Protestant (53 percent); one in five were Catholic and another one in five were unaffiliated.[8]

Over two-thirds of the Muslim participants in our study are black or African-American. If we were to judge wholly on the basis of that percentage, we would have to conclude that Islam draws disproportionately on the black population in the US for its new converts. That is largely true, and while Islam in the US is racially diverse, with no one racial group forming a majority, Muslims born in the US are far more likely than Muslim immigrants to identify as black (32 percent vs. 11 percent).[9] Indeed, "fully half of Muslims whose families have been in the US for at least three generations are black (51 percent)."[10] At the same time, the percentage (not the total number) of African American Muslims is shrinking as the number of immigrants from Muslim-majority countries increases in the US.[11]

---

4. Pew, "America's Changing Religious Landscape," 50. For Christians it is 49, for Jews it is 50, and for Buddhists it is 39.

5. Pew, "U.S. Muslims," 120.

6. Ibid.

7. Ibid., 30.

8. Ibid., 119.

9. Ibid., 35.

10. Ibid.

11. Ibid., 37.

Sixty percent of the persons in our study claimed that converting to Islam was a gradual process, and the median length of time it took was about a year. The other 40 percent said their conversion was sudden enough that they could put a date on it. For both groups, the path to Islam typically involved influential encounters with other Muslims (often one's spouse, partner, or friends) followed by an exploration of Islam for themselves through prayer, reading, and study.

Why convert?

A little over two-thirds of the Muslims in our study said they converted to Islam because they found truth and meaning in its teachings, both intellectually and spiritually. A few explicitly mentioned their dissatisfaction with Christianity, and their desire to have a direct relationship with God, which they did not find in Christianity (where Christ is typically understood as mediator). In some cases, the draw to Islam came through study, research, or going to services. Some attributed their decision to credible or inspiring examples of Muslims they knew, and, for several, it just felt like the right time, or "it just made sense." About one in ten of our participants converted for the sake of their spouse (or future spouse). That is about the same percentage as the Pew Research Center found nationally at 9 percent (Figure 8.1). About nine in ten Muslims in the US marry other Muslims, since many Islamic traditions do not condone Muslim women marrying non-Muslims. Muslim men are permitted to marry outside the faith, but based on Quranic teaching, they may only marry Christians and Jews—other persons "of the book."

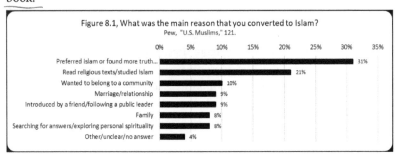

Figure 8.1, What was the main reason that you converted to Islam?
Pew, "U.S. Muslims," 121.

Preferred Islam or found more truth...	31%
Read religious texts/studied Islam	21%
Wanted to belong to a community	10%
Marriage/relationship	9%
Introduced by a friend/following a public leader	9%
Family	8%
Searching for answers/exploring personal spirituality	8%
Other/unclear/no answer	4%

Forty percent of the Muslims in our study had taken instructional classes as part of their conversion, which is significantly lower than we found in other religious traditions. All of those who took such classes found them helpful, though. When asked how they signaled their new faith commitment, virtually all said they did so by reciting the *shahaadah*, the testimony of faith that is taken publicly and is the first of the five pillars of Islam: "*I bear witness that there is no deity except Allah, and I bear witness that Muhammad is the messenger of Allah.*"

What does it mean to be Muslim?

When new Muslims were asked what it means to be Muslim, three primary themes emerged: believing in God, affirming Muhammad as God's prophet, and living a moral life. This is entirely consistent with what we know about Muslims more generally in the US (not just new converts). According to the 2017 Pew study mentioned earlier, 85 percent of US Muslims say "believing in God" is essential to being a Muslim, 72 percent say "loving the Prophet Muhammad," and 69 percent say "working for justice and equality in society" (Figure 8.2). The first of these two affirmations, of course, are the primary claims of the *shahaadah*. The oneness of God was stressed by the participants in our study, just as it is in Islam more generally, and often our respondents asserted this explicitly in opposition to the Christian belief in the Trinity.

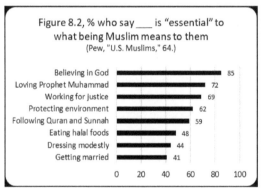

Figure 8.2, % who say ___ is "essential" to what being Muslim means to them
(Pew, "U.S. Muslims," 64.)

Believing in God	85
Loving Prophet Muhammad	72
Working for Justice	69
Protecting environment	62
Following Quran and Sunnah	59
Eating halal foods	48
Dressing modestly	44
Getting married	41

When it comes to living a moral life, Muslims found a variety of ways of expressing this, though mostly in general terms such as the golden rule, being good and kind, and treating others well. Again, this is consistent with other research. Their responses frequently connected the moral life to belief in and submission to God (Islam means "submission" or "surrender"). One middle-aged woman, for example, spoke of her personal *jihad*, a word that means struggle, or the struggle of faith. And though the primary context of Muslim *jihad* is one's daily life—being gracious for what one has, avoiding envy of others, remaining patient and calm—she noted how unfortunate it is that this term has been reduced simply to "war" within the political rhetoric of US culture.

Drawn in by Others or Active Seekers?

Muslims in our study had among the highest percentages of those who said they were drawn in by others without actively seeking (60 percent) and, conversely, the lowest rates of those who said they were active seekers (43 percent).[12] The high incidence of becoming converted for a spouse accounts for some of this, but certainly not all. If the persons in our study are an indication of larger trends, then Muslims are clearly taking an active initiative in inviting others to faith within the US context.

Religious or Spiritual?

Muslims were fairly evenly split between describing themselves as "religious" (44 percent) and "both spiritual and religious" (38 percent). Only a minority said they were "spiritual but not religious" (19 percent). No one claimed to be "neither spiritual nor religious." We can compare this with the 2017 Pew study, but that study only offered four categories, and did not offer the category "religious," which, interestingly, was the one most of our participants chose. Half of the Muslims in the Pew study claimed to be "religious and spiritual." As with our study, they also found that 19 percent claimed to be "spiritual but not religious." They found a much higher percentage (20 percent) than we did (we found none) of those who claimed to be "neither religious nor spiritual." But then we were studying only those who had recently converted to Islam while they were studying the wider Muslim population in the US, and there lies the difference.

FACTORS LEADING TO FAITH

We asked Muslims to identify both the primary factor in coming to faith and as many supporting factors as they wished. Scripture and one's spouse or partner stand out as especially important factors for Muslims, though a good number also identified religious activities and their imam, the congregational, worship, and prayer leader of the mosque (Figure 8.3).

When we combine supporting factors with the primary factor, we get the fuller picture shown in Figure 8.4. The picture changes only slightly. Scripture is still mentioned most frequently followed by spouse or partner and religious activities. The percentage of those listing a congregation or friends increases substantially when we add supporting factors.

12. Muslims were second only to Evangelicals in reporting that they were drawn in by others without actively seeking.

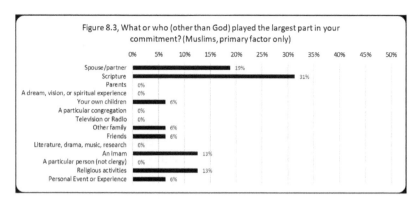

Figure 8.3, What or who (other than God) played the largest part in your commitment? (Muslims, primary factor only)

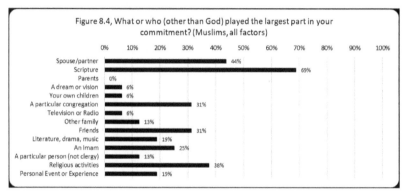

Figure 8.4, What or who (other than God) played the largest part in your commitment? (Muslims, all factors)

Scripture

Scripture surfaced over and over as the most important factor for Muslims in their conversion. It was the primary factor for almost a third of our participants and a primary or supporting factor for over two-thirds. Persons stressed its truth, divine origin, factuality, practicality, and its resonance with their minds and hearts.

> *After reading Quran and other Islamic books, it most closely identified with me and my beliefs. I liked what I read, especially the miracles within the Quran. I concluded that this was the word of God and the true religion.*

> *As I read the Quran I realized how strongly I agreed with Islam.*

> *For me, I just feel like everything in the Quran and hadiths are fact. Everything makes sense and isn't bogus.*

> *It had in it everything I needed to know and do.*

The Qu'ran answered questions I had never gotten the answers to in Christianity.

Spouse or Partner

A considerable number of Muslims come to faith for the sake of their spouse—19 percent of our Muslim participants cited their spouse or partner as the primary factor and 44 percent as either a primary or supporting factor. For some, the conversion was to ensure a Muslim marriage, but it was rarely that simple. For most of our respondents, their spouses or fiancés provided a deeper influence, answered questions, and modeled Islamic faith and practice.

> *My husband actually does practice what he preaches and I did see him pray, whether we were on the beach or at my parent's house he prayed. The fact that he did not put any pressure on me to convert, now that I have fully experienced his family's culture was amazing. In the 3rd chapter of the Qur'an, God clearly states, "There is no compulsion in religion" and my husband followed that.*

> *I was not looking for anything in the spiritual realm of things when I got married. Had I not married my wife, I would not be a Muslim today.*

> *He introduced me to it and answered the questions I had.*

> *He is a practicing Muslim and seeing him in daily pray and live calmly in the world helped me understand Islam better.*

Other persons

Few Muslims referenced their children, parents, or other family members as influential in their conversion. Those who did, however, reported that family members had a profound effect on them by living out Islamic teachings and practices in a way that left them wanting what they saw. Over a third of the Muslims in our study identified friends and other persons who were not family or clergy as either a primary or supporting factor in coming to faith. They found those friends to be role models, and they experienced their invitational warmth, love, and respect without pressure or compulsion.

> *I was welcomed into a group of women that gave me what my family never did, love and it felt right.*

I couldn't say which factor was most important to me. I derived a lot of benefit from seeing Muslims practicing their faith in my local mosque and I think their example and their outreach to me just as friends and fellow students made me feel like a Muslim even before I knew I had accepted the faith.

The friends I made at the local mosque were from all different places. Many were from the U.S. and had converted to Islam. I had never met people like me who had converted to Islam. I made friends with the Muslims at the mosque and began to see myself as one of them.

My friend also helped me quite a bit with my questions and helped guide me.

My friend is a hijabi from graduate school who was so profoundly gentle, calm and a wonderful presence. She alone was a beautiful source of dawah [invitation] Masha'Allah [praise be to God].

The Congregation and its Activities

Though none of our Muslim participants identified their mosque or congregation as the primary factor in coming to faith, 31 percent said it was a supporting factor. Most of those persons also cited religious activities such as prayer, classes, and social gatherings as supporting factors, and a few even listed religious activities as primary. Persons experienced their congregations as receptive, welcoming, and peaceful. They found there a diverse community united by faith and practice that expanded their horizons and reinforced their journey of faith.

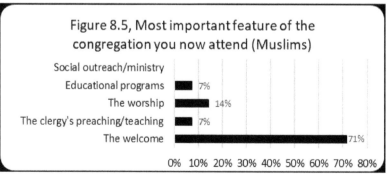

Figure 8.5, Most important feature of the congregation you now attend (Muslims)

The welcome received from a congregation was far and away the most important feature of the particular congregation attended by the Muslims participating in our study (Figure 8.5). When asked to list all of the features of their congregation that participants found important (including the primary one), the teaching and preaching of the imam rose to second in importance (Figure 8.6).

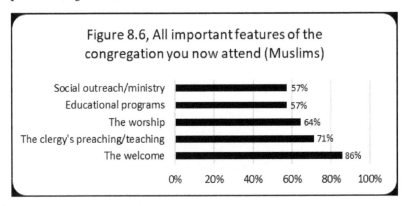

Figure 8.6, All important features of the congregation you now attend (Muslims)

Choosing a Congregation

Over half said proximity was the most important factor in choosing the particular congregation they now attend, with several persons noting that there was only one mosque in town, so it's not like they had a lot of choice. The remainder identified some special feature of the congregation that was important to them—for example, their mosque was the only one that offered classes for new converts, it responded actively to their requests for information or provided assistance, or the mosque was open and friendly.

The Imam

A quarter of the new Muslim converts in our study said their imam was either the primary or supporting factor in coming to faith. As leader of the mosque, the imam offered welcome from the outset, answered questions and cleared up misconceptions, put Islamic doctrine into accessible terms, and modeled key Islamic values such as peace, compassion, and mercy.

OBSTACLES?

Most of the Muslims who spoke with us did not claim there were significant obstacles in the process of conversion. Those that identified obstacles focused very little on beliefs and teachings of Islam and more on practices such as eating halal meat, needing to know Arabic, or abstaining from alcohol. Several women mentioned the practice of modest dress and wearing hijab, or head-scarf (four in ten Muslim women always or usually wear hijab in the US).[13] There were clearly those who experienced Islam as too strict for them—citing the disciplines of fasting for Ramadan, giving money to charity, or praying five times a day (and trying to find a location to do that while at work or in public). Most have adapted to these practices or they continue to struggle with them.

WHAT WAS MOST APPEALING?

Among the beliefs Muslims found most appealing, we heard repeatedly about the "oneness" of God and the attractiveness of the personal and direct relationship to God they experienced without the need for a "middle man," as one person put it, referring to Jesus. Persons spoke of the "wholeness" of Islam and its view of God, and the integration of belief in God with a daily spiritual practice. Many of the Muslim women in our study spoke of the respect for and rights of women that they found in Islam as most appealing. This included a decreased sexualization of women and an emphasis on modesty.

WHAT CHANGED?

Attendance

According to the 2017 Pew study on US Muslims, about two-thirds claim that religion is very important in their lives, and about four in ten say they attend a mosque on a weekly basis. Four in ten also report that they pray all five *salah* (prayers) daily.[14] We saw similarly high levels of religiosity as measured by such things as prayer, attendance, Scripture reading, and involvement in religious and social activities in the Muslims who participated in our study. In fact, one of the greatest changes accompanying conversion was increased attendance at religious services. As Figure 8.7 shows, prior to conversion, over three-fourths attended only several times a year or less, and most of those attended less than once a year. After conversion, two-thirds

13. Pew, "U.S. Muslims," 111.
14. Ibid., 105.

now attend at least once a month, and that percentage rises to 86 percent who attend two to three times a month or more.

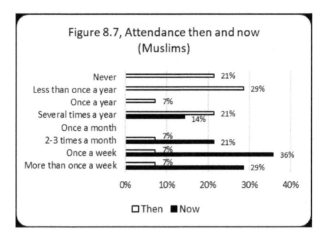

Figure 8.7, Attendance then and now (Muslims)

Other Involvement

New Muslim converts reported being very involved in their faith communities. A third of the persons in our study said they were "very" involved in the life and activities of their mosque while a half said they were "somewhat" involved. A minority said they were "not very" involved, nor were they happy about that low level of involvement, hoping to become more active in the future.

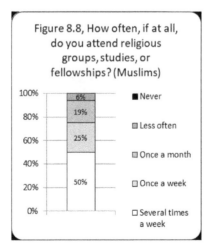

Figure 8.8, How often, if at all, do you attend religious groups, studies, or fellowships? (Muslims)

As shown in Figure 8.8, three-quarters of Muslim participants attend various activities and meetings at least once a week. This involvement includes congregational prayer (*jumu'ah*) each Friday, but also conferences, lectures, language study, classes for new converts, interfaith groups, and *halaqas* (gatherings for study and discussion of the Quran and other topics in Islam).

Multiple Religious Belonging

Muslims in our study did not belong to other faith traditions, as that would very much go against the teachings of Islam. However, participation in interfaith events was mentioned often; indeed, it was mentioned as much as or more than we found in persons from other faith traditions.

Reading Scripture

Given the fact that Scripture was the most frequently cited factor in coming to faith for new Muslims, we would expect to see that importance show up in their report of how frequently they read Scripture—and that is indeed the case. New Muslims were already reading Scripture frequently during the process of their conversion—60 percent report that they did so several times a week (Figure 8.9). That increased to 69 percent after conversion, and those reading Scripture several times a month increased from 7 to 25 percent.

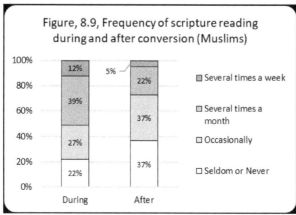

Figure, 8.9, Frequency of scripture reading during and after conversion (Muslims)

God

The vast majority (80 percent) of the Muslims in our study had thought a lot about God prior to the time of their conversion, and we did not hear reports of much shifting in their views of God after conversion. Indeed, half said their view of God was unchanged. The other half, however, reported shifts in their thinking that emphasized the oneness of God (again, in contrast to trinitarian views they formerly held) or that centered on God's compassion and mercy instead of God's anger and distance.

Other Changes

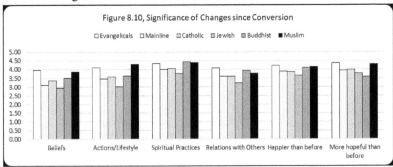

Figure 8.10, Significance of Changes since Conversion

□ Evangelicals   □ Mainline   □ Catholic   □ Jewish   ▨ Buddhist   ■ Muslim

Figure 8.10 illustrates our Muslim participants' understanding of changes in their life after conversion in comparison with Jewish, Buddhist, and Christian responses. Overall, Muslims appraise changes in their lives as being fairly significant, especially in relation to their actions and lifestyle, where they report more significant change than persons from the other three traditions. New Muslims also rate highly the significance of changes in their spiritual practices (including especially prayer, attendance at services, Scripture reading, and study). By most measures, Muslim converts rated the changes in their lives more highly than any other group except Evangelicals.

When Muslims in our study were asked to report in their own words what the main difference that becoming a Muslim has made in their lives, about half described that change with reference to their belief in or relationship to God. The other half focused more on changes in attitudes, dispositions toward others, or way of life. These often overlapped or were connected to each other. For the first half, we heard repeatedly about how they were more aware of God and close to God. The accent here was not simply on changed belief, but rather a reliance on God that brought confidence and happiness, reinforced daily through prayer.

> *Made me more conscious of God in all aspects of my life and that I am accountable to Him.*

> *I feel closer to Allah.*

> *More peace, happiness and closeness with God.*

Well it has given me the one shot at salvation and the attainment of paradise. God/Allah is free to have mercy upon whomever He chooses but Islam is the only acceptable religion to God.

For the other half, their outlook on life had changed as had their approach to daily living. For several of the females, wearing the hijab (headscarf) was identified as a significant change. In some situations, it elicited respect from other persons; in other situations, it occasioned curiosity or judgment.

It has forced me into a routine of rigorous rhythm and productivity for the sake of that only, removing ego and self-interest from tasks have allowed me to seamlessly blend into a team player role.

I have stopped drinking and sleeping around and am overall much happier and more stable than before.

The most obvious difference is that I wear a headscarf now. In this way my religion is more apparent than it was before, . . . so the main difference for me is the social difference and how this affects my interactions with others.

I feel less anxious and just content.

Social Issues

We did not see many 180-degree changes in attitudes or positions on social issues from recently converted Muslims. However, Muslims were overwhelmingly supportive (or became even more supportive) of women's equality, racial justice, care for the natural environment, and economic justice for the poor. They were also against war at a higher percentage (85 percent) than Buddhists, Jews, or any Christian tradition, contrary to the picture many Americans have of Muslims. The majority of Muslims (57 percent) were against abortion and tended to be against same-sex marriage rather than supportive of it (43 percent vs. 29 percent).

Figure 8.11, How have your attitudes and positions on the following social issues changed, if at all, since making your new commitment or recommitment?" (Muslims)

	Already opposed, became more opposed	Already opposed, remain just as opposed	Now become opposed	No opinion/ Don't know	Now became supportive	Already supported, stayed just as supportive	Already supportive, became more supportive
Right to an Abortion	14%	43%	0%	7%	7%	21%	7%
Gay Marriage	14%	29%	0%	29%	7%	14%	7%
Gun Control	8%	8%	0%	8%	0%	50%	25%
War	15%	69%	0%	0%	0%	8%	8%
Women's Equality	0%	0%	0%	0%	0%	69%	31%
Racial Justice	0%	8%	0%	8%	0%	31%	54%
Economic Justice for the Poor	0%	0%	0%	0%	8%	38%	54%
Care for the Natural Environment	0%	0%	0%	0%	0%	46%	54%

Converting to Islam would be a fairly radical change for most persons in the US, regardless of whether they come from a Christian, Jewish, or other religious background, or no religious background at all. But that is even more the case since 9/11; the rhetoric, discrimination, and hate crimes against Muslims are well documented.[15] But perceptions of Muslims in the US as violent or war-loving just don't match what we saw in our study. On the contrary, we heard story after story about persons being drawn to the peacefulness of Islam. Likewise, we were captivated by the consistency of female testimonies to the respect they experienced as women in a way that runs refreshingly counter to the hyper-sexualizing of women in US culture.

What we saw in the Muslims who participated in our study is a passion for the practicality and truth of Islam as a holistic framework for living

15. Corbin, "Terrifying Reality."

and believing in the modern world. Persons who come to faith as Muslims are welcomed and attracted by the warmth and authenticity of personal encounters, and they are guided by their own study, research, Scripture reading, and prayer. While converting to Islam is a major shift in lifestyle, including things like daily and weekly calendar, eating patterns, or even dress, we were impressed by the number of people who talked about how organic and entirely natural it felt to them. If Islamophobia is on the rise in the US, so are conversions to Islam. And if the converts in our study are any indication of the attractiveness and power of Islam to bring people into an empowering and enlivening relationship with God and each other, that will continue to be the case in the US.

9

Unitarian Universalists and Quakers

IN THIS CHAPTER, WE turn to two faith traditions with long histories in the United States, each of which embrace considerable religious diversity and openness—Unitarian Universalism and the Religious Society of Friends, commonly known as Quakers. Both traditions emphasize individual truth and conscience rather than assent to ecclesiastical authority or religious dogma. Both traditions are known for their commitments to peace, nonviolence, equality of all persons, social justice, and social service. While both traditions have Christians among their ranks, they afford us insight into faith traditions in the US that represent something very different from what we see in other world religions, including Christianity.

UNITARIAN UNIVERSALISTS

Unitarian Universalists (UUs) originated in the US as a merger in 1961 of two traditions: Unitarianism and Universalism, each with long histories in the nation. The Universalist Church of America was founded in 1793 and the American Unitarian Association started in 1825. Together, they are now the Unitarian Universalist Association.[1] Though they make up only .3 percent of the US population, UUs have a wide appeal, intentionally drawing on multiple religious traditions with a posture of openness and tolerance, emphasizing choice in matters of religious faith. A total of 90 Unitarian Universalists participated in our study, which is disproportionately high

---

1. Unitarian Universalist Association, "History of Unitarian Universalism," para. 1.

given their numbers nationwide, but we were glad to receive such robust participation.

Age and Education

The median age of the UU participants is 48, slightly younger than the median age of Unitarian Universalists in the United States, which is 54.[2] Overall, UUs tend to be an aging religious group. Unitarian Universalists are reported to be one of the most educated groups in the US, and that was true for our participants.[3] Eighty-six percent of the UUs in our study had graduated with at least a bachelors degree (higher than any other group in our study) and 60 percent with a post-graduate degree.

Coming to faith

Seventy-two percent of the UUs in our study were first-timers and had not always been UU prior to their new commitment. Fifteen percent had always been UU, but were less committed and wanting to take a new step. Thirteen percent were returning after a time away. A little over half of all the UUs in our study were not previously affiliated (agnostic, atheist, no religion) and just under a third were previously Christians. The remaining 10 percent came from Jewish, Buddhist, Pagan, and other traditions.

Seventy-two percent of the UUs in our study claimed that making their new commitment was a gradual process, and the median length of time it took was about three years, the same as we saw with Christians and Buddhists. The other 28 percent said that their commitment was sudden enough that they could put a date on it. For those coming to faith gradually, the process varied, but when asked if there were any particularly important incidents during the process, well over half cited their participation in a particular congregation. One-fourth mentioned the birth of a child or the fact that their children had gotten to the age where religious education was now a high priority. Some said there had been difficulties in their lives ranging from marital problems to health issues to deaths of loved ones. A few became disillusioned or angered by Christianity in some way. For the most part, however, the incidents they cited were positive and charted a course of moving toward faith rather than a reactive turn away from something else. For those coming to faith more suddenly, the responses overwhelmingly

2. Public Religion Research Institute, "America's Changing Religious Identity," 21.
3. Ibid., 8.

pointed to their experiences in congregations. They talked of searching for just the right church, and then, through research, church shopping, or sheer chance, landing on a church that made all the difference.

Why make this new commitment?

When new Unitarian Universalists were asked why they decided to make this commitment, about half mentioned their desire for community or having found what they were looking for within their congregation. Some described this in more social and relational terms, others in spiritual terms, and others in more intellectual terms (for example, finding those who were "like-minded"). But those descriptions often overlap and blur together. About a third said they made their new commitment because they agreed with the beliefs, principles, values, and commitments (especially social justice commitments) of the Unitarian Universalist church. Unitarian Universalists allow and encourage tremendous latitude in what persons believe or how they practice their faith. We found several persons in the study who made their new commitment within the UU church precisely because it is non-creedal, so that they didn't have to subscribe to any particular set of beliefs. One in ten said they took this new step for the sake of their children; another one in ten said they wanted to publicly formalize their membership and participation; and 7 percent accounted for their decision in terms of needing a change, most often from their Christian past.

When asked how they signaled their new faith commitment, almost all of the UU respondents said they did so through reception into membership, and a great number of those specifically mentioned the widespread UU practice of publicly signing a "membership book." A few others made some form of public declaration or oath. A little over three quarters of the UUs in our study had taken instructional classes as part of their conversion, about the same as we found with Christians. Almost all (97 percent) of those who took such classes found them helpful.

What does it mean to be a Unitarian Universalist?

Persons making a new commitment in the Unitarian Universalist tradition talk frequently about their "seven principles":

> (1) The inherent worth and dignity of every person; (2) Justice, equity and compassion in human relations; (3) Acceptance

of one another and encouragement to spiritual growth in our
congregations; (4) A free and responsible search for truth and
meaning; (5) The right of conscience and the use of the demo-
cratic process within our congregations and in society at large;
(6) The goal of world community with peace, liberty, and justice
for all; and (7) Respect for the interdependent web of all exis-
tence of which we are a part.[4]

While almost all of the responses emphasized these principles in some
way or another, they were rarely stated by simply quoting them. But over
and over we saw an emphasis on a freedom of beliefs, tolerance of others,
and an engaged faith that is committed to equality, diversity, and social justice in the world. A few responses accentuated being part of a community,
but for the most part the UU principles form the foundation for the new
commitments we saw in this study.

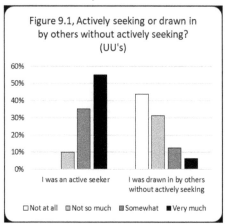

Figure 9.1, Actively seeking or drawn in by others without actively seeking? (UU's)

Drawn in by Others or Active Seekers?

On the whole, Unitarian Universalists are persons who are actively seeking
faith and spirituality rather than being drawn in or invited by others. In this
respect, they resemble the Buddhists in our study. Seventy percent of new
UUs say they were not drawn in by others while only 24 percent say they
were (Figure 9.1). Conversely, 76 percent say they were active seekers, and
only 22 percent say they were not.

4. Unitarian Universalist Association, "The Seven Principles."

Religious or Spiritual?

The UUs in our study were not at all attracted to the label "religious," and instead over half considered themselves "spiritual but not religious" (54 percent), the highest percentage of persons to choose that descriptor of any religious group we studied, including Buddhists, who had the next highest percentage at 47 percent. Close to one-fifth said they were "both spiritual and religious" and another one-fifth had no opinion. That fits very closely with what we heard overall about the very nature of Unitarian Universalism as a faith tradition—it provides a home for those who are seeking spiritual growth and community but who are less inclined to be drawn to traditional religious beliefs and authority structures.

Factors Leading to Faith

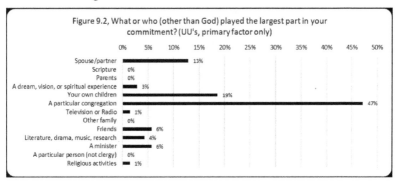

Figure 9.2, What or who (other than God) played the largest part in your commitment? (UU's, primary factor only)

Spouse/partner	13%
Scripture	0%
Parents	0%
A dream, vision, or spiritual experience	3%
Your own children	19%
A particular congregation	47%
Television or Radio	1%
Other family	0%
Friends	6%
Literature, drama, music, research	4%
A minister	6%
A particular person (not clergy)	0%
Religious activities	1%

Based on the answers to other questions, it may be no surprise that most Unitarian Universalists identify the congregation as the primary factor in their new commitment. They repeatedly extol its significance as a community of like-minded persons devoted to respect, diversity, compassion, justice, tolerance, and freedom of conscience. Almost half (47 percent) of all UUs say the congregation is the primary factor (Figure 9.2). With no other religious group did we see that high a percentage of responses going to any one factor as primary. Moreover, the percentage soars to 79 percent when we include those who also list the congregation as a supporting factor (Figure 9.3). Children and spouse or partner are also significant factors, and half of all UU respondents say the minister was a supporting factor.

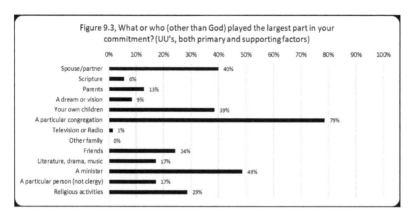

Figure 9.3, What or who (other than God) played the largest part in your commitment? (UU's, both primary and supporting factors)

Spouse or Partner

The spouse or partner is the primary factor for 13 percent of new Unitarian Universalists, and a primary or supporting factor for 40 percent more. Despite these high percentages, we don't find here the sense of obligation to convert for the sake of the spouse that we found in the case of Jews and Muslims. Instead, the rationale reflected in UU responses parallels what we also saw in their choice of the congregation as primary—persons drawn to the UU faith are looking for companionship on their journey, a fellowship of diverse but like-minded persons who share the same fundamental commitments and want to help each other grow.

Among the persons in our study, it was often the case that one's partner was of a different faith—for example, one an agnostic and another a Buddhist—but the UU tradition provided them common ground on which they could be who they are, and yet be together—a feature they extolled repeatedly.

> *I wanted to find a place that my husband and I could share and both be a part of.*

> *My wife felt that our relationship would improve if we could share a common experience, esp. one that would require commitment over a period of time.*

> *We believe the same things and finding a church that appealed to both of us was critical.*

> *We are a wonderful couple but are different people with different spiritual backgrounds. We needed a place that we could be together and both enjoy the experience.*

My husband is an avowed atheist. When I first started going to church, he refused to come with me, but after some time started coming occasionally, then more and more regularly. It was easier for me to feel at home and part of the group when he was with me, and it is satisfying to find a place that welcomes all belief systems.

Children

Concerns about raising children and how they will be formed and educated are critically important to UUs. Nineteen percent say their children were the primary factor in their new commitment and 39 percent say children were either a primary or supporting factor. Several new UUs were concerned about providing their children a non-dogmatic, progressive, and justice-oriented faith that might help "inoculate" them (as one person put it) against the conservativism in their communities. Peer pressure can be strong among youth, and UU parents are concerned that their children be able to think for themselves while at the same time being immersed in a community that celebrates diversity and is committed to the principles of equality, tolerance, and freedom of conscience.

It is important to me that my children receive religious education that is free from dogma or creeds. They need to be able to evaluate information and decide for themselves what they believe without being told they are wrong or immoral. It is also important to me that liberal principals of fairness, equality and community service are reinforced through religious education.

I want my child growing up in a religious liberal environment. He needs to be taught to think for himself, and that everyone is important no matter their beliefs.

I wanted a place my children could grow and be allowed to ask questions and explore without ridicule. They needed to understand the religions around them so that they could learn every life and path is unique and has honor and dignity. I didn't want them to be forced into a place they didn't fit in.

I want my son to be exposed to ideas of faith and covenant and social justice. I want him to be afforded the opportunity to grow up in a thoughtful, justice-seeking community.

Parents

While no UUs in our study said their parents were the primary factor, 13 percent said that parents were a supporting factor in their decision. In those cases, this was largely due to the influence of parents in raising them within the UU tradition or at least with a particular set of progressive religious commitments that later made the UU tradition attractive.

Friends and other persons in particular

Only 6 percent of new UUs identify friends as the primary factor, though 24 percent say friends were a primary or supporting factor. An additional 13 percent claim some other particular person was a supporting factor. Respondents in our study were about equally divided in describing the nature of that influence. In some cases, they were invited to attend a UU church by friends or other persons. In other cases, it was the witness of those other persons' lives that was important. And in still other cases, friends or other individuals gave valuable support and encouragement along the way.

The Congregation

As already noted, 47 percent of all new Unitarian Universalists say the congregation was the primary factor in their commitment and 79 percent say it was either a primary or supporting factor. They most often mention the importance of having a community of shared commitments and values without rigidity or uniformity in beliefs. They also value the welcome and warmth they experience in their congregations. UUs were drawn to the activities, actions, and outreach of the congregation, whether those were religious, educational, or social in nature. While the minister of the congregation is treated below in a separate category, it is clear from the responses that the minister was often closely connected to what they loved most about the congregation, so that it is difficult to separate those two.

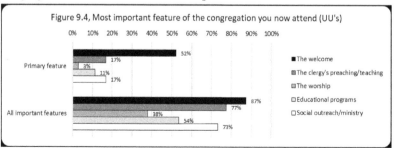

Figure 9.4, Most important feature of the congregation you now attend (UU's)

When asked to rate the most important feature of the congregation they now attend, the welcome of the congregation was rated primary by just over half of all UU respondents (Figure 9.4). When respondents were invited to identify as many features as they wished, the welcome rose to 87 percent, while the teaching and preaching of the minister and the social outreach and commitment to social justice work also claimed over three-quarters of all the responses.

The UU congregation is very welcoming and friendly. There is no fear of hell. They live by the Golden Rule. Deeds before creeds!

This church made me feel welcome. No pressure to commit unless I wanted. Very friendly people, very open principles toward religion. I even started going out to lunch after services with a group from church so I felt connected. Love the community and really love the clergy.

I think that the biggest part in my decision to become a member of the church was the realization that I was home. The community gave me a sense of belonging, a sense of purpose, and a sense of acceptance, for just exactly who I am. I had known for a long time that I agreed with the church's values. It was really just about knowing that this was where I belong.

Welcoming community with exceptional minister who provided thought provoking Sunday sermons.

Everyone was welcoming no matter what your financial status, community status, if you were LGBTQ, what faith background you brought with you or ideas you had. It was refreshing to find others with as many questions as we had.

Choosing a Congregation

Just under half of all new Unitarian Universalists chose the particular congregation they now attend on the basis of its proximity (Figure 9.5), though they were often looking for a UU church in their area, not just choosing any church that was close by. The next most important reason was their attraction to some feature of the congregation, usually its compatibility with their beliefs and commitments, or its programs and activities.

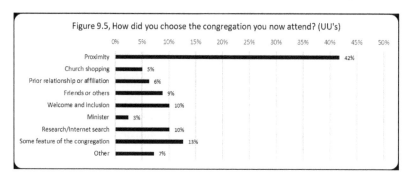

Figure 9.5, How did you choose the congregation you now attend? (UU's)

Religious Activities

About 30 percent of new Unitarian Universalists cite religious activities as a supporting factor in making their new commitment (only a very few say such activities were a primary factor). Again, the focus for the most part among UUs is on religious education and social justice activities, both of which Unitarian Universalists are well known for. Other significant and influential activities include discussion and support groups for various constituencies, worship services, the arts, and social gatherings.

The Minister

The minister and ministerial staff come up often from new UUs as highly influential, inspirational, and formative. While only 6 percent say the minister was the primary factor in their commitment, almost half say the minister was a supporting factor. The most commonly reported features of UU ministers in relation to finding faith are the combination of providing understanding and grounding within the UU tradition while creating a space for a wide range of doubts, questions, and beliefs ranging from atheism to Buddhism to paganism to indigenous traditions, just to name a few. And, as we have seen with other faith traditions, the minister is also important in relationship to preaching, leading worship, and providing care, support, and welcome.

> She has a way of providing the insightful answer or support you need. She has delightful sermons that touches on all faiths from Atheist to Buddhist (how refreshing).

> I like her energy and lack of sanctimony.

> Felt a personal connection; helped me understand the broader faith tradition and the local church.

The pastor at the Unitarian Universalist church embodies the approach to faith and religion's role in daily life that I was looking for (principles and core values, without creeds and doctrine).

My minister is committed to social justice and is amazing at connecting people together to do the work.

She was extremely accepting and open and warm, and seemed to genuinely want me to be part of the community. She made me feel like my presence mattered.

Scripture, Literature, Music, and Media

Not very many Unitarian Universalists cite Scripture as influential in their new commitment, though for those who do, a plurality of Scriptures from across various faith traditions was important to them. The fact that the Unitarian Universalist tradition takes a non-literalist, non-exclusivist approach to Scripture gets mentioned frequently as significant by new UUs. Within our study, other literature beyond Scripture (especially writers with UU connections such as Ralph Waldo Emerson or Louisa May Alcott) were mentioned as influential. Several persons counted the music of their congregation and participation in the choir as supportive in their journey of faith.

Obstacles?

When asked if they found any UU teachings, practices, persons, or institutions to be an obstacle in making their new commitment, only 22 percent identified anything—the lowest percentage of any group we studied. On the contrary, new UUs generally find it easy to adopt their tradition. One of the most common obstacles was that UU services can be a bit boring or its meetings and actions overly focused on procedure—too cerebral and "not enough soul," as one person put it. Others mentioned a fundamental conflict they experienced between wanting to be tolerant and, at the same time, fighting against those who are intolerant in the larger society, for example concerning LGBT inclusion or reproductive rights. We heard a somewhat different example of this tension from those who said they continue to be irritated when someone persists in using God language even though many of the members in the congregation are atheists. But they know that this comes with the territory for a tradition that seeks to be open and inclusive.

What Was Most Appealing?

Given what has been said thus far, it will probably be easy to figure out what new Unitarian Universalists find appealing in their tradition. What attracts them most are the seven principles in some way or another—the lack of dogma, freedom of conscience, the commitment to social justice, and the tolerance, respect, and inclusivity they find there. They find appealing the fact that services aren't "preachy," but informative and thought-provoking. They appreciate that they are encouraged to draw from wisdom wherever they may find it. They might hear a Buddhist sermon one week and a Jewish sermon the next, without feeling the need to choose one or to call one right and the other wrong. That kind of openness and flexibility is very much at the heart of why persons adopt the UU faith as their own.

What Changed?

Attendance and Involvement

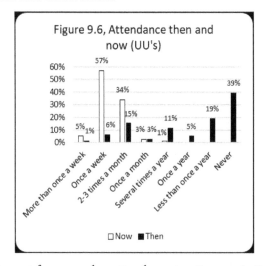

Figure 9.6, Attendance then and now (UU's)

New UUs went from very low attendance to 96 percent attending at least two to three times per month, with most of those attending at least once a week (Figure 9.6). Nine out of ten say they are "somewhat" or "very" involved in the life and activities of their congregation, the highest level of involvement reported of any group we studied (though Evangelicals and Buddhists come close). This accords with the importance of the congregation and religious activities in their lives, as we have already seen. Eighty-three percent say they are happy with their level of involvement. At the same

time, UUs are not as highly involved in religious groups, studies, or fellowships (Figure 9.7), and in this respect they are similar to Catholics and Jews.

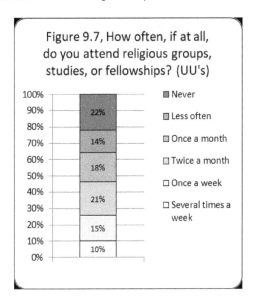

Figure 9.7, How often, if at all, do you attend religious groups, studies, or fellowships? (UU's)

Multiple Religious Belonging

Three-quarters of the UUs in our study said they do not participate in
religious services or activities from another religion, but that still leaves a
substantial number who do. Buddhist meditation, yoga, or the occasional
Christian or Jewish Shabbat service were mentioned with the most frequency. This is consistent with the Unitarian Universalist premise of looking for
truth wherever it is to be found.

Reading Scripture

As already mentioned, when the UUs in our study were asked about Scripture, we learned it was significantly less important to them than for other
religious groups in our study. This is largely because there is no single Scripture that is authoritative within their tradition, and instead Unitarian Universalists draw from many sources of religious wisdom in their worship,
education, and formation activities. Before making a new commitment, 89
percent of UUs reported seldom or never reading Scripture and that remained largely unchanged afterwards (87 percent). When asked how important Scripture is to their faith, 59 percent say "not at all," 24 percent say

"not very," and 17 percent say "somewhat." None of the respondents claimed that Scripture was "very" important.

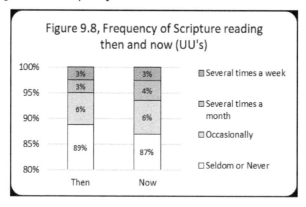

Figure 9.8, Frequency of Scripture reading then and now (UU's)

God

Over 60 percent of the UUs in our study were unchanged in their thinking about God after their new commitment, but the solid majority of those were either atheists or agnostics (in about equal proportions) both before and after. Several of those persons, moreover, mentioned that their move toward atheism or agnosticism was the catalyst for their interest in Unitarian Universalism rather than the other way around. Of the other 40 percent, about half described their view of God as having changed substantially—whether toward a more loving and universal presence or force in the universe, a mystery, or toward atheism or agnosticism. The other half (or about 20 percent of the whole) continued to believe in God, for the most part, but their notions of a personal God had largely begun to morph into a higher power, a presence in the universe that connects us, or "a guiding spirit."

Social Issues

We found that Unitarian Universalists do not tend to change their social positions radically as a result of a new faith commitment. More often than not, they choose this faith tradition partly because it aligns with their stances on social issues. Other than Quakers (as we shall see later in this chapter), no group we studied was more consistently or more thoroughly in favor of reproductive rights, same-sex marriage, women's equality, racial justice, economic justice for the poor, and care for the natural environment (Figure 9.9). And no group was more consistently against war (though around 10 percent already supported war and remained unchanged in that support).

We also saw no religious tradition in our study where fewer "no opinion" or "don't know" answers were given (though, again, Quakers are fairly similar). Unitarian Universalists may place a high premium on tolerance for the views of others, but they are not wishy-washy and know pretty clearly where they stand.

Figure 9.9, How have your attitudes and positions on the following social issues changed, if at all, since making your new commitment or recommitment?" (UUs)	Already opposed, became more opposed	Already opposed, remain just as opposed	Now become opposed	No opinion/Don't know	Now became supportive	Already supported, stayed just as supportive	Already supportive, became more supportive
Right to an Abortion	0%	0%	0%	3%	4%	77%	16%
Gay Marriage	0%	0%	0%	0%	3%	57%	41%
Gun Control	3%	12%	0%	3%	6%	58%	19%
War	13%	57%	4%	16%	0%	9%	1%
Women's Equality	0%	1%	0%	0%	3%	71%	25%
Racial Justice	0%	0%	0%	1%	1%	63%	34%
Economic Justice for the Poor	0%	0%	0%	3%	3%	51%	44%
Care for the Natural Environment	0%	0%	0%	0%	5%	62%	33%

To further emphasize this last point, when asked to rank the significance of changes in their lives using the same categories we offered to others in the study (see Figure 9.10), Unitarian Universalists reported the least change of any group we studied. Unitarian Universalists were drawn to their tradition precisely because it already fit with their own spiritual journey and their intellectual and social positions. Only a very few UUs talked about what was happening in their lives as a "conversion." Most did not talk that way and instead spoke powerfully about having arrived at a point in their lives where they had come to find a group of like-minded persons with shared commitments.

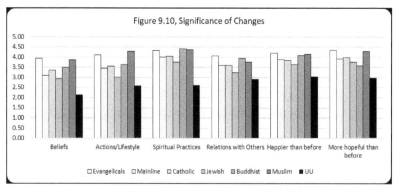

Figure 9.10, Significance of Changes

In fact, when UUs in our study were asked to report in their own words what the main difference that becoming UU made in their lives, half mentioned the importance of community, of no longer feeling alone, or of feeling connected. They spoke about wonderful conversations they were now having, of having persons they could turn to, and of finding a group of people with whom they could explore their faith and engage the world. About 25 percent of the UU respondents described the change as something that had happened to their attitude and outlook. They spoke about being peaceful, more balanced or centered, whole, authentic, happier, and less angry. Twenty percent talked about changes in how active and engaged they now were, especially in relation to seeking social justice, but also in their church and community. Another 20 percent spoke of the change in their lives as a matter of finding purpose and meaning, of feeling anchored and at home in a religious tradition where they could be themselves with integrity.

QUAKERS

It is estimated that there are around 400,000 Quakers in the world, with 19 percent of those in the United States (most are in Africa).[5] There are many different types of Quakers, all tracing their roots to the original seventeenth-century movement started by George Fox in England. Though Fox was a Christian, not all Quakers are. The Quaker Information Center identifies four main branches in the US: Liberal, Conservative, Pastoral, and

5. Friends World Committee for Consultation, "How Many Quakers Are There in the World?"

Evangelical. The differences between these groups pertain to (1) whether their worship is led by a pastor and thus "programmed" or whether it is silent, without pastoral leadership, and thus "unprogrammed"; (2) whether they place their theological emphasis on the authority of Christian Scripture or on the authority of the Inward Light ("Orthodox" on one end of the spectrum and "Liberal" on the other); (3) whether missionary and evangelistic work is carried out in addition to social service work or whether it is not; and (4) with which larger Friends organizations they affiliate, if any.[6] These differences show up to a fair degree in the responses we received from the Quakers in our study.

Thirty-one Quakers (or "Friends," as they are also called) participated in our study, a relatively small population, but a group that represents a good deal of the breadth and diversity of the Quaker movement in America. Some identified as Christians, though certainly not all. Those that did identify as Christians were included also among the Christian responses in the first chapters of this book. We saw tremendous diversity among the Quakers in the study. Some did not specify any particular group with which they identify in the Friends community and many described themselves as "unprogrammed." Some said they were liberal, some conservative, and some left that unspecified. Because of the relatively small number of Quaker participants in the study, I will exercise reserve in making generalized conclusions about coming to faith as a Quaker. Yet we still found their experiences illuminating in our attempt to paint as wide a picture as possible of how persons find faith today in the US.

Coming to faith

About two-thirds of the Quakers signaled their new commitment by reception into membership, while others cited the fact that they had simply begun attending regularly or made this commitment in their heart. Several spoke of having met with a "clearness committee," which helps persons gain clarity about such things as membership and leadership roles. Half received some sort of instructional class, and the other half did not.

For 85 percent of the Quakers who participated in our study, this was their first time to be a Quaker. Only a few were previously Christians, and the remainder had not been religiously affiliated, though several mentioned being spiritual or spiritual seekers. For eight out of ten, the process was gradual, and the median length of time it took was about five years. But, again, the sample size is far too small to generalize from that to what may

6. Quaker Information Center, "Branches of Friends Today."

be true for most new Quakers. In response to the question of whether they were active seekers, 60 percent of the new Quakers in our study said "very much" and another 28 percent said "somewhat." Only 8 percent said "not so much." Conversely, just under three-quarters of the group said they were "not at all" or "not so much" drawn in by others. Even with our small sample size, it is pretty clear that persons in the US who end up making a new commitment as Quakers tend to be persons who are actively seeking a spiritual home.

Why make this new commitment?

The Quakers in our study decided to make this commitment for a variety of reasons. One mentioned the support and care she received from the local Quaker meeting during a crisis ("meeting" is the term Quakers use to describe a particular faith community or congregation, as well as a more informal gathering of Quakers). Several said they were looking for spiritual growth, wholeness, and purpose in their lives, and another group said they found Quakerism a better fit with their beliefs and commitments. A few just wanted to formalize their participation in Quaker meetings, which had been taking place for some time, and a couple mentioned the importance of making this commitment for raising their children. Right at half of all the new Quakers, however, talked about the importance of the fellowship that they were seeking and had now found, repeatedly using the word "home" to describe their experience of the community of which they were now a part.

What does it mean to be a Quaker?

Quakers often speak of the "five testimonies" as a way of summarizing the kinds of commitments to which they are dedicated: simplicity, peace, integrity, community, and equality. When asked what it means to be a Quaker, new members spoke regularly of these in some form, even if they did not recite them (though several did). Quakers in our study highlighted the importance of seeing God in each person, listening carefully for truth, looking inward, and being open to mystery. But they also spoke of working for peace and justice, of loving others, and of exercising patience and gratitude in their daily lives. Those who were Christians often mentioned explicitly the importance of Scripture and following the example of Christ in their lives.

Half of the Quakers in our study described themselves as "spiritual but not religious," almost as high a percentage as the UUs we saw earlier in this chapter. Another quarter said they were both "spiritual and religious."

Factors Leading to Faith

It is impossible to summarize the primary factors in coming to faith for Quakers with the fourteen categories we used for other religious traditions. While around 10 percent of Quakers listed their children as the primary factor and over 20 percent listed their faith community as primary, over half of the respondents chose "other," unsatisfied with the options we provided. That in itself was highly unusual. But there was a common theme that ran through most of these "other" responses—and that was the Quaker meeting itself—the way persons in the fellowship interacted, the silence and quiet meditation, the openness, and the spiritual depth. As one person put it, "The experience was an overwhelming feeling that went beyond emotions to what I believe is a spiritual place." That said, the congregation to which individuals belonged was still ranked highly by Quakers—22 percent cited it as the primary factor and 63 percent cited it as either the primary or supporting factor. Yet it is hard to escape the fact that Quakers wanted to identify something deeper in their experience of the faith community that transformed them.

Quakers resembled UUs in relation to the importance they placed on their children as a factor in coming to faith (10 percent chose children as the primary factor and 33 percent chose children as either primary or supporting). As with UUs, Quakers wanted a type of formation for their children that would provide an alternative to the consumerism, violence, and injustices of the wider society. While only one Quaker cited a friend as the primary factor in coming to faith, one-third claimed that friends were at least a supporting factor.

Choosing a Congregation

About half of the Quakers in our study chose the particular congregation they now attend on the basis of its proximity or because it was the only Quaker meeting in their town. We heard a variety of other reasons, of course, and interestingly many of those noted the serendipity of having walked by a Quaker meeting house and deciding to go in, or accidentally encountering some Quakers and being impressed by their witness. Since Quakers do not have clergy in the traditional sense (or as one respondent put it, "we have no laity!"), they tend to rely instead on voluntary leadership. So we did not hear much about the influence of ministers or pastors.

When asked to rate the most important feature of the congregation they now attend, half of the Friends in our study said it was the welcome they experienced while most others said it was the worship, the silence, and the openness that characterized the community and their meetings. When persons were asked to identify as many features as they wanted to, rather than only the primary feature, all of the Quakers identified the worship and the welcome; and over half said the social outreach and ministry of the congregation. One-third identified the educational programs as important.

Obstacles?

When asked if there were any obstacles in the process of making this new commitment, only a very few participants identified any; the vast majority said no. Among the few obstacles that were mentioned, we heard some of the downsides of Quaker openness and the unusual style of their meetings, which feature silence until someone rises with something to say. One person was used to music in worship, and just had to get used to its absence. Another found the Quaker desire to be all things to all persons a bit hard to get used to and inevitably bound up in contradictions. One person described how miserable it was when the same person got up each week and gave twenty-minute monologues without a point to them. And one person found the requirement of going through a "clearness committee" more regimented than Quaker general practice. But all of the respondents pressed on, and while they identified these obstacles as initial impediments, that did not stop them from making their commitments.

What Was Most Appealing?

As has already been mentioned, the Quakers in our study were most attracted to the contemplative and open style of Quaker meetings. But they were also drawn to the fact that Quakers strive to be non-hierarchical, trust the "inner teacher," and have no doctrines or creeds. At the same time, they were pulled toward the fact that Quakers have fundamental commitments to simplicity, peace, integrity, community, and equality. In trying to hold this tension, Quakers remind us very much of the Unitarian Universalists. Friends repeatedly highlighted how much they appreciate the consensus approach to decision-making in their faith communities and the respect for individual conscience and experience.

What Changed?

The number of Quakers who attended services at least a few times a month almost doubled after their commitment (from 44 percent to 84 percent). Sixty-four percent now attend at least once a week, which is comparable to the 62 percent we found among UUs (though still considerably lower than the 84 percent of Evangelicals, 82 percent of Catholics, and 75 percent of Mainline Protestants). Eight out of ten said they are "somewhat" or "very" involved in the life and activities of their congregation. We also saw relatively high involvement in religious groups, studies, or fellowships, with two-thirds participating twice a month or more. Several of the Quakers in our study mentioned that they participate from time to time in Buddhist meditation, Christian services, or interfaith gatherings, which would be consistent with the openness that characterizes many Quaker communities.

God

When asked about their views of God, the Quakers in our study had not changed much since making their new commitment. They instead found the Quaker tradition compatible with, or at least open to, their current views. At the same time, several had made some substantial shifts away from the remote, judgmental, and largely absent God of their upbringing. Virtually none of the Quakers in our study talked about the traditional deity of Judaism, Islam, or Christianity. Instead they consistently made reference to the God within them, and within each of us—the "inner light" or "inner voice" that requires silence and discernment in a community.

Social Issues

In response to our questions about their positions and attitudes on social issues, few reported much change since making their new commitment. We saw new opposition to war and new support for gay marriage and women's equality. But in regard to most other social issues, we only heard about positions remaining unchanged or growing stronger. On the whole, as Figure 9.11 demonstrates, the Quakers in our study were among the most socially progressive, or liberal, of any religious group we studied.

Figure 9.11, How have your attitudes and positions on the following social issues changed, if at all, since making your new commitment or recommitment?" (Quakers)						
	Already opposed, became more opposed	Already opposed, remain just as opposed	Now become opposed	No opinion/ Don't know	Now became supportive	Already supported, stayed just as supportive	Already supportive, became more supportive
Right to an Abortion	4%	0%	4%	9%	0%	78%	4%
Gay Marriage	0%	0%	0%	0%	8%	67%	25%
Gun Control	4%	0%	0%	17%	4%	43%	30%
War	48%	28%	8%	8%	0%	0%	8%
Women's Equality	0%	0%	0%	0%	8%	68%	24%
Racial Justice	0%	0%	0%	0%	0%	48%	52%
Economic Justice for the Poor	0%	0%	0%	4%	0%	36%	60%
Care for the Natural Environment	0%	0%	0%	4%	0%	40%	56%

Finally, when Quakers were invited to put into their own words the difference their new commitment has made, half talked about their new community and of how helpful it is to have a group of compatible persons with whom to share experiences, seek answers, and achieve good in the world rather than trying to do all that solo. They felt grounded, deepened, and full of potential because of these experiences of community. The other half focused their responses on personal characteristics that had altered, such as feeling more at peace, finding more purpose and intentionality in their lives, and experiencing more connection with and sensitivity toward others.

Excursus on Hinduism, Jainism, and Sikhism

Before proceeding to some final conclusions and summary observations, it may be helpful to say a word about the status of three religious traditions that have a significant presence in the US context, but do not feature as prominently in our study because of the very small number of persons we could locate who had recently converted to those traditions. In this chapter, we will look briefly at Hindus, Jains, and Sikhs. While we were not able to secure sufficient participation to form substantial conclusions about finding faith in these traditions, we expect that will change within a few more decades. If Indian immigration patterns continue as they have in recent decades, we will undoubtedly see continued exposure to these religious traditions, more learning about them through friendships and other workplace or even romantic relationships; and inevitably we will see more conversions. Already, for example, on college campuses, students are increasingly becoming exposed to Hindu, Jain, and Sikh practices, dance, art, and festivals.

Hindus

Out of almost 1,800 persons in our study, only six persons identified as Hindu. People in the US do convert to Hinduism, of course, but the numbers are small and there are no data available to give us an estimate. In addition, some persons celebrate Hindu holidays and festivals, study with a guru or yogi, read Hindu Scripture, or engage in Hindu practices such as worship, chanting, meditation, or yoga—all without disaffiliating from their own faith tradition (if indeed they belong to one). Yet there are several reasons for not finding as many new Hindus in the US context to participate in this study.

First, their demographic characteristics make that something of a challenge. Hindus now make up 0.7 percent of the US population, about the same as the number of Buddhists. Hindus, moreover, have grown in the past decade from 0.4 percent of the US population in 2007.[1] However, the pool of converts to Hinduism in the US is relatively small compared to the other religious traditions we have looked at thus far. Nine out of ten Hindus were raised Hindus;[2] indeed, 96 percent of American Hindus are either immigrants or come from immigrant families.[3] Hindus in the US also have the highest retention rate (80 percent) of any American religious group and the fewest religious intermarriages (9 percent).[4] We knew early on that it was going to be very difficult to recruit new Hindu converts for our study.

Second, one does not find in most US expressions of Hinduism the formal processes of signaling a conversion that one finds in other religious traditions. One might, for example, simply begin studying its teachings or experimenting with its practices. Persons may visit an ashram or temple, pray, meditate, or hear a lecture there, all without any need (or pressure) to convert or become a member. Likewise, in most cases there is no centralized religious authority or structure, or mandatory requirements for becoming a Hindu. So, for example, even among the few Hindus who did participate in the Finding Faith Today project, when asked how they signaled their new commitment, they gave answers like: "participation in service projects for the welfare of all beings and the planet"; "by practicing the religious beliefs, continued meditation, yoga and fasting and being a vegetarian after listening to the holy scriptures"; and "internal commitment, no other ritual needed."

Lastly, Hindus do not have a robust history of proselytizing or sending missionaries in the way that other religious traditions do, such as Christianity. Nor is it a principle of their faith to be concerned with seeking new conversions. For some, it is even considered a violation of the Hindu faith to do so, and perhaps many would stand by Gandhi's words, "I disbelieve in the conversion of one person by another. My effort should never be to undermine another's faith but to make him a better follower of his own faith. This implies belief in the truth of all religions and therefore respect

1. Pew, "America's Changing Religious Landscape," 4.
2. Ibid., 39.
3. Ibid., 53.
4. Ibid., 47.

for them."[5] For some Hindus, then, there is no such thing as conversion to Hinduism. There are certainly exceptions to this, and groups related in some ways to Hinduism, such as the Hare Krishnas or the school of Transcendental Meditation, have been more active in recruiting or spreading their practices.

Jains

The situation with Hindus in the US is similar to Jains, a much smaller group globally than Hindus (though also originating in India), with around 100 temples in the US and around 100,000 adherents (only four Jains participated in our study).[6] As with Hindus, the vast majority of Jain adherents are born into the faith and one does not find in Jainism the culture of conversion found in some other religious traditions. Jains for the most part do not try to convert others, nor are there the same types of "entry" rituals within Jainism one finds in other religions. There is certainly no way to estimate how many persons have converted recently to Jainism in the US.

The Jain commitment to nonviolence and non-injury (both toward one's self and all other living beings) expressed not only in its pacifism but in vegetarianism, forgiveness, and self-control can seem quite ascetic and demanding to Americans. Jains sometime speak of their faith as a "way of life" rather than a religion, and as therefore open to being practiced without being religiously "converted." But for various reasons—mostly because of its small numbers but partially because of its austerity and perhaps partially also because it does not seek converts—Jainism is not as popular in the US as other Asian religious traditions that have made their way west, such as Hinduism or Buddhism.

Sikhs

Sikhism is yet another religion native to India but with a substantial presence in the United States, where Sikh population estimates range from 279,000 to 700,000.[7] Only eleven Sikhs participated in our study. While it is safe to guess that most people in the United States would not be able to describe Sikhism, even in broad strokes, it is the fifth largest religion in the world and

5. Tendulkar, *Mahatma*, 2:450.

6. Lee and Nadeau, eds., *Encyclopedia*, 487.

7. The 279,000 figure comes from Johnson and Grim, eds., *The World's Religions in Figures*, 49. The Sikh American Legal Defense and Education Fund claims there are 700,000: "Who Are Sikh Americans?," para. 1.

has more adherents globally than Judaism.[8] As with Hinduism and Jainism, in Sikhism one does not find a robust culture of seeking converts. Sikhs tend to be born into the tradition rather than to convert in, and many Sikhs talk about their tradition as a way of life to be practiced. Thus, most of the new Sikhs participating in our study, when asked how they signaled their new commitment, said they learned about it, studied, and simply started practicing it. None of the eleven took instructional classes as part of the process. But in some Sikh communities there are initiation rituals such as the Amrit Sanchar ceremony for those being baptized into the Khalsa order, mentioned by two of the Sikh participants in the study.

Though few in number, the Sikhs in our study were remarkably unified in emphasizing the oneness of humanity, the universality of Sikh truth, and the importance of humbly serving the whole human race. They expressed great respect for the teachings of the gurus and for the path of honest seeking that is central to Sikhism. We saw among them a strong impetus toward seeing God in everything, and they consistently reported changes in their lives that emphasized a new calm, patience, kindness, and compassion that had begun to characterize their lives thanks to the spiritual practices they had taken up.

Sikhs have no clergy or central governing bodies, so it will likely remain a challenge to locate and study Sikh converts in a comprehensive or systematic way via its institutions in the US. But, again, we expect that to change in the coming years as we see continued exposure to Sikhs and Sikhism throughout the US.

8. Johnson and Grim, eds., *The World's Religions in Figures*, 48.

10

Concluding Observations

THE FINDING FAITH TODAY project is an attempt to understand the experiences of adults who come to faith in the United States as signaled by some form of public commitment, membership, ritual of initiation, vow, or profession of faith. In reflecting on the many and varied ways people come to faith, the first and most important observation is that faith identity powerfully shapes the process of coming to faith. So, for example, what it means *to be* a Jew powerfully shapes how one comes to faith *as* a Jew. That may sound obvious, but it warrants emphasis. One of the most important questions we asked was the question, "What do you think it means to be a [Christian, Buddhist, Muslim, etc.]?" That answer helps us to understand and frame almost every other answer. Religious traditions vary greatly from each other, and it is simply not the case that they are interchangeable "brands." Nor are they just different species of the same genus, "religion." In fact, it is not always clear that a single word like *religion* or *faith* can apply to them all, at least not in the same way.

SO, FOR EXAMPLE, JUDAISM and Islam—and Catholicism to a great extent— have deep cultural and social dimensions, almost as if they were ethnic groups (and indeed for Jews that is actually the case). For the most part, persons do not become Catholic, Muslim, or Jewish solely by undergoing an experience of the heart or professing a belief, as one might within Evangelicalism. Nor does one simply become inducted as a member on a given Sunday, as one might within a Mainline church, or sign a membership book, as one would in a Unitarian Universalist context. On the contrary, conversion means adopting a new set of cultural and social behaviors—for example, distinctive dress or dietary observances; a new daily, weekly, or annual calendar; or perhaps even learning a new language. It is no wonder that one's spouse, partner, and family are such significant factors in those traditions—largely because of the enculturation processes that are entailed in coming to faith. By contrast, we find something altogether different in Buddhism, which offers a new mindfulness and awareness that can only come through taking up certain practices such as meditation. Naturally, adopting this religious tradition is going to be quite different from any of the other paths we looked at. Each tradition must be understood on its own terms, and there are significant limitations to superficial comparisons.

There is no "one-size-fits-all" process of coming to faith in the United States. Evangelicals prioritize certain beliefs, practices, and experiences in describing what it means to be a Christian that are not at all the same as what Quakers or Jews prioritize within their traditions. Likewise, the kinds of changes we see in persons' lives vary tremendously from tradition to tradition, and even within each tradition, though there remain distinct "family" resemblances (religiously speaking).

A second summary observation is that for many religious traditions, people may experience themselves as members of a religious group for several years before formally affiliating, converting, or making a commitment. This is especially the case with a religion such as Christianity where, because of its long history and cultural dominance in the United States, persons might think of themselves, at least nominally, as Christians all their lives without actually making a formal faith commitment. But the same is true in a different way and to a lesser degree for minority religions such as Judaism, Buddhism, or Islam. Even though most of the persons we heard from in those traditions were converting from outside the faith, we encountered several who had been participating for a long time, but now wanted to formalize the identity they had already begun to assume.

Third, and closely connected to the previous point, it is worth emphasizing the journey-like nature of coming to faith for most persons in the U.S. Even those who are first-timers to a faith tradition are likely to take one to three years. For a significant number, the journey is even longer than that, and several persons claimed the process is ongoing, if not lifelong. For faith communities interested in ministries of invitation, outreach, and inclusion, that means emphasis should be placed on accompaniment, formation, and education rather than solely on tactics to get people in the door. In contrast to some traditional religious approaches that emphasize conversion, and make incorporation and assimilation secondary, it is abundantly clear from our study that people *belong before they believe* rather than *believing before they belong.*

Fourth, most persons who end up making a faith commitment are active seekers. As Appendix E demonstrates, in all of the religious traditions we studied except Islam, no less than 70% of new adherents claim to have been an active seeker either "somewhat" or "very much." There are, of course, a good number of persons who claim to have been "drawn in by others without actively seeking." But for the most part, that number is relatively low, while those who say they were not drawn in by others without actively seeking is relatively high.

So what are we to make of this point? One might conclude that many religious communities tend to be insular, not doing much by way of reaching out or actively attempting to draw others in. Perhaps that is true, at least to some extent, though strictly speaking our data do not lead inevitably to that conclusion. The more important take-away is to recognize that, despite the increase in the percentage of "nones" in the US, there remains a significant number of people who are actively seeking some sort of new spiritual home, purpose, outlook, recovery, or healing in their lives. While it is ever important that faith communities offer warmth and hospitality, reaching out beyond their four walls to extend invitation and welcome, it is also critical that those interested in reaching others recognize they need not beg, entice, badger, and cajole persons into making a new faith commitment. A good number of persons are already seeking, and they are looking for a faith community that is responsive, generous, open, and able to accompany them on their journey, even if that takes many years.

This connects to a fifth concluding observation—the incredible importance of congregations, temples, mosques, synagogues, and sanghas in the process of coming to faith. While in Islam, the congregation is a primary or supporting factor for just 31 percent, the percentage is 43–55 percent for Catholics, Evangelicals, and Jews, and 63–79 percent for Quakers, Mainline Protestants, Buddhists, and Unitarian Universalists. When we include other factors associated directly with the congregation, such as ministers, laity, worship, educational programs, social service work, and other religious or social activities, the percentages skyrocket.

And this brings me back to one of the early observations of the book—people reach people. For all the importance of other forms of outreach (literature, media, events, campaigns, and activities), it is still human relationships that are the number one factor for persons finding faith—whether by offering support, answering questions and challenging assumptions, offering community or, perhaps most importantly, providing a credible witness and example of lived faith.

Moreover, as we saw repeatedly in our study, faith communities have theological and not merely strategic importance in the process of finding faith. Or to put it another way, the faith that people are finding is inherently *social.* In traditions like Christianity, Judaism, and Buddhism, for example, the church, synagogue, or sangha is more than just an instrument for finding faith. For Jews, God's purpose in history is the creation of a chosen people that is God's offer of salvation to the world. To become Jewish is to be made part of a "people." Christians hold that God's offer of peoplehood has been messianically extended through Christ, but they also affirm that to be a Christian is to be formed into "the body of Christ," the church. Indeed, they go so far as to affirm (in the Apostles' Creed and the Nicene Creed) that they "believe" in the church as an article of faith. Likewise, Buddhists "take refuge" in the Sangha as one of the three jewels of Buddhism. The Buddhist community is, in other words, intrinsic to Buddhist "faith" (if we can use that word). Even Unitarian Universalists, though non-creedal, identify the congregation as the primary or supporting factor in finding faith with a higher percentage of responses than any other group we studied. If persons in our study have found faith, for most that means finding a faith *community.*

Previously, I said that persons *belong before they believe.* But the word "believe" is pretty bad shorthand for an experience as complex as coming to faith, and we use it only because in English we don't have a good, simple verbal form for the word "faith" (most people don't go around talking about "faithing," or claiming that they "faithed"). So we use the word "believe." But that changes things pretty drastically. In truth, coming to faith in our time is, for most persons, not primarily about new "beliefs." When we study what changes most for persons who find faith, it is a robust constellation of beliefs, actions, spiritual practices, relations with others, attitudes, lifestyle, and outlook. In other words, for most persons, coming to faith is about one's entire identity. It is the acquisition of a form of life, a material formation into a new set of habits, commitments, values, and social patterns.

Appendix A

Christian Representation in the Survey

	U.S. Christians[A]	Survey Responses
Catholic	30.5%	20.0%
Evangelical Protestant	37.2%	31.2%
Baptist	13.5%	4.7%
Free Church	0.4%	0.9%
Holiness	1.0%	1.2%
Lutheran	2.2%	2.3%
Methodists/Pietist	0.6%	0.8%
Non-Denominational/Nonspecific	9.4%	14.4%
Pentecostal/Charismatic	5.3%	2.7%
Presbyterian/Reformed	1.6%	3.4%
Restorationist	2.3%	0.4%
Adventist	0.9%	0.3%
Mainline Protestant	21.5%	35.7%
Baptist	3.1%	0.3%
Dual		0.3%
Episcopal	1.8%	10.9%
Free Church	0.7%	0.7%
Lutheran	3.1%	1.4%
Methodists/Pietist	5.7%	14.7%

Non-Denominational/Nonspecific	4.0%	
Restorationist	0.4%	0.7%
Presbyterian/Reformed	2.8%	6.6%
Historically Black	9.5%	1.3%
Orthodox	0.7%	1.1%
Other Christian	0.6%	0.1%
Unknown		10.6%
	100.0%	100.0%

A. Pew, "America's Changing Religious Landscape," 50.

Appendix B

Factors in Coming to Faith by Tradition

Primary Factor in Coming to Faith								
	Main-line	Evan-gelical	Cath-olic	Juda-ism	Bud-dhism	Islam	UU	Quaker
Spouse/ partner	20%	17%	28%	43%	9%	19%	13%	0%
Scripture	1%	8%	2%	0%	3%	31%	0%	0%
Parents	4%	7%	2%	0%	2%	0%	0%	0%
A dream or vision	2%	1%	3%	13%	3%	0%	3%	4%
Your own children	10%	10%	14%	13%	0%	6%	19%	11%
A congregation	28%	13%	11%	6%	23%	0%	47%	22%
Television/ Radio	0%	1%	1%	0%	0%	0%	1%	0%
Other family	2%	3%	4%	0%	1%	6%	0%	0%
Friends	2%	9%	5%	6%	5%	6%	6%	4%
Literature/ drama/music	3%	2%	4%	2%	13%	0%	4%	0%
A minister/ teacher	19%	17%	11%	4%	18%	13%	6%	0%
An evangelis-tic event	1%	1%	1%	0%	0%	0%	0%	0%

Some other person	4%	9%	8%	0%	6%	0%	0%	0%
Religious activities	4%	3%	5%	13%	11%	13%	1%	0%
Personal Event/ Experience					5%	6%		4%
Other								56%

Primary or Supporting Factor in Coming to Faith							
	Main-line	Evan-gelical	Cath-olic	Juda-ism	Bud-dhism	Islam	UU	Quaker
Spouse/ partner	48%	45%	56%	66%	30%	44%	40%	11%
Scripture	32%	54%	43%	36%	31%	69%	6%	11%
Parents	18%	25%	15%	9%	8%	0%	13%	7%
A dream or vision	12%	14%	15%	23%	15%	6%	9%	7%
Your own children	32%	40%	34%	40%	6%	6%	39%	33%
A congregation	68%	48%	43%	55%	63%	31%	79%	63%
Television/ Radio	4%	9%	6%	19%	4%	6%	1%	0%
Other family	11%	15%	20%	21%	9%	13%	0%	15%
Friends	29%	35%	32%	28%	34%	31%	24%	33%
Literature/ drama/music	16%	20%	18%	57%	45%	19%	17%	4%
A minister/ teacher	60%	58%	46%	66%	68%	25%	49%	4%
An evangelis-tic event	3%	11%	3%	0%	0%	0%	0%	0%
Some other person	13%	22%	23%	9%	28%	13%	17%	11%
Religious activities	23%	25%	32%	47%	52%	38%	29%	15%
Personal Event/ Experience					37%	19%		19%

Other								63%

*Not all surveys contained the "personal event/experience choice."
**Because of the number of Quakers who chose "Other," we report that for them as its own separate category.

Appendix C

Changes in Attitudes and Positions on Social Issues

	Already opposed, became more opposed	Already opposed, remain just as opposed	Now become opposed	No opinion/Don't know	Now became supportive	Already supported, stayed just as supportive	Already supportive, became more supportive
Right to an Abortion							
Evangelicals	24%	35%	14%	14%	1%	11%	1%
Mainline	3%	18%	5%	19%	2%	49%	3%
Catholics	19%	27%	17%	18%	2%	17%	1%
Jews	0%	0%	0%	8%	0%	88%	4%
Buddhists	0%	2%	2%	12%	2%	76%	7%
Muslims	14%	43%	0%	7%	7%	21%	7%
UU's	0%	0%	0%	3%	4%	77%	16%
Quakers	4%	0%	4%	9%	0%	78%	4%
Gay Marriage							
Evangelicals	22%	31%	9%	15%	4%	16%	3%

Mainline	3%	10%	2%	13%	10%	43%	19%
Catho-lics	12%	18%	5%	23%	1%	34%	7%
Jews	0%	0%	0%	4%	0%	84%	12%
Bud-dhists	0%	0%	0%	4%	3%	73%	19%
Muslims	14%	29%	0%	29%	7%	14%	7%
UU's	0%	0%	0%	0%	3%	57%	41%
Quakers	0%	0%	0%	0%	8%	67%	25%
Gun Control							
Evan-gelicals	8%	21%	2%	24%	8%	29%	8%
Mainline	6%	20%	1%	21%	4%	38%	10%
Catho-lics	5%	20%	3%	28%	3%	34%	7%
Jews	0%	4%	0%	12%	4%	52%	28%
Bud-dhists	11%	12%	1%	13%	4%	43%	17%
Muslims	8%	8%	0%	8%	0%	50%	25%
UU's	3%	12%	0%	3%	6%	58%	19%
Quakers	4%	0%	0%	17%	4%	43%	30%
War							
Evan-gelicals	10%	21%	6%	39%	2%	20%	1%
Mainline	11%	41%	5%	26%	2%	13%	2%
Catho-lics	15%	38%	6%	30%	1%	10%	1%
Jews	8%	36%	0%	24%	8%	24%	0%
Bud-dhists	32%	39%	4%	11%	7%	7%	0%
Muslims	15%	69%	0%	0%	0%	8%	8%
UU's	13%	57%	4%	16%	0%	9%	1%
Quakers	48%	28%	8%	8%	0%	0%	8%
Women's Equality							
Evan-gelicals	1%	4%	1%	21%	3%	55%	15%
Mainline	0%	0%	0%	7%	2%	68%	22%
Catho-lics	1%	2%	1%	13%	4%	66%	14%

Jews	0%	0%	0%	0%	0%	92%	8%
Bud-dhists	0%	1%	0%	3%	1%	71%	24%
Muslims	0%	0%	0%	0%	0%	69%	31%
UU's	0%	1%	0%	0%	3%	71%	25%
Quakers	0%	0%	0%	0%	8%	68%	24%
Racial Justice							
Evan-gelicals	3%	5%	0%	18%	5%	53%	17%
Mainline	0%	1%	2%	10%	3%	61%	24%
Catho-lics	1%	3%	1%	10%	3%	67%	14%
Jews	0%	0%	0%	0%	4%	76%	20%
Bud-dhists	0%	1%	0%	3%	0%	67%	30%
Muslims	0%	8%	0%	8%	0%	31%	54%
UU's	0%	0%	0%	1%	1%	63%	34%
Quakers	0%	0%	0%	0%	0%	48%	52%
Economic Justice for the Poor							
Evan-gelicals	2%	5%	0%	24%	11%	40%	18%
Mainline	0%	1%	1%	12%	6%	44%	36%
Catho-lics	2%	1%	1%	17%	5%	46%	29%
Jews	0%	0%	0%	4%	12%	64%	20%
Bud-dhists	0%	0%	0%	4%	2%	56%	38%
Muslims	0%	0%	0%	0%	8%	38%	54%
UU's	0%	0%	0%	3%	3%	51%	44%
Quakers	0%	0%	0%	4%	0%	36%	60%
Care for the Natural Environment							
Evan-gelicals	2%	3%	0%	20%	9%	49%	17%
Mainline	0%	0%	0%	12%	4%	58%	25%
Catho-lics	1%	2%	0%	15%	5%	56%	21%
Jews	0%	0%	0%	0%	8%	76%	16%
Bud-dhists	0%	0%	0%	3%	3%	48%	47%

Muslims	0%	0%	0%	0%	0%	46%	54%
UU's	0%	0%	0%	0%	5%	62%	33%
Quakers	0%	0%	0%	4%	0%	40%	56%

Appendix D

Most Important Feature
of the Congregation

Most Important Feature of the Congregation You Now Attend								
	Main-line	Evan-gelical	Cath-olic	Juda-ism	Bud-dhism	Islam	UU	Quaker
The Welcome	29%	20%	31%	51%	27%	71%	52%	53%
The Preaching & Teaching	30%	49%	23%	9%	40%	7%	17%	5%
The Worship	21%	18%	32%	23%	8%	14%	3%	37%
Educational Programs	5%	0%	2%	14%	5%	7%	11%	0%
Social Outreach/ Ministry	9%	4%	3%	3%	3%	0%	17%	5%
Meditation Practice					18%			

All Important Features of the Congregation You Now Attend								
	Main-line	Evan-gelical	Cath-olic	Juda-ism	Bud-dhism	Islam	UU	Quaker
The Welcome	77%	73%	73%	91%	77%	86%	87%	89%
The Preaching & Teaching	81%	84%	59%	49%	78%	71%	77%	11%

The Worship	69%	74%	70%	51%	28%	64%	38%	100%
Educational Programs	35%	33%	34%	57%	38%	57%	54%	32%
Social Outreach/ Ministry	53%	40%	38%	51%	21%	57%	73%	58%
Meditation Practice					24%			

Appendix E

Active Seekers or Drawn in by Others Without Actively Seeking?

Active Seeker?					
	Not at all	Not so much	Not sure	Somewhat	Very Much
Evangelicals	6%	14%	8%	33%	38%
Mainline	2%	9%	5%	32%	52%
Catholics	4%	7%	5%	31%	53%
Jews	8%	5%	3%	26%	58%
Buddhists	5%	12%	3%	26%	53%
Muslims	21%	21%	14%	0%	43%
UU's	9%	13%	3%	34%	42%
Quakers	0%	8%	4%	28%	60%

Drawn in by Others Without Actively Seeking?					
	Not at all	Not so much	Not sure	Somewhat	Very Much
Evangelicals	18%	17%	6%	36%	24%
Mainline	26%	26%	5%	25%	19%
Catholics	25%	20%	9%	32%	13%
Jews	26%	32%	9%	26%	6%

Buddhists	43%	31%	3%	12%	10%
Muslims	36%	14%	0%	36%	14%
UU's	39%	31%	6%	17%	7%
Quakers	40%	30%	10%	15%	5%

Appendix F

Significance of Changes

On a scale of 0 to 5 (with 5 being "very significant"), estimate how significant have been the changes, if any, in your life since making your new commitment or recommitment?						
	Beliefs	Actions/ Lifestyle	Spiritual Practices	Relations with Others	Happier than before	More hopeful than before
Evangelicals	3.95	4.11	4.33	4.06	4.21	4.35
Mainline	3.09	3.45	4.00	3.61	3.89	3.93
Catholic	3.36	3.56	4.05	3.60	3.85	3.98
Jewish	2.93	3.00	3.76	3.23	3.64	3.76
Buddhist	3.50	3.63	4.42	3.94	4.09	3.58
Muslim	3.86	4.29	4.38	3.77	4.14	4.29
UU	2.13	2.57	2.59	2.90	3.03	2.97
Quaker	2.76	2.69	3.52	3.09	4.60	3.05

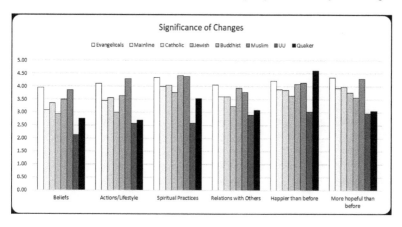

Bibliography

Ammerman, Nancy T. "Golden Rule Christianity: Lived Religion in the American Mainstream." In *Lived Religion in America*, edited by David Hall, 196–216. Princeton, NJ: Princeton University Press, 1997.

Center for Applied Research in the Apostolate. "Frequently Requested Church Statistics." http://cara.georgetown.edu/frequently-requested-church-statistics/.

Corbin, Theresa. "The Terrifying Reality of Converting to Islam in America Right after 9/11." *Washington Post* (December 30, 2015). https://www.washingtonpost.com/posteverything/wp/2015/12/30/the-terrifying-reality-of-converting-to-islam-in-america-right-after-911/?utm_term=.4834e3ff209e.

Finney, John. *Finding Faith Today: How Does It Happen?* Stonehill Green: British and Foreign Bible Society, 1992.

Friends World Committee for Consultation. "How Many Quakers Are There in the World?" (September 16, 2016). http://quakerspeak.com/how-many-quakers-are-there-in-world/.

Gallup. "Support for War Modestly Higher Among More Religious Americans" (February 27, 2003). http://news.gallup.com/poll/7888/support-war-modestly-higher-among-more-religious-americans.aspx.

Granqvist, Peter, and Berit Hagekull. "Religiousness and Perceived Childhood Attachment: Profiling Socialized Correspondence and Emotional Compensation." *Journal for the Scientific Study of Religion* 38 (1999) 254–73.

Granqvist, Peter, and Lee A. Kirkpatrick. "Religious Conversion and Perceived Childhood Attachment: A Meta-analysis. *International Journal for the Psychology of Religion* 14 (2004) 223–50.

Ingraham, Christopher. "Nearly One Third of the American Labor Force Works on the Weekend." *Washington Post* (September 8, 2014). https://www.washingtonpost.com/news/wonk/wp/2014/09/08/nearly-one-third-of-the-american-labor-force-works-on-the-weekend/.

Johnson, Todd M., and Brian J. Grim, eds. *The World's Religions in Figures: An Introduction to International Religious Demography*. Malden, MA: Wiley-Blackwell, 2013.

Kennedy, John W. "The 4–14 Window." *Christianity Today* 48:7 (July 2004) 53.

Kirkpatrick, Lee A. "God as a Substitute Attachment Figure: A Longitudinal Study of Adult Attachment Style and Religious Change in College Students." *Personality and Social Psychology Bulletin* 24 (1998) 961–73.

Lee, Jonathan H. X., and Kathleen M. Nadeau, eds. *Encyclopedia of Asian American Folklore and Folklife.* Santa Barbara, CA: ABC-CLIO, 2010.

National Association of Evangelicals. "When Americans Become Christians" (Spring 2015). https://www.nae.net/when-americans-become-christians/.

Peterson, Kristin. "You Can Go Home Again: Catholic Return to the Church." *U.S. Catholic* 75:7 (July 2010) 18–22.

Pew Research Center. "5 facts about prayer" (May 4, 2016). http://www.pewresearch.org/fact-tank/2016/05/04/5-facts-about-prayer/.

———. "America's Changing Religious Landscape" (May 12, 2015). http://www.pewforum.org/2015/05/12/americas-changing-religious-landscape/.

———. "Belief in Heaven." http://www.pewforum.org/religious-landscape-study/belief-in-heaven/.

———. "Different Faiths, Different Messages" (March 19, 2003). http://www.people-press.org/2003/03/19/different-faiths-different-messages/.

———. "Faith in Flux: Changes in Religious Affiliation in the U.S." (April 2009). http://assets.pewresearch.org/wp-content/uploads/sites/11/2009/04/fullreport.pdf.

———. "Participation in Electronic and Offline Religious Activities" (November 5, 2014). http://www.pewforum.org/2014/11/06/religion-and-electronic-media/pf_14-11-06_faithsocial-01-2/.

———. "A Portrait of Jewish Americans" (October 1, 2013). http://www.pewforum.org/2013/10/01/jewish-american-beliefs-attitudes-culture-survey/.

———. "Religion and Electronic Media" (November 6, 2014). http://www.pewforum.org/2014/11/06/religion-and-electronic-media/.

———. "The share of Americans who leave Islam is offset by those who become Muslim" (January 26, 2018). http://www.pewresearch.org/fact-tank/2018/01/26/the-share-of-americans-who-leave-islam-is-offset-by-those-who-become-muslim/.

———. "U.S. Muslims Concerned About Their Place in Society, but Continue to Believe in the American Dream" (July 26, 2017). http://www.pewforum.org/2017/07/26/demographic-portrait-of-muslim-americans/.

Poston, Larry. "The Adult Gospel." *Christianity Today* (January 1, 2002). http://www.christianitytoday.com/ct/2002/januaryweb-only/32.0.html.

Public Religion Research Institute. "America's Changing Religious Identity" (September 6, 2017). https://www.prri.org/wp-content/uploads/2017/09/PRRI-Religion-Report.pdf.

Quaker Information Center. "Branches of Friends Today" (May 26, 2011). http://www.quakerinfo.org/quakerism/branches/today.

Roof, Wade Clark. *A Generation of Seekers: The Spiritual Journeys of the Baby Boom Generation.* San Francisco: Harper & Row, 1994.

Sikh American Legal Defense and Education Fund. "Who Are Sikh Americans?" http://saldef.org/who-are-sikh-americans/#.WoL7DKinGUk.

Smith, Christian. *Soul Searching: The Religious and Spiritual Lives of American Teenagers.* Oxford: Oxford University Press, 2005.

Stetzer, Ed. "If it doesn't stem its decline, mainline Protestantism has just 23 Easters left." *The Washington Post* (April 28, 2018). https://www.washingtonpost.com/news/acts-of-faith/wp/2017/04/28/if-it-doesnt-stem-its-decline-mainline-protestantism-has-just-23-easters-left/?utm_term=.ba4ab8edb325.

Tendulkar, D. G. *Mahatma, Life of Mohandas Karamchand Gandhi.* Bombay: Vithalbhai
K. Jhaveri & D. G. Tendulkar, 1953.
Unitarian Universalist Association. "History of Unitarian Universalism." https://www.
uua.org/beliefs/who-we-are/history.
———. "The Seven Principles." https://www.uua.org/beliefs/what-we-believe/principles.